TO
WALLACE E. LAMBERT

FOREWORD

Language learning is a much more complex activity than most people realize, especially if it involves large numbers of people, as it does when it enters the educational or administrative systems of a nation. Also language learning has wider ramifications than is usually recognized. It can be the factor which determines whether a country disintegrates or keeps together, remains a pastoral society or becomes an industrial state, stays isolated and aloof, or influences and is influenced by other nations.

Language learning can keep a nation together, and the lack of it can rend it asunder. In Canada, for example, a hundredfold increase in the scope and level of the learning of French as a second language in key areas of the society could be one of the most important factors in keeping that country together whereas a comparable decrease could contribute to the creation of two independent states. Analogous cases may be found in Belgium, tropical Africa, and India, to name only these.

Language learning can determine a nation's future. In Africa, for example, in many nations the scientific, administrative, and technical personnel must learn one of the great international languages in order that their tribal and underdeveloped economy may be converted into that of a modern state. In fact, the change from tribalism, which is largely language based, to nationalism, which supposes the mutual comprehension of at least one common language, is largely dependent on the learning of that common language, at least by the governing and administrative personnel. In some countries like Nigeria, where more than a hundred tribes speak as many mutually incomprehensible languages, the problem is one of gigantic proportions.

Language learning helps one country influence or be influenced by another country. A country may be desirous of extending its influence abroad through treaties, pacts of friendship, and mutual assistance or agreements on cultural exchange. But it cannot and does not assume that the other country receiving its gifts has also a knowledge of the giver's language. The gifts or assistance of exchange may have a much greater effect if offered and presented in the language of the receiver as, for example, when experts or technicians sent abroad speak the language of the area in which they are to serve.

These are just a few examples of the importance of language learning in national and international development. Few countries in the world today can afford to be without some sort of language policy.

A language policy determines which languages are important, the areas of activity in which they may be involved (and to what extent), which percentage of the national budget should be devoted to language and how it should be distributed among the various language needs, which language aims should be achieved and by what date. Language policy, however, cannot be divorced from general government policy or from the needs of the society which will supply the language learners.

If a government decides that the national interest is served by promoting friendship with another country, it might try to encourage its nationals to learn the language of that country and to promote the exchange of persons between both countries. On the other hand, a nation may decide to promote its own language abroad as a vehicle for the transmission of its national culture. An example of this was the founding of the Alliance française at the end of the last century, followed by the creation of similar French government agencies, some of which became the instruments for the application of language policies. As a result, thousands of persons throughout the world have learned French at the expense of the French government.

At the same time—also at the expense of the French government—many thousands of French citizens through their national schools have learned other languages. These languages were not necessarily those of the people who have learned French as a result of France's language policy abroad. They are languages which the French government, through its Ministry of Education, has considered useful to promote at home, either because of the proximity of the peoples speaking the language, because of the economic or scientific importance of the language, or even because an important sector of French society has traditionally considered the language as indispensable to a general education.

The government may be responsible not only for which languages are learned and by whom, but for when and how they are taught and by whom. It may also determine which elements of the language are learned and at which level. It will do this through the language curriculum branch of its Ministry of Education, which may even carry on or commission research to determine which elements of the language should form the basis of the curriculum. An example of this is the *français fondemental* project which elaborated a basic grammar and word list for use throughout the world.

When a government is directly or indirectly involved in teaching its national tongue abroad, it may do so through certain methods for the use of which carefully selected teachers may be specially trained. The methods and materials themselves may have been made by one of the language agencies of the government or under government contract.

When we realize that the target of all this expensive hierarchical activity is the foreign language learner, it is surprising that so little scientific attention has been devoted to the process through which he learns or does not learn the language. True, there exists a vast professional literature for the foreign language teacher; but it is almost entirely devoted to the teaching process or to the "best" methods to teach a foreign language, which are quite separate from what foreign language learning is and what it implies. In fact, there has always been an inexplicable confusion between language teaching and language learning, even in the titles of books on language learning which deal exclusively with what the teacher does.

It was in an effort to put a little order into the field that *Language Teaching Analysis* was conceived as a first approximation to a framework into which variables could be pigeonholed, talked about, analyzed, and eventually measured for purposes of planning and research. Details in the analytic framework were intentionally limited to the variables found in the activity of language teaching, as distinguished from those involved in language learning–limited, that is, to the variables found in the teaching of foreign languages (*T*) and those within the methods and materials used (*M*). The relationship of all three, teaching, method, and learning (*I, S, L*) are in the diagram at the end of this foreword.

In addition to the analysis of language teaching and language teaching methods, we now have an analytical study, also a first approximation, of the variables in foreign language learning. It includes the learning or instruction (*I*) and is a function of method (*M*) and teaching (*T*). It also comprises the effects of the sociolinguistic environment (*S*) on the learning of the learner as manifested by what he does and says (*L*) as the result of the reaction of all these forces upon his psychological make-up, as illustrated in the diagram. This study goes a long way to completing the picture of what a general framework of foreign language acquisition (policy, teaching, learning) might look like, once tested and proved as being complete. It is essentially an interdisciplinary framework involving such sciences as psychology, sociology, anthropology, law, education, government, linguistics, and other ancilliary disciplines and technologies such as computer science and psychoacoustics. It can include much of the growing literature on language planning (Fishman, Rubin, et al.), studies of language laws (Kloss, Ostrower, et al.), and psycholinguistics (Carroll, Lambert, et al.), to name only these.

It is the psycholinguistic dimension of the language acquisition framework that Léon Jakobovits has elaborated. Since the psycholinguistic dimension is composed largely of human variables, it is more complex and more difficult to analyze than are the methods and materials variables, which can be reduced to textual and hence stable elements that can be classified and counted.

The learning variables of our diagram in the *ISL* triangle are by their nature unstable not only because they are those of individual human beings but also because they form a complex web of interrelated habits the whole of which comes under the heading of language learning. These are habits which have to develop to a point where a language may be said to have been learned. What this point is remains one of the difficult questions for language learning analysis. Some of these habits, or families of habits, may be acquired independently of others. Reading (recognition of words and word groups and the understanding of their meaning within a context) may be acquired independently of the writing skill, but the converse is not true. Skill in understanding the spoken word can be acquired independently of skill in speaking it, but again the converse is not true. Another such dichotomy is that of competence and performance. Competence in the codes of the language may not be transformed into the performance skills of message production as heard in fluent speech and writing.

All this, and much more of what is involved in language learning, may vary according to the learner's age, his background, his aptitudes and attitudes, his motivation and cultural environment. The relationship between all this and factors of language teaching and language teaching methods and materials will remain unexplored, however, until we are able to measure objectively the kind and degree of learning achieved according to variations in the kind and degree of teaching as it affects the meanings and forms of the language and their comprehension and expression. Such objective measurement is one of the most ambitious objectives of the field of language testing, not only in relation to what has been taught but according to how much of the language itself has been mastered.

The achievement of this objective would lead the way to the discovery of how much of a language could be learned by whom and under what conditions. These conditions may not be those of the formal or classroom teaching of language, as the appended diagram indicates. They may also be those of the society in which a language is spoken. Any such knowledge may affect foreign language requirements and be fed back into the curriculum and methods of the system. It is therefore as part of a larger whole that the psycholinguistic dimensions of language learning are to be examined and appreciated.

Language Learning, Teaching, and Policy: An Interaction Model

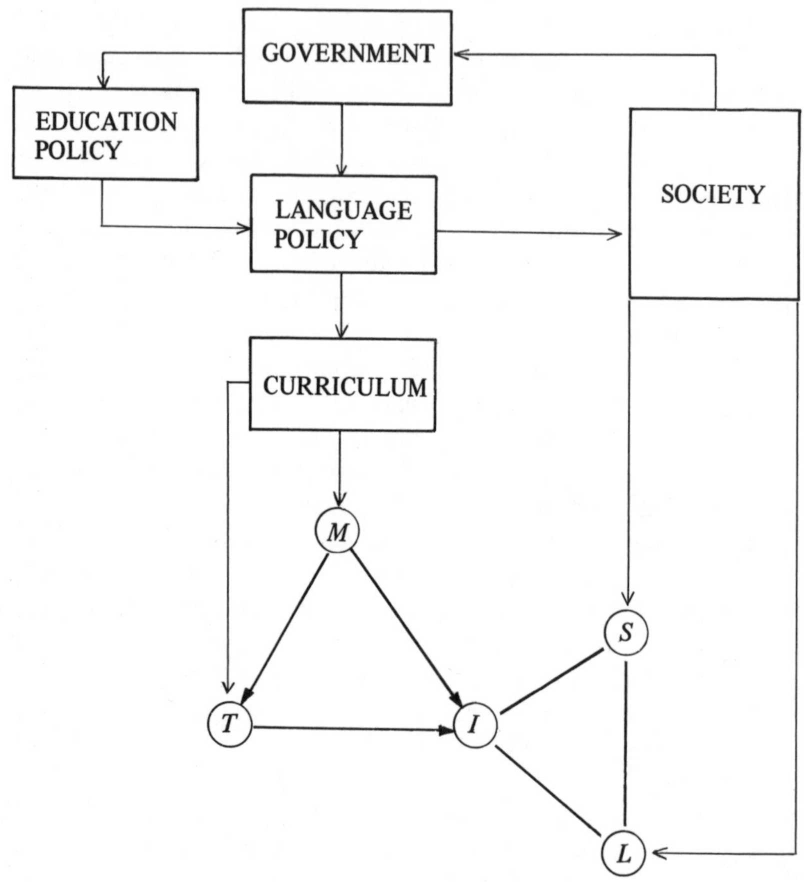

M = Method and material variables: texts, tapes, films (cf. *Language Teaching Analysis,* Part II)

T = Teacher variables: what the teacher does. (cf. *Language Teaching Analysis,* Part III)

I = Instruction variables: what the learner gets (cf. Jakobovits)

S = Sociocultural variables: what the environment does (cf. Jakobovits)

L = Learner variables: what the learner does (cf. Jakobovits)

This model indicates that the language instruction a learner gets (I) is a function of both teaching (T) and method (M), which in turn are functions of CURRICULUM and LANGUAGE POLICY operating not only in the field of education but in all activities in which the GOVERNMENT may exert its influence–the military, the courts, the parliament, administration, transportation and communications. This language policy may determine the curriculum directly or indirectly (or both) by being inserted into a general EDUCATION POLICY. The language policy may decide which and how many languages will be used and taught. It might consciously promote early training in the oral use of a second language with the intention of having it later used as a medium of instruction. Or it may limit the learning skill in the second language to a reading knowledge in order to weaken the incursions of a rival language, while preserving the advantages of being able to make use of everything produced in that language. The policy may also decide the amount of mass media to be used to propagate a language, the amount of money to be allocated to the research and preparation of language teaching materials, the amount and sort of training for language teachers and language inspectors, the amount of school time in years and hours to be devoted to language teaching, and the amount of bonus payments for language skills. It can do all this both through changes in the curriculum and modifications in the training of language teachers. The curriculum can determine what, how much, and how the learner learns through the methods and materials with which he comes in contact. Both what the method does and what the teacher does determine the instructional activity to which the learner must react.

But this instructional activity is not the learner's only source of language learning. There is also his linguistic role in SOCIETY as well as the sociolinguistic forces (S) exerted both upon him and upon his language learning activities.

William Francis Mackey

PREFACE

The purpose of this volume is to bring together various materials I have prepared dealing with psychological aspects of foreign language learning and bilingualism. While this edition does not intend to be a fully integrated text on the subject, the materials herein have been useful in my course on Second Language Acquisition and provide the basis for a text in preparation.

Some of the materials in this volume have been distributed by request to foreign language teachers, researchers, and administrators; others are being made available for the first time. All of them have been arranged here for the use of persons interested in what I call "Compensatory Instruction" in foreign languages.

Compensatory Instruction involves the notion of adjusting the teaching activities to the needs of individual students. In Chapter III I outline in specific terms what the student factors are in foreign language learning and how they are to be diagnosed and treated by the teacher. Chapter V presents various questionnaire forms that the teacher may use in identifying attitudinal and motivational problems among students and their parents. The other chapters offer a critical examination of the implications of recent psycholinguistic developments for the learning and teaching of a second language. Much of this material is polemical in nature and I have made no attempt to present all sides of the issue. Rather, I have tried to make as good a case as I could, at this stage, for what many would see as the new "liberal" approach to language teaching. This approach regards the student as the most important contributor to the learning process. Throughout, I have argued that the teacher, rather than the academic researcher, is best qualified to decide upon the innovations in instructional procedures and materials which are to render foreign language teaching more effective than it presently is. In order to be able to play this role and not relinquish it to others, the teacher must come to have a proper understanding not only of psychological theory and research per se, but of the process whereby psychologists themselves come to formulate these theories.

Psycholinguistics, being a relatively new but vibrant field, will change during the coming years. I believe that this change will noticeably affect foreign language teaching and all persons involved with the acquisition and maintenance of language in a professional capacity. I believe that the effects will be beneficial to all and I trust that this volume will hasten and increase that benefit.

I hope that this volume will become a link between myself and the readers who share my desire to see an improvement in foreign language curricula in our schools. I should like to develop any such link and I encourage every reader, especially foreign language teachers and administrators, to share with me your ideas and experience. I invite you to write directly to me:

February, 1970

Leon A. Jakobovits
Department of Psychology
University of Hawaii
Honolulu, Hawaii

ACKNOWLEDGMENTS

Chapter 1 is based on "Implications of recent psycholinguistic developments for the teaching of a second language" previously published in *Language Learning* (1968, Vol. XVIII, 89-109). Chapter 2 is based on "The physiology and psychology of second-language learning" previously published in the *Britannica Review of Foreign Language Education* edited by Emma Birkmaier (Vol. 1, Encyclopaedia Britannica, 1969). Chapter 3 is based on a previously unpublished manuscript entitled "A psycholinguistic analysis of second-language learning and bilingualism" originally prepared in 1969 under the sponsorship of the International Center for Research on Bilingualism, Laval University (W.F. Mackey, Director). Chapter 4 is based on the following three previously published articles: "A functional approach to the assessment of language skills" (*Journal of English as a Second Language,* 1969, Vol. IV, 63-76); "Dimensionality of compound-coordinate bilingualism" (*Language Learning,* 1968, Special Issue No. 3, 29-55); "Second language learning and transfer theory: A theoretical assessment" (*Language Learning,* 1968, Vol. XIX, 55-86). Chapter 5 is based on the following three sources: "Research findings and foreign language requirements in colleges and universities" (*Foreign Language Annals,* 1969, Vol. 2, 436-456); "Illinois Foreign Language Attitude Questionnaire–Forms S_1 and S_2" (Copyrighted by the Board of Directors of the Northeast Conference on the Teaching of Foreign Languages and by the author); and part of the Appendix to "Aptitude, attitude, and motivation in second-language acquisition," an unpublished doctoral dissertation by H. J. Feenstra (University of Western Ontario, 1968).

All these materials were used with the permission of the publishers and Dr. Feenstra, and to them I hereby express my sincere thanks.

CONTENTS

CHAPTER IV
PROBLEMS IN ASSESSING LANGUAGE PROFICIENCY 149

CHAPTER V
FOREIGN LANGUAGE APTITUDE AND ATTITUDE 223

Chapter 1

PSYCHOLINGUISTIC IMPLICATIONS FOR THE TEACHING OF FOREIGN LANGUAGES

This chapter attempts to summarize some recently developed notions about the language acquisition process and makes some preliminary suggestions about the implications of these ideas for the problem of teaching a second language. The original impetus in demonstrating the shortcomings of traditional psychological and linguistic theories in the understanding of the processes of language structure and language acquisition must be credited to Chomsky (1957; 1959) who also developed new theories to cope with the problem. Subsequent writers have elaborated upon this new outlook pointing out the various specific inadequacies of the earlier notions and making concrete suggestions for new approaches (see Miller, 1965; Katz, 1966; McNeill, 1966; Lenneberg, 1967; Slobin, 1966; and the contributions in Bellugi and Brown, 1964). To appreciate fully these new developments it is necessary to consider briefly the nature of the inadequacy of the earlier notions on the language acquisition process.

1.1 FROM SURFACE TO BASE

The traditional psychological approach to the language acquisition process was to view it within the framework of learning theory. The acquisition of phonology was viewed as a process of shaping the elementary sounds produced by the infant through reinforcement of successive approximations to the adult pattern. Imitation of adult speech patterns was thought to be a source of reward to the babbling infant and repeated practice on these novel motor habits was thought to serve the function of *stamping in* and automatizing them.

From these elementary phonological habits the words of the language were thought to emerge through parental reinforcement. It was said that the child could better control his environment by uttering words to which the parents responded by giving the child what he wanted. The child learned the meaning of words through a conditioning process whereby the referents which the word signalled appeared in contiguity with the symbol thus establishing an association. The acquisition of grammar was conceptualized as learning the proper order of words in sentences. Generalization carried a heavy theoretical burden in attempts to explain novel uses of words and novel arrangements of sentences. Perceptual similarity of physical objects and relations, and functional equivalence of responses were thought to serve as the basis for generalizing the meaning of previously learned words. Similarly, generalization of the grammatical function of words was thought to account for the understanding and production of novel sentences.

Two aspects of this approach are noteworthy. One is that the burden of language acquisition was placed on the environment: the parents were the source of input and reinforcement was the necessary condition for establishing the *habits.* The child was merely a passive organism responsive to the reinforcement conditions arranged by agencies in the environment. The second aspect to be noted was the relatively simplistic conception of the knowledge to be acquired: sentences were conceived as orderings of words, arranged in sequential probabilities that could be learned then generalized to novel combinations. A general characterization of this overall approach would be to say that the process of acquisition was from surface to base; that is, the knowledge represented by language learning at all levels–phonological, semantic, syntactic–was entirely based on the relations contained in the overt speech of the parents. The new approach to be discussed below can be characterized by saying that it reverses this order; that is, the burden of acquisition is now placed on the child with relatively minor importance attached to the environment as a *reinforcing* agency. Furthermore, the approach minimizes the relations contained in the surface of language, attributing the significant information to be acquired to the underlying structure of language which is not contained in the surface input. However, before taking up this new approach I shall point out the specific inadequacies of the earlier approach.

1.1.1 The Acquisition of Phonology

The notion that the child first learns the constituent elements of the adult phonemic structure and then produces speech by associating these elements appears to be contrary to fact. In the first place it is doubtful that speech is made up of a concatenation of physically unique sound elements. A sound typewriter which would convert each physically different sound into a different orthographic type would not produce a very readable record (Lenneberg, 1967), because speech recognition is not simply a process of identifying physical differences in sounds. In fact it requires overlooking certain acoustic differences as unimportant and paying attention to certain other features in relation to the acoustic context in which the sound is imbedded. In other words, the "cracking" of the phonological code of a natural language involves a process of pattern recognition and equation, not simply learning the identity of constituent elements. The first recognizable words of a child are not composed of acoustically invariant speech sounds (see Lenneberg, 1967). Therefore, a description of phonological acquisition in terms of learning individual speech sounds which are then combined into words must be false. Furthermore, it is not clear how a notion of shaping by successive approximation can ever account for the acquisition of sound pattern recognition and the discovery by the child of phonological structure of a hierarchical nature.

1.1.2 The Acquisition of Meaning

It is an indication of the simplistic character of previous behavioristic views of language that they have concerned themselves with the problem of reference to the almost total exclusion of the semantic interpretation of utterances. Reference deals with the relation between words and objects or aspects of the environment. Psychological theories of meaning (or reference) were based on a philosophical system of conceptualization which now appears to be false; namely the notion that "words tag things" in the physical environment. The adoption of such a view led to elementary descriptions whereby a particular combination of sounds (a word) was conditioned to an object or set of objects. When a new object having certain physical similarities to the one previously conditioned was encountered, the learned verbal response was said to have generalized to this new instance. More elaborate versions of this form of theorizing were developed to account for the obvious fact that familiar words would be used in connection with objects or situations which had no physical similarity to the originally conditioned object. However, due to the requirements imposed by viewing meaning as a conditioned response to a stimulus, these later elaborations merely pushed back the locus of the similarity from the external physical object to an internal (even though functional) representation of that object. Thus an individual's capacity to understand the extension of the word *eye* in *the eye of the needle* was thought of as arising from the fact that the internal conditioned responses elicited by the word *eye* in the above phrase are similar in some (unspecified) manner to the responses originally conditioned to the word *eye* in such instances as *this is your eye, these are my eyes, this is the doggy's eye,* etc. The total inadequacy of this kind of approach as an explanatory device is this: it leaves obscure the specific nature of the similarity of the conditioned response from the original to the extension, and it is incapable of specifying the nature of the extension and cannot predict it until after it has occurred. Thus the view of reference as a conditioning process has the same shortcomings for semantics as the view of conditioning of sequential probabilities of parts of speech has for syntax. That is, the creative and novel use of words which is so characteristic of language remains completely beyond its explanatory range.

The difficulties attached to these behavioristic explanations of meaning can be resolved by abandoning the notion that "words tag things" in favor of the view that "words tag the processes by which the species deals cognitively with its environment" (Lenneberg, 1967, p. 334). This view reverses the order between the object-stimulus and its conditioned response-process. That is, rather than saying that the concept-meaning involved in the use of the word *eye* is a conditioned process (external, internal, or cortical) developed as a result of tagging various objects having certain characteristics and experiences relating to them, this view says that the word *eye* tags a class of cognitive processes developed through a categorization and differentiation process which is independent of verbal labeling. When a child (or adult for that matter) is confronted with a new word, the new word acquires meaning only in the sense that it comes to refer to a class of cognitive processes already possessed by the individual. Novel uses of words, such as metaphoric extensions, are understandable to others by virtue of the fact that human categorization and differentiation processes are similar across the species, the word merely serving as a convenient tag whereby these processes can be labeled. The language of stimulus-response theory does not seem to offer any particular advantages when conceptualizing the problem in this fashion.

A conception of meaning such as the one just outlined has certain implications for a theory of semantics which it might be important to state explicitly. Meaning becomes a purely cognitive concept (as linguists of a generation ago used to believe) and semantics represents the linguistic expression of these cognitive operations. The problem of the development of meaning becomes the problem of cognitive development, which is to say that the dimensions of meaning–how the human species categorizes and differentiates the universe–*antedate* the dimensions of semantics–how cognitive categories and relations find expression in linguistic terms. An adequate theory of meaning must be able to characterize the nature of this relation, namely the mapping of cognitive to linguistic processes. Note that this theory includes not only lexical (vocabulary) items but also the morphophonemic and inflectional system of language, since the latter contain cognitive differentiations such as present vs. past, animate vs. inanimate, definite vs. indefinite, mass vs. count, male vs. female, plural vs. singular, and so on. It follows that an adequate theory of semantics must concern itself not only with the vocabulary of a language and the relation between words and things (reference) but also with the manner in which the syntactic component of a language allows the expression of cognitive relations (meaning). While the first aspect may be conceptualized as a closed system such as that represented by a dictionary of a language, the second aspect is an open system that cannot be described by a taxonomy of properties or relations. In other words, while it is possible to make an inventory of all the words in a language, it is impossible to make an inventory of all the possible usages of any single word (with the exception perhaps of most function words). An adequate semantic theory must therefore contain at least the following two things: (a) a model of human cognition specifying a finite set of dimensions or features, probably in the form of a generic hierarchy of increasing inclusiveness as we move up the tree, and (b) a set of finite rules (or transformations) specifying the possibilities of manipulations of the elements in the tree. The description of (a) must be a general psychological theory and is made up of "psychological or cognitive universals" as defined by the biological capacity of the human species. The description of (b) must be a cultural and individual psychological theory as defined by individual differences in general intelligence and in personal experiences.

1.1.3 The Acquisition of Syntax

The failure of behavior theory to account in any significant manner for the problem of the acquisition of syntax can be interpreted as stemming from a failure to recognize the complexity of the syntax of language. As long as sentences are viewed as a sequential ordering of words or categories of words and the phenomenon to be explained as a problem in the learning of sequential probabilities of items or classes of items, no meaningful progress can be made. The relations among the following eight sentences taken from Lenneberg (1967, pp. 273-275) illustrate the complexities of the problem to be dealt with:

(1) colorless green ideas sleep furiously
(2) furiously sleep ideas green colorless
(3) occasionally call warfare useless
(4) useless warfare call occasionally
(5) friendly young dogs seem harmless

(6) the fox chases the dog
(7) the dog chases the fox
(8) the dog is chased by the fox

If one compares sentence (1) and (2) it is evident that (1) is grammatical while (2) is not. The difference cannot be entirely in their meaning for, although sentence (1) is more likely to have some meaning than sentence (2), nevertheless sentence (1) will be judged more grammatical than sentence (2) even by the most prosaically inclined person. Nor can it be said that the reason sentence (1) is more grammatical than sentence (2) is that it is more familiar, since both sentences had a frequency of zero until linguists began to use them a short while ago to make the kind of point that is being made here. The ungrammatical string (4) has the same order of parts of speech as the grammatical string (1), namely (adjective + noun + verb + adverb). Similarly, the grammatical and semantically interpretable sentence (3) has the same order of parts of speech as the ungrammatical and semantically uninterpretable string (2), namely (adverb + verb + noun + adjective) [Sentence (3) might occur, as Lenneberg points out, "in an instruction booklet on pacifistic rhetoric" 1967, p. 274]. Consequently, the transitional probability of parts of speech in a sentence cannot account for either their grammaticality or their susceptibility to semantic interpretation. The same is true for the order of morphemes in the sentence as shown by the fact that sentence (5) which is both grammatical and meaningful uses the same order of bound morphemes (-ly, -s, -less) as sentence (2) which is neither grammatical nor meaningful. Sentences (6) and (7) demonstrate that the particular words used offer no clue to the meaning of the sentence. Sentence (8) can be recognized as having the same meaning as sentence (6) even though the order of subject and object is the same as that of sentence (7) showing that directional associations between the ordered elements are irrelevant to the understanding of the sentence.

These various examples should suffice to convince one that the process of acquiring language must involve a much more complex analysis procedure than that offered by such surface relations of sentences as order of elements and word-associations. As if this were not enough, we are confronted with the added complication that the child is continuously exposed to both well-formed and semiformed and semigrammatical sentences in the ordinary speech of adult speakers. Out of this confused input he has to be able to separate the false clues from the correct ones, yet he demonstrates this ability and succeeds in the relatively short period of 24 months (roughly from age one-and-a-half to three-and-a-half). Let us now turn to these newer formulations of child language acquisition.

1.2 FROM BASE TO SURFACE

If we discard earlier theories of language acquisition as unproductive, it is necessary to start anew right from the beginning. The study of the acquisition of grammar usually begins when the child is at about a-year-and-a-half, the time when he begins to use two word combinations. Prior to that it is difficult to study the child's grammatical competence since he uses single words, and techniques have not as yet been developed to study the child's grammatical comprehension at that early age. Speech records of a child over successive periods offer a picture of a changing grammar which the psycholinguist attempts to characterize in formal terms by giving a description of its structure at each period. This approach is necessarily limited since an inference of grammatical competence must be made from the child's speech performance, the latter being affected by a number of variables that are not directly relevant to grammatical competence (e.g., memory span, temporal integration, inattention, etc.). Given this limitation we can nevertheless inquire as to the kind of developmental picture that emerges.

1.2.1 Differentiation of General Classes

Children's earliest utterances of two words (or more) exhibit nonrandom combinations of words. Some examples from the speech of three children reported in the literature are the following (McNeill, 1966, Table 1): *big boy, allgone shoe, two boot, that baby, here pretty.* Distributional analysis of these two-word combinations reveals that the words the child uses at this earliest stage fall into two categories in terms of their privileges of occurrence. One of the two classes contains a small number of words each having a relatively high frequency of occurrence. Examples of this class include *allgone, big, my, see* in one child's speech, *my, two, a, green,* in a second child's speech, and in a third, *this, a, here.* The second class contains a larger number of words and additions of new words to this class occur at a higher rate (some examples are: *beat, Mommy, tinker-toy, come, doed*). Words in this second class occur by themselves or in combination with words from the first class, whereas words in the first class never occur alone. For these reasons the first class was named the *pivot* class (P) while the second class was named the *open* class (O). A shorthand expression of these facts can be represented by the following notation.

$$S \rightarrow (P) + O$$

This notation implies that the child's competence includes a rule which says that a sentence, S, can be produced by combining any two words from class P and class O (in that order) or, alternately, by using any single word from class O. The rule excludes such sentences made up of two words from the same class, or a sentence made up of a single word from the P class.

It is to be noted that the rule[1] for constructing this earliest sentence cannot have been developed as a result of direct mimicking of adult sentences. Many of the two-word combinations that this rule generates are in the wrong order from the point of view of adult speech (e.g., *allgone shoe* vs. the likely adult model of the *shoe* is *allgone*). In addition, it permits combinations that are unlikely to occur in adult speech at all (e.g., *big milk*). Such novel (and non-adult) combinations and the ready substitutability of words within each category are convincing arguments that these word combinations could not be memorized imitations of adult speech.

[1]The concept of a grammatical "rule" as used in generative transformational linguistics in no way implies that the individual is consciously aware of what he is doing. "Rule" is to be understood in its formal (mathematical) sense as an expression that generates a set of operations of defined elements.

Distributional analysis of successive speech records of the children that have been studied shows that the words in the original pivot class begin to subdivide into progressively more differentiated categories in a hierarchical manner that can be represented as follows:

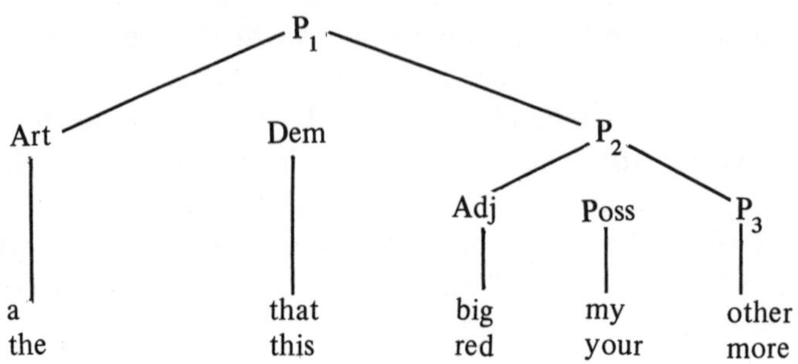

(based on McNeill)

This representation shows that the original pivot class (P_1) subdivided into three classes of words: Articles, Demonstrative Pronouns, and all the rest (P_2). Subsequently P_2 subdivided into three further classes: Adjectives, Possessive Pronouns, and all the rest (P_3).

The implications of this picture are extremely important. Note that there is no logical necessity for the development of grammatical distinctions to assume this particular form of development. The child could have made up categories of words on a trial and error basis, continually rearranging them on the basis of evidence contained in adult speech. He could thus isolate a category of words that correspond to adjectives, or articles, or possessives, until he gradually homes in on the full fledged adult pattern. However, instead of making, as it were, a distributional analysis of adult speech, he seems to have come up with a progressive differentiation strategy that has the peculiar property of being made up of a *generic* class at each point: that is, the original pivot class must already honor in a generic form all the future distinctions at level 2; the undifferentiated pivot class at level 2 (P_2) must contain in a generic form all the future distinctions at level 3, and so on. In other words, the child seems to honor grammatical distinctions in advance of the time they actually develop. How is this possible?

McNeill's conclusion is as bold as it is inevitable: the hierarchy of progressive differentiation of grammatical categories "represents linguistic universals that are part of the child's innate endowment. The role of a universal hierarchy of categories would be to direct the child's discovery of the classes of English. It is as if he were equipped with a set of templates against which he can compare the speech he happens to hear from his parents. . . . We can imagine, then, that a child classifies the random specimens of adult speech he encounters according to universal categories that the speech exemplifies. Since these distinctions are at the top of a hierarchy that has the grammatical classes of English at its bottom, the child is prepared to discover the appropriate set of distinctions" (1966, pp. 35-36).

The assumption of innate language universals is sure to be unacceptable to current behaviorist theories. Someone is bound to point out that one does not explain the *why* of a complex phenomenon by saying it is innate. The fact of the matter is, however, that the complex behavior system of any organism is bound to be dependent upon the structural and functional properties of its nervous system. Language is a product of man's cognition, and, as Lenneberg (1967, p. 334) points out, "man's cognition functions within biologically given limits." Granting the innateness of language universals, we are still left with the task of explaining the *how* of language acquisition. The scientific investigation of language, both from the linguist's and the psycholinguist's point of view, is to give an adequate characterization of the structure of the child's innately endowed "language acquisition device," the nature of its universal categories and their interrelations.

1.2.2 The Development of Transformations

The ability to manipulate transformations constitutes an essential part of linguistic competence according to the linguistic theory developed by Chomsky, and Lenneberg (1967) argues convincingly that transformations are an essential aspect of categorization processes of all biological organisms. An insight into the nature of linguistic transformations can be gained by considering the manner by which the following two sentences are understood by an adult speaker (based on Lenneberg, 1967, pp. 286-292):

(1) they are boring students
(2) the shooting of the hunters was terrible

Both sentences are semantically ambiguous. The ambiguity in sentence (1) can be resolved by a process of "bracketing" which reveals that its constituent elements can be broken up into two different "phrase markers,"[2] as follows:

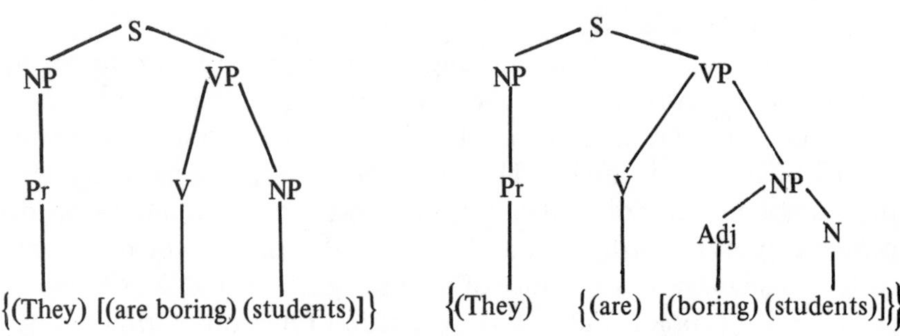

This phrase marker shows that the ambiguity of the sentence lies in the fact that the word *boring* functions in one case as an inflected verb-form, and in the other case, as an adjective modifying the word *students.* Now consider sentence (2): it is ambiguous in at least two ways (one could say that either the hunters need more practice or they need a funeral!). Only one phrase marker description is possible for this sentence, so we need some other process to explain its ambiguity. One interpretation is related to the sentence *hunters shoot inaccurately,* the other, to the sentence *hunters are shot.* The reason we understand the ambiguity of sentence (2) may thus be attributed to the fact that we are able to recognize the relation between it and two other sentences each of which has its own distinct phrase

[2] A phrase marker is simply a graphic representation of the constituents of a sentence. "Bracketing" shown at the bottom of this figure is an alternative method of accomplishing the same thing.

marker. This type of relationship is the essence of transformations: they are laws that control the relations between sentences that have "grammatical affinity."

The early stages of child language competence does not apparently include the ability to perform transformations, according to McNeill (1966) who relates the impetus for acquiring transformations to the cumbersomeness of having to manipulate the elementary forms of sentences in the underlying structure of language ("base strings"). (Since more extensive discussion on the development of transformations is not possible here, the reader is referred to McNeill, 1966, pp. 53-65.)

1.3 IMPLICATIONS FOR SECOND LANGUAGE TEACHING

The view on language acquisition that has been outlined may at first appear frustrating to those whose inclination and business it is to teach language. The claim that a child has achieved linguistic competence by age three-and-a-half is likely to be scoffed at by the elementary school teacher in composition. At the claim that grammatical rules are discovered by the child through linguistic universals, the foreign language teacher is likely to wonder what happened to this marvelous capacity in the foreign language laboratory. In this section I would like to examine the implications for language teaching of the views outlined earlier on the language acquisition process. I shall discuss a number of topics including the role of practice and imitation, the distinction between competence and performance, and the nature of skills involved in foreign language acquisition.

1.3.1 The Role of Practice and Imitation

The assumption that practice plays a crucial role in language acquisition has been central to earlier speculations. To behaviorists it is almost an axiom not to be questioned. This view rests on the basic assertion that there exists a fundamental continuity between language acquisition and the forms of learning studied in the psychological laboratory. Chomsky (1959), Miller (1965), Lenneberg (1967), and others have questioned this view on general grounds and McNeill (1966) questions it on more specific and reduced grounds. If we grant that the language acquisition process is guided by the child's innate knowledge of language universals, does practice theory explain how children go about finding out the locally appropriate expression of the linguistic universals?

Practice theory leads to two possible hypotheses about language acquisition: one is that when the child is exposed to a novel grammatical form he imitates it; the other is that by practicing this novel form, he *stamps it in.* The evidence available indicates that both hypotheses are false. A direct test of children's tendency (or ability) to imitate adult forms of speech shows that children almost never repeat the adult sentence as it is presented. A child does not readily "mimic" a grammatical form that is not already in his repertoire as evidenced by his own spontaneous utterances. Direct attempts by the child at imitation of adult sentences end up as recodings, as the following examples taken from Lenneberg (1967, p. 316) illustrate:

Model Sentence	*Child's Repetition*
Johnny is a good boy.	Johnny is good boy.
He takes them for a walk.	He take them to the walk.
Lassie does not like the water.	He no like the water.
Does Johnny want a cat?	Johnny wants a cat?

It has been estimated that only about ten percent of a child's *imitations* of adult speech are *grammatically progressive,* that is, embody a form novel to the child.

Whatever the means by which novel forms enter the child's speech, does practice strengthen these responses? The evolution of the child's command of the past tense of verbs provides negative evidence to this question. In the child's early language the past tense of the irregular strong verbs in English (*came, went, sat*) appears with high frequency relative to the regularized /d/ and /t/ forms of the weak verbs. Thus, we would expect that these much practiced irregular forms would be highly stable, more so than the regular forms. Yet evidence shows that they are in fact less stable than the less practiced regular form, because at a certain point in the child's development he suddenly abandons the irregular form in favor of the regularized form and produces *comed, goed, sitted.* This kind of discontinuity shows that the practice model is not applicable here; rules that the child discovers are more important and carry greater weight than practice. Concept attainment and hypothesis testing are more likely paradigms in language development than response strength through rote memory and repetition.

This realization ought not to lead us to pessimism about the potential usefulness of language *teaching.* There is strong evidence that the attainment of grammatical rules can be facilitated by proper presentation of speech materials. Observation of children's speech during play interaction with an adult (usually the mother) shows that up to half of their imitations of adult expansions of children's speech are grammatically progressive (McNeill, citing data by Slobin, 1966, p. 75). An expansion is an adult's *correction* of the child's utterance. The advantage expansions seem to hold over other samples of adult speech may be attributable to the fact that expansions exemplify a locally appropriate expression of a linguistic universal at a time when the child is most ready to notice such a distinction. For example, if the child says *Adam cry,* and the mother expands this by saying, *Yes, Adam cried* (or *Yes, Adam is crying*—depending on her understanding of what the child intends), the child is thereby given the opportunity to discover the specific manner in which the past tense form (or progressive form) is expressed in English at a time when this distinction is maximally salient to him. The faster development of language in children of middle-class educated parents may be attributable to a tendency on the part of these mothers to expand to a greater extent than other parents. However, this hypothesis needs further investigation.

1.3.2 On the Distinction between Competence and Performance

This distinction has been recognized by all psychological theories, including behavioristic ones (see Hull's, 1943, distinction between $_SH_R$ and $_SE_R$). A confusion that may arise in language behavior comes from the fact that *understanding* is usually (if not always) superior to *speaking* and one might want to equate understanding with competence and speaking with performance. However, this cannot be the case. Both understanding and speaking must be viewed as instances of performance since the nonlinguistic factors that affect speaking (e.g., memory span, temporal integration, inattention, etc.) are equally likely to affect understanding. We are thus confronted with the fact that one type of performance, understanding, appears to develop before another type of performance, speaking. What may be responsible for this?

McNeill (1966) examines the specific claim that every grammatical feature appears first in understanding and second in speaking and is led to the conclusion that the overall parameters of conversion from competence to performance are simpler, easier, and less complex in the case of understanding. In order to account for this fact he postulates three kinds of memory span of different size or length, in the following order of decreasing magnitude: phonological production, grammatical comprehension, and grammatical production. He postulates these kinds to account for some data by Fraser, Bellugi, and Brown (1963) showing that a child can repeat a longer sentence than it can either understand or produce spontaneously, and also that it can understand a longer sentence than it can produce spontaneously. The difficulty with McNeill's hypothesis is that it equates sentence length with sentence complexity. It would seem that it is easier to understand a long but simple sentence than a short but involved one. It would also appear that one can understand a sentence too long to be repeated. Children show evidence of having understood sentences they cannot (or will not) repeat (see Lenneberg, 1967, p. 316). The problem may be conceptualized in a different way, as illustrated by the following diagram:

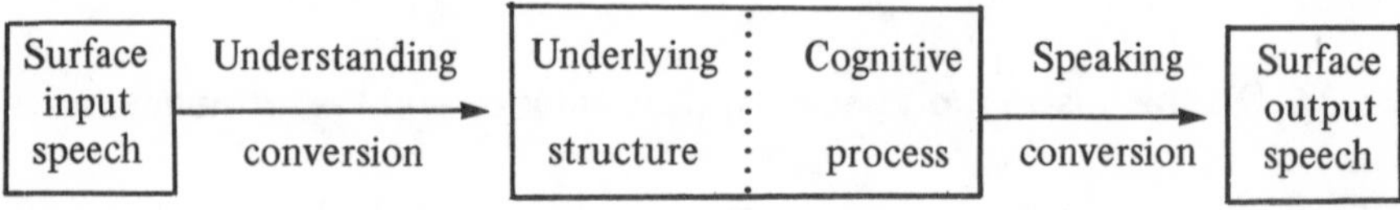

The asymmetry between the capacity to perform the understanding conversion as opposed to the speaking conversion may be related to the fact that the former requires an analytic approach while the latter demands a synthetic capability. It may be that for humans analytic processes are easier than synthetic ones. One might say that it is easier to learn the art critic's job than the artist's.

1.3.3 The Acquisition of Foreign Language Skills

Let us raise the question of the specific relevance of our discussion on first language acquisition for an understanding of second language learning and teaching. What are the parallels to be considered? First, let us look at the argument for the differences. Assuming second language acquisition which takes place after the age of four, one may point out the following: (a) the individual's cognitive development is at a later and more advanced stage; (b) he is already in possession of the grammatical structure of a language which may serve to facilitate the acquisition of a second one through transfer; (c) he already possesses concepts and meanings, the problem now being one of expressing them through a new vocabulary.

The importance of the first argument would seem to depend on the relevance of cognitive development for the acquisition of language. The view outlined in this paper is that the necessary knowledge for language acquisition cannot be gained from experience with the outside world and that language acquisition is dependent on an innate endowment which constitutes the knowledge of language universals. Hence the imputed advantage of advanced age and cognitive development is a dubious proposition. The two other arguments are based on the assumption of the operation of transfer in grammatical structure and in reference (vocabulary). What is the evidence in support of this assumption? It is necessary to distinguish between two claims about transfer theory. One refers to the general expectation that new forms of learning do not go on independently of what the organism has learned before. The truth of this statement would seem fairly obvious and need not concern us further. The second and specific claim expresses the expectation that the learning of certain specific and identifiable elements in Task B is facilitated (or hindered) by the previous learning of certain specific and identifiable elements in Task A. The status of this strong claim for any type of complex learning outside the laboratory is unknown. A serious test of it in second language acquisition would require the prior analysis of the two languages in a form which would identify the specific elements to be transferred at the grammatical and lexical levels. On *a priori* grounds we would expect negative transfer as much as positive transfer, assuming that transfer is relevant to the problem. Carroll (1966b) claims that the Modern Language Aptitude Test designed for English speakers predicts success in a foreign language equally well regardless of the particular language involved. This fact is difficult to explain if transfer has any overall relevance to the language acquisition process. Nevertheless, some phonological studies on contrastive analysis reviewed by Carroll would seem to indicate the operation of negative transfer effects. He cites Suppes et al. (1962) who "claim to be able to predict quite precisely from mathematical learning theory what [phoneme] discrimination problems will arise" (Carroll, 1966a, p. 16).

The problem is complicated still further by the possibility that transfer effects might affect performance and competence factors in different ways. Or the various performance factors themselves (understanding, speaking, reading, writing) may be affected to different degrees. The same comment might be made for different levels of performance, that is phonology, vocabulary, and syntax. A further aspect to this problem is the consideration of whether transfer effects are necessary processes or whether the extent of their operation is dependent on the strategy with which the learner attacks the new task. An individual who tries to "fit in" the dimensions of the new task into the old structure may encounter different problems from the individual who inhibits the interaction of the two tasks, if we assume that the latter strategy is possible. Finally, the fact that it is possible to predict errors of confusion, as in contrastive analysis of phonology, is not necessarily an indication that transfer effects will operate in the acquisition of the new task. Thus, the fact that the [l] and [r] sounds are predictable areas of confusion for a Japanese learning English says nothing about the way in which he will eventually learn the distinction. It is unlikely that this distinction is learned in isolation. Instead, it is more likely that the confusion will disappear when the overall structure of English phonology is internalized. (For a more extensive discussion on transfer see Chapter 4 Section 4-7.)

The above considerations lead to a number of implications for the teaching of a second language which I shall now take up.

1.3.4 Teaching the Knowledge of Structure

Since it is clear that knowledge of language at all levels consists of knowing patterns of relations rather than constituent elements, the usefulness of efforts to teach the latter is in doubt. Examples of such efforts include teaching specific sound discriminations, *shaping* phonological production, increasing vocabulary through association of translation equivalents, and practicing specific morphological and inflectional examples. Pointing to individuals who successfully acquired a foreign language in a course using these methods has no force of argument, for it is quite possible that their success occurred despite these methods rather than because of them.

1.3.5 Teaching Successful Strategies of Acquisition

Carroll (1962) has isolated a number of factors which are predictive of success in a foreign language. These factors may offer clues about the strategies that a successful learner uses with the possibility that such strategies may be taught to those who normally make no use of them. One of the abilities Carroll has identified deals with verbalization of grammatical relations in sentences. The successful foreign language learner is apparently capable of the following task: given a word italicized in one sentence (e.g., "The man went into the *house.*") he can identify that word in another sentence which has the same grammatical function (e.g., picking one of the italicized words of the following sentence: "The *church* next to the *bowling alley* will be built in a new *location* next *year.*"). We know of course that the individual is capable of recognizing the grammatical relations in the second sentence (otherwise he could not give it a semantic interpretation), so the ability must be one of explicit verbalization of implicitly known rules and relations. Verbalizing a grammatical relation can take two forms; one refers to the type of statement that can be found in a grammar book that includes technical terms (relative clause, head noun, modifier, predicate phrase, etc.); the second refers to a statement of equivalence or relation expressed in any convenient way using whatever terms are available to the individual, whether technically correct or not. The teaching of such verbalizations therefore ought to facilitate foreign language acquisition.

Another variable identified by Carroll "is the ability to 'code' auditory phonetic material in such a way that this material can be recognized, identified and remembered over something longer than a few seconds" (1962, p. 128). We do not know at present the specific strategy that may be employed in facilitating this kind of coding. Whatever the strategy may be, it seems unlikely that the superior person in this task derives his advantage from a special innate capacity. In the first place the strategy is not related to the ability to perceive phonetic distinctions, and second, given the biological foundations of language capacity (see Lenneberg, 1967), we would not expect innate differences in the general capacity of coding phonological material.

Contrastive analysis of grammatical structure would not seem to offer particular advantages beyond those provided by verbalization of grammatical relations and by attention to a grammatical distinction at a time of saliency (see the effects of *expansion,* discussed above). The expectation that the advantage of contrastive analysis lies in making the contrast per se is based on an assumption of transfer for which evidence is lacking. At any rate the pointing up of the *contrast* may just as well lead to negative transfer by facilitating the assimilation (or "fitting in") strategy. I know of no evidence that emphasizing distinctions of incompatible responses, especially those that are automatized, leads to a decrease in incompatibility.

1.3.6 Teaching Habit Integration and Automaticity

Temporal integration of phonological skills, both of understanding and production, is a problem independent of the knowledge of the phonological structure and transformations of a language. It would seem likely that sensory and motor integrations of this type can be automatized through practice and repetition. The more interesting problem would relate to the time at which automaticity practice is likely to be valuable and to the form it is to take. Reading represents a different aspect of phonological production skill than speaking, as is well known, and practice in reading does not represent a sufficient or necessary condition for achieving automaticity of phonological production in speaking.

The factors that enter into the problem of automatizing grammatical habits are not very clear. Tests of speech comprehension under conditions of noise (see for example Spolsky et al., 1966) seem to be quite sensitive to the level of automaticity and degree of integration achieved by a foreign language speaker. They show that the problem of integration goes deeper than high proficiency in understanding and speaking demonstrated under ordinary conditions. At the moment we do not have available a psychological theory of sentence understanding or production. The relevance to this problem of recent experiments on latency of various grammatical manipulations still remains to be shown. Many language teachers seem to be convinced that pattern drills serve to automatize grammatical habits. However, it is difficult to justify this expectation on theoretical grounds. I have already argued that the semantic interpretation of a sentence cannot be viewed as a process of sequential analysis of categories of words. Thus, pattern drills, at best, can serve only to automatize phonological production skills, and for this latter purpose other methods may prove equally, if not more effective. At any rate, if the pattern drill argument is taken literally, namely that the structure is automatized through practice of the specific pattern that is being repeated, then the learner could never achieve automatized speech. This consequence must follow since in ordinary speech we use an infinite variety of patterns, and therefore, since the second language learner could not possibly be drilled on an infinite variety of patterns, he could never develop automatized speech. Hence pattern drill cannot possibly do what it is supposed to do.

From a theoretical point of view the development of grammatical competence should be facilitated by getting the learner to perform a set of transformations on families of sentences (e.g., *I cannot pay my rent because I am broke; if I weren't broke I could pay my rent; Given the fact that I have no money, I cannot pay my rent; How do you think I could possibly pay my rent if I am broke; Since*

I am broke, the rent cannot be paid; To pay the rent is impossible given the fact that I have no money; etc.). The distinction between this exercise, which we may refer to as perhaps a "transformation exercise," and "pattern drill" is that the first deals with the competence involved in deep structure while the second focuses on surface structure. Rutherford (1968) has shown that surface structure similarities are completely unenlightening as to the semantic interpretation of sentences.

The notion of transformation exercises is equally applicable to phonology and vocabulary. Exercises in vocabulary transformations are more difficult to specify at this stage of our knowledge, but from our earlier discussion of meaning we can perhaps anticipate giving the student a task of this kind: "Change the following list of words using the gender transformation: *boy, father, bull,*"–which might yield: "*girl, mother, cow.*" Other examples might include asking the student to give opposites, similars, subordinates, superordinates, and so on, in a restricted word-association task. Semantic relations of this kind may be responsible for the well known psychological fact that in memory words are organized in clusters (see, for example, Deese, 1965).

1.3.7 On Semigrammatical Sentences

The fluent speech of most native speakers does not consist totally (or even in the majority of instances) of well formed sentences. One would imagine that the imposition of a requirement to utter exclusively well formed sentences would seriously hinder the fluency of most native speakers. The logical implication of this observation would be that no language teacher should ever force his pupils to use only well formed sentences in practice conversation whether it be in the classroom, laboratory or outside. This conclusion is not as odd as it might seem at first sight. After all, children seem to acquire the competence to produce well formed sentences despite the semigrammaticality of the adult speech to which they are continually exposed. It is important to note that semigrammaticality does not mean randomness. The reason that in most instances we are able to give a semantic interpretation to semigrammatical sentences lies in the fact that we have the capacity to relate these semisentences to their well formed equivalents. There must therefore exist lawful transformations between semisentences and well formed ones. We are able to understand the speech of children for the same reason: the grammar of their utterances is generic of the later grammar of well formed sentences. If it were not so, we would not be able to expand (hence understand) their utterances.

An important question poses itself at this juncture: should second language teaching take specific account of the developmental stages that are likelv to mark the acquisition of a language? By "specific account" I mean at least the following two propositions: First, to recognize and allow the production of semisentences on the part of the learner; and second, to expose the learner to utterances which are grammatically progressive at each stage but which fall short of having the full complexity of well-formed sentences. The first proposition may already be the policy in some modern and intensive courses which encourage active speech production "at any *cost*" [sic]. The second proposition is sure to be resisted by most teachers; yet the fact of the matter is that all *natural* language acquisition situations expose the learner to semigrammatical sentences more often than not. We do not know whether these are facilitative or retarding situations. Some parents tend to talk to their children by attempting to imitate their speech and it is sometimes said that this kind of "baby talk" retards acquisition. The evidence on this point is lacking. It may be of course that the fastest method of acquiring a second language need not be one that replicates the conditions existing under *natural* language acquisition. In fact various claims for highly intensive language courses followed by individuals with high foreign language aptitude put the time requirement for the acquisition of a foreign language at between 250 and 500 hours of study (Carroll, 1966a, b). Compare this figure with a minimum estimate of 3,000 hours for first language acquisition. This rough figure is arrived at by estimating the total waking hours of a child up to age three-and-a-half and taking thirty percent of that as an estimate of the amount of exposure to language. Of course the two situations are not directly comparable and the level of competence achieved may be different (especially by measures of automaticity and background noise, see Spolsky, et al, 1966); nevertheless, the comparison highlights the fact that certain aspects of the *natural* rate of language acquisition process can be greatly accelerated. It is important to note that although the language acquisition capacity per se must be viewed as an innate capability shared by all members of the species, the *rate* at which language is acquired, especially a second language, and the effectiveness with which language is used as a *communicative process* are performance factors that are affected by individual differences within the species (variations in general intelligence, in experiences, in physical health, in motivation, etc.). It is here that the concept of *teaching* may assume its full importance.

1.4 SUMMARY AND COMMENTS

Traditional psychological theories about language acquisition emphasize the role of reinforcement provided by environmental agencies and view language as a set of vocal habits that are conditioned to stimuli in the environment. Imitation and practice of new forms are the processes by which language behavior develops and generalization of learned forms is supposed to account for the novel uses of language. Recent developments in linguistics have influenced our conception of the structure of language, hence the nature of the knowledge that the child has to acquire. A radically new psycholinguistic theory of language acquisition has been proposed which emphasizes the developmental nature of the language acquisition process and attributes to the child specific innate competencies which guide his discovery of the rules of the natural language to which he is exposed. Imitation, practice, reinforcement, and generalization are no longer considered theoretically productive conceptions in language acquisition. The implications of these new ideas for the teaching of a second language lie in the need for controlled exposure of the student to linguistic materials in a manner that will facilitate his discovery of the significant features of the language. "Shaping" of phonological skills, discrimination training on sound "units" and pattern drills are rejected in favor of "transformation exercises" at the phonological, syntactic and semantic levels.

Probably the most controversial aspect of this chapter is the argument that "pattern drill cannot possibly do what it is supposed to do." The usual claim of the audiolinguist is that mere repetitive practice of patterns is sufficient for acquiring grammatical structure through a process of inductive reasoning subsequently followed by generalization to related patterns. This is essentially a one-factor theory of learning that proceeds from surface to base. This theory is rejected in favor of a two-factor acquisition theory that is composed of the following two steps: (a) the discovery of the underlying structure of the language by means of inductive and deductive inferences guided by (i) innate grammatical universals and (ii) sample linguistic data which are sentences and semisentences in the second language; (b) the automatization of the phonological surface transformations of this underlying knowledge through practice. Note that in step (a) exposure to the linguistic data is not a sufficient condition for acquiring the structure. Furthermore, at any one time in the acquisition process only those linguistic data will be relevant which are needed to test whatever particular hypothesis about underlying structure the learner is working on: the teacher cannot control the inference process directly by choosing the relevant linguistic data since he has no access to the learner's inferencing process (neither does the learner, since the process is unconscious). Note also that the automatization of speaking and understanding can come only *after* knowledge of the structure has been acquired. Thus, practicing sentence patterns whose structure is not yet understood would seem to be useless. In addition, the type of practice that leads to automatization in speaking is not repetition of sentence patterns *given* to the learner, but rather the phonological surface actualization of base sentences the individual produces *himself*.

This two-factor theory of language acquisition implies a very different teaching approach from that dictated by the audiolingual habit theory approach. First, it suggests that the learner should be exposed to the *full range* of linguistic data right from the beginning so as to give him maximum opportunity to test out his inferences about the underlying structure of the language. Second, he should be encouraged to produce any sentence, even if "incorrect," to enable him to practice phonological surface transformations of base strings; "correction" of such semisentences by the teacher is helpful only when they represent "expansions," as discussed in this chapter in connection with first language acquisition. Third, drills and exercises are of dubious utility unless they represent attempts to communicate freely (as opposed to practicing a grammatical rule artificially).

It would be extremely difficult (in my opinion impossible) to demonstrate "experimentally" the correctness of the two-factor theory over the audiolingual habit theory, but there are both empirical and theoretical considerations which argue persuasively to that effect. First, there is the evidence (see Chapter 2) which shows that the audiolingual method has failed to produce meaningful foreign language achievement in the vast majority of students exposed to it. Second, the two-factor theory appears to be a more correct description of what goes on under natural conditions of language acquisition, whether first or second. Third, intensive language courses, which follow the implications of a two-factor theory more closely than those of the one-factor theory, have been consistently successful in their goals of teaching communicative skills. Fourth, the recent developments in linguistic theory and the empirical work on language acquisition in children, as reviewed in this chapter, are consistent with the two-factor theory while they specifically deny the assumptions underlying the audiolingual habit theory. In the last analysis it will not be a *proof* that will resolve this argument but the realization on the part of language teachers that teaching methods which do not work should be abandoned.

Attacks on the audiolingual method, such as this one and others as well, have generated heated counterattacks on the part of devotees who have committed a life time of work to the method and feel that without "definitive proof" it should not be abandoned. Unfortunately, in the heat of this polemical debate we have allowed ourselves to be drawn into a power struggle of clashing personalities and personal threat to established power structures. Surely the proponents of the audiolingual method are not to be personally blamed for the inefficacy of their approach to Foreign Language (FL) teaching. At the time it became entrenched in the profession, it did seem to be the best possible strategy, and the proponents deserve credit for the forthrightness and purity with which the approach was developed and applied. But educational practices, no less than scientific theories, continually evolve and there are no absolute "truths." It is thanks to the consistency and purity with which the audiolingual method has been steadfastly applied that it has been possible to test out its ultimate inefficacy and which made it possible now to move on to something potentially better. And when these newer ideas are eventually put into practice and found wanting, as surely they must be, we will be able to move on to still other, hopefully better, approaches. Let us not forget that our goals coincide in the highest interest of the pupils in our charge—the effective teaching of FLs.

Chapter 2

PSYCHOLOGICAL AND PHYSIOLOGICAL ASPECTS OF FOREIGN LANGUAGE LEARNING

The amount of effort that is being expended in the teaching of foreign languages in this country has reached considerable proportions. According to various surveys conducted by the Modern Language Association of America, 80 per cent of public secondary schools offered FL courses in 1965 and more than one out of every four senior high school students were engaged in the study of a FL (Willbern, 1968). Some predictions estimate that by 1970 roughly half of all public school pupils will be engaged in the study of a language other than English. Most of the large universities in the country have either a college entrance requirement in their Liberal Arts and Sciences Schools or a college graduation requirement involving a FL.

There are powerful social pressures for the maintenance of such a large educational investment in the teaching of a second language which go beyond the traditional goals of FL study stated in terms of promoting the "cultured person." According to the 1966 Statistical Abstract of the United States there were in 1960 close to 24 million Americans in the category labelled "Native of foreign or mixed parentage," of which almost 10 million are foreign born. Over 18 million Americans claim that their mother tongue is not English (Fishman, 1966a). Considerable social effort is expended within a non-English medium of communication: over 500 periodicals are published regularly (including 61 daily newspapers); some 1,500 radio stations broadcast in a FL for several hours a week; there are approximately 2,000 ethnically affiliated schools of which more than half offer mother tongue (i.e., non-English) instruction; there exist at least 1,800 ethnic cultural organizations most of which favor maintenance of their FL (Fishman, 1966a).

An assessment of the present level of technology for teaching a second language is extremely difficult. Depending on the students involved, the available time for teaching, and the larger social context within which the instruction program is embedded, variable results have been achieved. On the higher end of success the results are impressive: with preselected students for high motivation and high FL aptitude placed in an intensive program of instruction involving anywhere from 6 to 14 hours of directed and individual study a day, day after day, meaningful levels of proficiency (e.g., fluent conversation with natives) can be insured within 30 to 40 days according to some lower estimates (Carroll, 1963) or six months according to some higher estimates (Mueller, 1967). Intermediate levels of success are achieved with FL majors in colleges (Carroll, 1967) where after several years of concentrated study audiolingual skills remain generally low. Much more modest levels of success are to be found in the massive educational effort of FL teaching in our high schools where the indications are that most of the students involved do not reach meaningful levels of proficiency.

In one sense the technology of teaching FL's has been solved. Given motivated and talented individuals we have the "know-how" to expose the individual to an instructional procedure that insures the learning of any FL within a matter of weeks or months. The fact that this success is limited to a preselected sample of individuals should not lead us to minimize this pedagogical achievement. It is far better than we knew how prior to the new techniques developed since World War II and it is comparable, and perhaps even superior, to most industrial training programs designed to impart skills of a much lesser complexity.

On the other hand, and from a quite different perspective, our ability to train successfully the multitudes of students in our public schools in the use of a FL is considerably less and by all indications does not compare favorably to the pedagogical achievements of teaching the three "R's." This sobering assessment is apparently shared by members of society at large: parents, students, school administrators, legislators responsible for appropriating educational funds, educators not directly involved in the teaching of FL's, all are increasingly engaged in asking a persistent and disturbing question: Why should so much effort be spent on the teaching of FL's when the results appear to be so meager? In a recent Gallup Poll Survey parents consistently expressed the opinion that FL courses represent the weakest part of the school curriculum and should be the first to go in any curtailment of efforts. There are signs that the largesse of federal grant assistance to the FL teaching effort is being tempered along with the general slow down of federal support for research and an increasing number of universities are "liberalizing" their FL requirements, which is to say, reducing them at both the undergraduate and graduate levels. One might say that the FL instruction establishment has been put in a defensive position. It must come up with good answers to the baffling problem that besets it today: How is FL instruction to be made more successful and more relevant to the aspirations of the "New Student" in an educational setting that competes for his attention and time?

The responses to this challenge are likely to come along three levels. First, on the technological side, better trained teachers using more advanced techniques (including both "hardware" and "software") are to come on the scene. Second, FL's are to be taught increasingly earlier (cf., FLES efforts: Foreign Language for the Elementary School) affording more cumulative time for study. Third, increasing efforts are to be made to improve the motivation of students by recognizing the social-psychological implications of FL study and taking into account the attitudinal and sociological matrix within which FL study and maintenance are embedded in the larger societal, national, and world contexts.

This chapter attempts to organize the main facts that have come to be known about the physiology and psychology of FL learning as they impinge upon the three-pronged attack of the problem just discussed. The main issues to be dealt with can be summarized as follows:

1. Theory and Practice in FL Teaching: Out of Step. This section examines the problem of how research efforts come to influence teaching practices. Several statements by authoritative persons and organized bodies (e.g., The Modern Language Association or MLA) concerning the "state of the art" of FL teaching are to be summarized and reviewed. The conclusion that will be presented will stress the fact that most of what we know about teaching comes not from the experimental laboratory but from the teacher's experience in the classroom. Here, as in other areas of education, practical knowledge by far outstrips the specific contribution of organized research. Given the relatively backward condition of social science and educational research, this state of affairs is unavoidable and though it is pointless to criticize it, this situation should nevertheless be clearly and explicitly recognized.

2. What is it to "Know a Language?" Everyone accepts the notion that language is a means of communication, but there is much less agreement about just what is involved in the ability to communicate. The distinction between "linguistic competence" and "communicative competence" is either not explicitly taken into account in the majority of FL courses or it is tacitly assumed that the former must precede the latter in such a way that a certain high level of linguistic competence must be achieved before attempting the functional use of the FL. Arguments will be presented which show the harmful consequences of this practice. "Liberated expression" and the practical use of a FL is both desirable and possible at even the very beginning stages of study. A new attitude to the assessment of communicative skills (rather than language skills) is long overdue in the language testing field.

3. The Physiology of Second Language Learning. Current efforts at FLES are often justified on the grounds that there is a biological timetable for language learning which makes it increasingly difficult to learn a second language after puberty at which time the brain allegedly loses "plasticity." The discussion in this section will question the validity of this argument and will examine other grounds for both the advantages and disadvantages of early versus late FL teaching.

4. Motivational Aspects of FL Study. The importance of the problem of knowing how to motivate the FL learner has been mentioned. This section will examine a number of issues relating to this pressing need: (a), the consequences of the fact that becoming bilingual entails becoming bicultural; (b), the attitude of the student towards FL study generally, the goals and purposes which he sees in it.

5. Summary and Conclusions. This final section will attempt to summarize the major points that are discussed in this chapter and will offer some thoughts on some possible and desirable developments in the FL teaching field that may take place in the immediate future.

2.1 THEORY AND PRACTICE IN FL TEACHING: OUT OF STEP

2.1.1 Current Theories and Practices

Two basic truths about the psychology of human learning are (a), that it is amazingly efficient and powerful—by such standards as the learning capacities of other living organisms or man-made automata and (b), that this learning goes on in ways that neither the individual learner nor the educator or social scientist can describe or explicate even in elementary and simplistic terms. Two outstanding instances which illustrate both truths are (i), the learning of a language and (ii), the learning of a culture during socialization or acculturation. Concepts such as "stimulus," "response," "reinforcement," "habit," which social scientists have invented to account for these accomplishments of the individual have such weak explanatory power that even in much simpler learning situations, such as a rat running a maze, they allow for such inadequate and impotent descriptions that psychologists in a narrow field of specialization disagree about them. The weakest aspect about these "scientific explanations" is that they attempt to describe the learning process through concepts that refer to external events (stimuli, responses, schedules of reinforcement, etc.), whereas what obviously accounts for the process is the internal mechanism of the brain, the capacities and workings of the human mind. (Jakobovits, 1968c).

Theories about the mind, theories about knowledge (as distinguished from theories about behavior), theories about capacities, about potentialities and competencies, have been proposed by many writers over the course of modern scientific history, but these occupy the back seat to the leading theories in the social sciences. The most influential and widespread approach to psychological explanation remains in the United States today, in education (cf., programed instruction), in clinical psychology (cf., behavior modification), in much of experimental psychology (cf., verbal conditioning), that of Skinnerian operant conditioning of behavior. The latter is widely claimed as being *sound* and *tough-minded* in research, while theories of the mind are presented to graduate students and future researchers in a shadowy and not quite respectable light; they are *soft, nonrigorous, wishy washy.*

In the field of FL teaching the trend is notably the same. The recent book by Wilga Rivers (1964), *The Psychologist and the Foreign-Language Teacher,* is often cited as the most advanced scientific achievement in the field. While Dr. Rivers herself shows awareness of the theoretical shortcomings of the *habit* approach to language, many language teachers are not so cautious: they take the *habit* notion of the audiolingual approach quite literally, deriving much self-assurance from the *scientific* and *rigorous* pretentiousness of concepts such as stimulus, response, conditioning, and the automatic establishment of habits.

This is a strange situation, indeed. Teachers and therapists are practical people by necessity and they ought not to be castigated for adopting methods which seem to work. The two most notable and successful accomplishments achieved by the Skinnerians are programed instruction and behavioral modification, yet the theoretical foundations from which they have sprung are simplistic and inadequate in the extreme (see Chomsky, 1969; Lashley, 1951; Lenneberg, 1967). This is a curious paradox wherein surely lies the bankruptcy of the modern social scientific enterprise: what seems to work best on practical grounds, should not, it seems on theoretical grounds, and the theories that appear to be more sophisticated and more powerful do not enable us to develop effective practical approaches. It would seem to be a betrayal of the intellectual spirit to accept that which works when it should not, yet it would be folly to reject that which works merely because on theoretical grounds it ought not.

The resolution of this difficulty would seem to lie in a change of attitude on the part of both the theorist and the practitioner. On the one hand today's theorist should give up any claim that his speculations have the scientific authority whereby he can make infallible pronouncements about the solution of practical problems. On the other hand the practitioner should give up his attempt to justify his activities in the classroom and clinic by appealing to competing *scientific* theories often outdated by the time the practitioner gets hold of them. Careful thinkers have recognized the abyss that separates theory from practice. Skinner himself has consistently claimed for over a quarter of a century that his concern is with behavior not with theory, and it is only when he strays into the morass of theoretical justification (as in some parts of his book on *Verbal Behavior,* 1957) that the shortcomings of his system become so apparent (see Jakobovits, 1968c, 1966b). One of the most authoritative experts in the area of learning has recently stated that "thus far, there is little empirical evidence in support of [the] assumption [that] forgetting outside the laboratory is a function of the same variables and represents the same processes as are observed in formal studies on interserial interference" (Postman, 1961, p. 166). In the area of language Chomsky (1968) stated that there is no evidence today in support of the view that the scientific endeavour will ever be successful in explicating the fundamental facts. Integrity dictates that we clearly recognize the inherent limitations of the social and behavioral sciences as we know them today and not to claim for them more than is reasonable.

When this limitation is accepted, as it surely must be, then the interplay between theoretical and practical concerns can become more honest and possibly more rewarding. Experimenters can tackle practical problems by relaxing their unrealistic insistence on experimental controls and statistically *adequate* designs. Practitioners such as the teacher and the therapist need not feel the need to take sides in theoretical controversies or to justify their practices by appealing to particular theories; instead, they can adopt a healthy functional attitude concerning the effects of their methods of approach, *concentrating on developing and constantly using realistic evaluation criteria that would dictate maintaining or altering their activities in accord with the results they achieve.* In subsequent sections of this chapter, such an attitude will be repeatedly advocated.

2.1.2 The Audiolingual Method

The most widespread method of FL teaching today, the so-called "New Key" approach prevalent since the 1940's, is the audiolingual approach which claims to have largely displaced the earlier *traditional* method of grammar-translation. The proponents of the audiolingual approach base their claim of correctness on *sound* psychological theory as well as on efficient results. The purpose of this section is to show that both of these claims are questionable. In the following quotation an eminent figure in the FL field questions the first of these claims:

> "Let me point out that neither the audiolingual habit theory nor the cognitive code-learning theory is closely linked to any contemporary psychological theory of learning. The audiolingual habit theory has a vague resemblance to an early version of a Thorndikean association theory, while the cognitive code-learning theory is reminiscent of certain contemporary gestaltist movements in psychology which emphasize the importance of perceiving the "structure" of what is to be learned, without really relying on such movements. Actually, neither theory takes adequate account of an appreciable body of knowledge that has accumulated in the study of verbal learning. Among these facts are the following:
>
> a. The frequency with which an item is practiced per se is not so crucial as the frequency with which it is contrasted with other items with which it may be confused. Thus, the learning of items in *pattern-practice* drills would be improved if instead of simple repetition there were a constant alternation among varied patterns.
>
> b. The more meaningful the material to be learned, the greater the facility in learning and retention. The audiolingual habit theory tends to play down meaningfulness in favor of producing automaticity.
>
> c. Other things being equal, materials presented visually are more easily learned than comparable materials presented aurally. Even though the objective of teaching may be the attainment of mastery over

the auditory and spoken components of language learning, an adequate theory of language learning should take account of how the student handles visual counterparts of the auditory elements he is learning and help to prescribe the optimal utilization of these counterparts, such as printed words, phonetic transcriptions, and other visual-symbol systems.

d. In learning a skill it is often the case that conscious attention to its critical features and understanding of them will facilitate learning. This principle is largely ignored by the audiolingual habit theory; it is recognized by the cognitive code-learning theory. It would imply, for example, that in teaching pronunciation an explanation of necessary articulatory movements would be helpful.

e. The more numerous kinds of association that are made to an item, the better are learning and retention. Again this principle seems to dictate against the use of *systems* of language teaching that employ mainly one sensory modality, namely, hearing. A recent experiment performed at the Defense Language Institute, West Coast Branch (Army Language School, Monterey, California) seems to show that dramatic facilitation of language learning occurs when words denoting concrete objects and physical actions are associated with actual *motor* performances involving those objects and actions. Thus, the student learns the meaning of the foreign language word for *jump* by actually jumping! Language teaching becomes a sort of physical exercise both for the students and for the instructor whose actions they imitate.

These then are a few examples of theory-derived principles that, if further examined and verified, could contribute to more effective ways of teaching foreign languages. It would be trite to say at this point that 'more research is needed,' although it is obviously the case. Actually, what is needed even more than research is a profound rethinking of current theories of foreign language teaching in the light of contemporary advances in psychological and psycholinguistic theory. The audiolingual habit theory which is so prevalent in American foreign language teaching was, perhaps, fifteen years ago in step with the state of psychological thinking at that time, but it is no longer abreast of recent developments. It is ripe for major revision, particularly in the direction of joining with it some of the better elements of the cognitive code-learning theory. I would venture to predict that if this can be done, then teaching based on the revised theory will yield a dramatic change in effectiveness." (Carroll, 1966a, pp. 104-106).

Carroll's statement agrees with the assessment that theory and practice in FL teaching are out of step but he appears to believe that "contemporary advances in psychological and psycholinguistic theory" are necessarily relevant to FL teaching. As stated earlier, there are no good grounds for such optimism. Note that the five *facts* which he reviews and which he urges the FL teacher to consider are in the nature of empirical generalizations not theoretically derived principles. His call for "more research" can be welcomed as long as it is understood that this is to refer to efforts in the development of evaluation criteria of the effectiveness of teaching practices in terms of functional or terminal behaviors on the part of the learner (What can the learner *do* with the knowledge he has acquired?).

2.1.3 Experiments

There are two principal reasons for the weakness of currently known and practiced experimental techniques: the difficulty (practical impossibility) of controlling a large number of simultaneously varying and interacting factors and the fact that the individual's learning strategy is largely independent of the teacher's manipulative efforts even though it is a factor that greatly influences the learning process.

With respect to the first difficulty we are confronted with a double bind which is this: carefully controlled small-scale laboratory experiments yield generalizations whose extrapolation to the real learning situation, where *all things are not equal,* is a dubious activity; large-scale experiments on contrasting teaching methods which have, at least potentially, direct relevance for classroom practices leave so many factors uncontrolled that the conclusions are either unconvincing on the strength of the data or the results are more often than not contradictory (see the reviews by Carroll, 1965, 1966b).

The second difficulty, the contribution of the individual himself to the learning process, is inherent to the nature of the mind as an information processing and storing device about which little of substance is known today. To the chagrin of many teachers the individual is not a habit forming automaton who can be conditioned by carefully arranging the presentation of stimuli and rewards contingent upon overt responses. Passive learning is immeasurably inferior to active learning and, although we have been able to measure general learning capacities with intelligence tests, these not only represent weak predictors in specific learning situations but are also unenlightening concerning the processes that underlie individual learning strategies and how to influence or manipulate them. The teacher may spend a lot of effort in arranging sequences of materials to be presented at various stages but he has no control over what in fact the individual does mentally with them: how well he remembers them, whether he focuses on just the intended distinction, whether he tries to assimilate the new material to the old, how much of it he will transfer to new situations, whether he inductively arrives at generalizations, and so on.

2.1.4 Computer Based Programs

Development of computer based programed instruction in language (such as the PLATO system at the University of Illinois, Urbana) offers the possibility of a real alternative to the present inadequate policy of basing teaching practices on theoretical generalizations gained from laboratory experiments. Computer based individuated instruction, when fully developed, will not represent a *teaching method* as this is understood today. Rather it will consist of a conglomeration of many techniques and combinations thereof, fitted to the individual learner in terms of his own learning strategies, learning capacities, interests and goals. Each student will be taught by a different *method* when one considers the total teaching process from beginning to end, that which is most effective for him and most consistent with the goals he has for learning the language. Until computer based programed instruction is a reality for every pupil in the United States we must make do with the present less effective educational means at our disposal. There is much that can be done even during this stopgap interval to render the teaching of FL's more effective. The next section will review some such attempts which have been suggested by authoritative figures and bodies in the FL teaching field.

2.1.5 Foreign Language Teaching Today

The following extended statement by Professor Alfred S. Hayes represents in his words, "a summary of the state of foreign language teaching in the United States today:"

> "Traditional foreign language instruction in the United States was dedicated to the teaching of reading, approached through the study of the rules of grammar. The basic approach, with only minor variations, was extensive translation. But recent years have witnessed a shift of emphasis, since it has become a matter of national self-interest to increase the number of American citizens who can understand and speak a foreign language. This shift of emphasis is paralleled by recent advances in linguistic science and allied fields, which have contributed to a new view of language and language learning. This view is best characterized as a view of language as spoken communication, as signalling behavior, as a system of habits, which must be acquired to the point of automatic production of, and response to, the structure of the language as isolated by linguistic science, to the point where novel utterances acceptable to a native speaker are freely generated by the learner. Grammar is thus by no means discarded, as is sometimes supposed, but the emphasis is on internalizing it through practice, rather than discussing it. Gaarder (1961, pp. 171-172) gives a striking point-by-point comparison of language learning with learning to play a musical instrument.
>
> There is reasonably general agreement on the following points in first-level foreign language-instruction, although, in practice, procedures vary widely:
>
> 1. Learning proceeds in this order: (a) hearing and understanding; (b) speaking; (c) usually much later–reading; (d) writing. The tendency is, therefore, away from *book-centered* materials, and toward extensive audiolingual practice designed to develop a new set of habits.
> 2. Instruction proceeds in the initial stages without reference to the printed word.
> 3. Teaching pronunciation requires extensive *hearing* of the new sounds, preferably contrasted with similar sounds both in the foreign language and the language of the learner, followed by careful drill in their production.
> 4. Spoken language is initially presented and practiced in what are called pattern sentences or model sentences. Each pattern sentence contains a productive structure, i.e., one which, when mastered,

will permit the generation of *new* utterances by substituting new vocabulary; e.g., subject–verb–object in English. Pattern sentences are subsequently manipulated in drills designed to highlight changes in form or order which occur within the structures. Such drills are called pattern drills or structure drills.
5. Pattern sentences may or may not be presented originally in dialogue form.
6. Pattern sentences are practiced to the point of "overlearning," i.e., until they become reflex-like habits.
7. The amount of vocabulary which must be acquired is severely restricted until a large number of structures have been mastered.
8. Translation back and forth between the foreign language and the native language is avoided.

Controversy exists on these points:

1. Ways and means of narrowing the gap between *manipulation* and *communication.*
2. The teaching of *meaning* and the use of English in the classroom.
3. The role of grammatical statements and summaries.
4. The handling of extensive vocabulary acquisition in the later stages of instruction.

A basic tenet of the audiolingual approach has been the assumption that students so trained will not only be able to understand and speak the foreign language, but will eventually achieve skill in reading and writing at least comparable to and possibly superior to that of students trained by traditional methods. Until recently no experimental evidence existed to substantiate this claim. But now a small-scale experiment by Pimsleur and Bonkowski (1961) offers modest support, while a large-scale classroom experiment by Scherer and Wertheimer (1962) offers convincing confirmation of this view.

The language laboratory, an electromechanical installation generally consisting of multiple facilities for student listening and responding to recorded lesson materials, usually on tape, is coming into widespread use, supported in part by funds made available to the several states under Title III of the National Defense Education Act (NDEA). These facilities are intended to relieve the teacher of some of the drudgery of repetitive drill and to furnish authentic models for imitation and practice (see Hutchinson, 1961, and Hayes, 1962).

The principles of programed instruction discussed above are being applied to the problems of foreign language learning. The resulting programs, designed for presentation through the language laboratory, or through similar audio or audiovisual devices of varying complexity, are thus far only in limited experimental use, and show great promise. Some thirty-five to forty research projects are presently active in this field (see again Hayes *et al.*, 1962).

The teaching of foreign languages in the elementary school (FLES) is spreading rapidly but is severely hampered (as is the entire field) by lack of qualified teachers and by frequent failure to provide an adequate continuing program for children so trained. For a survey and evaluation of results to date see Alkonis and Brophy (1961). The research evidence supporting the notion of FLES is extremely slender (Carroll, 1960).

Teaching foreign languages by television is receiving strong support but results have been dubious because of the questionable methodological soundness of certain programs, the impossibility of getting feedback from the learner, and the implication that classroom work following the TV presentation can be handled by teachers with no foreign language training or experience (see Reid, 1961).

To help cope with the problem of retraining high school teachers to understand and use audiolingual methods, Summer Institutes have been operated by many colleges and universities pursuant to contracts with the U.S. Office of Education under Title VI of the NDEA. By the end of 1962 some 10,000 such teachers will have attended a total of 216 Institutes. It is chiefly among the products of these institutes that the awakening Miss F's are to be found. Preservice teacher training programs in colleges and universities are barely in the beginning stages of revision. Two new series of tests designed to measure teacher proficiency and student achievement respectively, developed under NDEA Title VI auspices, will eventually help training institutions to evaluate their products.

A broadly based program of research in problems of foreign language teaching, as well as the construction of teaching materials predominantly in *critical* but seldom taught languages, Language and Area Centers offering advanced study in such languages, and fellowship awards to students entering upon such advanced study, are likewise supported by Title VI of the NDEA.

The large foundations are providing increasing support for projects involving the teaching of foreign languages or research therein. Serving as a respected neutral intermediary in language matters of interest to government, military, the academic world, the foundations, and industry alike, the Center for Applied Linguistics in Washington, D.C., an arm of the MLA supported by the Ford Foundation, is having an impact which is rapidly becoming world-wide. One of its major interests is the teaching of English as a second language.

The implementation of audiolingual teaching has caused an upheaval in the publishing industry, which must now supply and is supplying completely new materials which provide the extensive pattern practice and drills required, plus tapes for the language laboratory and even phonograph records for home practice. It was inevitable that certain publishers should give the impression of *conversion* by offering tapes to accompany traditional texts, a confusing and ill-advised practice. A recent publication of the MLA provides criteria for the evaluation of materials (Allman, 1962).

Language teaching in the United States is in a state of transition. Audiolingual teaching in high schools, variously understood and administered by teachers, is widespread, but commonest in the large urban centers. Thinly disguised traditional teaching clings in many conservative colleges and universities, where the language laboratory tends to provide misleading superficial evidence of change. So radical is the nature of the change in progress that this situation must be regarded as expected and unavoidable. The pot, however, is boiling. But a more general understanding of language as signalling behavior is a necessary precursor to further progress in cross-cultural communication." (Hayes, 1964, 150-152).

2.1.6 Suggestions for Teachers and Learners

The Modern Language Association of America sponsored a conference in 1964 which resulted in a statement entitled "Advice to the Language Learner" (MLA, 1966). The 1964 statement was revised "in the light of comments from many teachers and linguists" and thus purports to represent the distillation of knowledge about the "state of the art." The following ten claims about the psychology of FL learning have been extracted from the 1966 revised statement:

a. Learning a FL facilitates subsequent learning of another FL thanks to the acquisition of "techniques of FL study" (see Carroll, 1963).

b. "Any intelligent student" can learn a FL provided there are present "hard work," "a good teacher," and "a good textbook" (for a discussion on FL aptitude see the review by Carroll, 1965).

c. A helpful strategy in learning a FL is to avoid making direct comparisons between it and English (for a detailed discussion see Chapter 4, Section 4.7).

d. "Learning a language means learning a whole new pattern of habits," . . . "a little like learning to play the piano or the violin, except that it is easier." Therefore, it is important to practice, to practice, and to practice still more. Practice should be "intensive and enthusiastic," "in class and out," silently and out loud, to oneself while reading, and to fellow students. Involve "all your senses as you learn a language by using your ears, mouth, eyes, fingers. Use your imagination. Pretend that you are an actor whose lines you are learning" (for a discussion on "language is a habit" see Chapter 3).

e. "There are three techniques in language learning: imitation, analogy, and analysis." Imitation consists of repeating "what you hear as closely as you can" by listening "carefully to your teacher and the other models." "Learning how to create by analogy is the purpose of pattern drills and other exercises." As one grows older, he begins "to lose [the] capacity for easy imitation" but he gains "the advantage of being able to reason: [to] analyze language." "Information of this sort given in grammatical explanations or rules can help you to learn the language faster." (See Section 2.3 for a discussion on age and language learning.)

f. Memorizing sessions should be broken up into several intense short periods of 15-20 minutes (see Carroll, 1963).

g. Reading and writing are learned more easily if one first learns to speak the language. Even if one is not interested in the spoken language, one "can not learn to read it without using *some* kind of pronunciation, even if it is only a silent one you invent. So, it makes sense to learn the normal pronunciation." (No evidence available.)

h. Practicing to speak should be done right from the start.

i. When reading a FL, one should at first read only what has been previously practiced, and do so out loud (for a contrary opinion, see Burling, 1968). Later, when reading new materials silently, one should underline new words, pronounce new phrases over and over, later returning to the underlined words.

j. English translations of words or phrases should never be written on the page in the reading book. "Doing so puts the emphasis on the English equivalent and not on the foreign word, which is the word that you must learn" (again, see Burling, 1968).

2.1.7 An "Ideal" FLES Program

Working Committee I of The Northeast Conference on the Teaching of Foreign Languages in 1964 outlined "an ideal FLES program." The statement was reprinted in Michel (1967) and the main points made by that influential committee of experts are summarized below. The ideal FLES program is one which:

a. introduces the FL in Grade III;

b. has a specially qualified teacher who serves as an excellent model, who motivates the children constantly, who corrects errors immediately;

c. exposes the children daily to FL instruction: 15-min. periods in Grades 3 to 5, longer in Grade 6; 45-min. periods, three times a week in Grades 7 and 8 or 30 min. periods daily; 45-min. periods, five times a week in Grades 9 to 12;

d. has a coordinated program throughout to insure proper sequencing for continuity;

e. has proper background support to insure success: parental support, qualified teachers for given languages, adequate budgetary provisions for continuity of program;

f. uses dialogue and structure drills in combination with careful introduction of new words; the selection of materials and their sequencing are such as to clearly point out some given grammatical principle and to avoid confusion;

g. devotes the first two-and-one-half years to the listening-speaking skills with no attention given to reading and writing;

h. is careful to avoid boredom due to repetitious drills;

i. induces the student to realistically act out dialogues;

j. makes judicious use of audio-visual aides (especially pictures and tape recorders); (but because of the limited time available the use of mechanized teaching aids is curtailed);

k. introduces reading after two-and-one-half years (in Grade 5), and writing after three years (in Grade 6); the materials for these should at first consist of items already familiar from the audiolingual training; major emphasis still remains on the speaking-listening skills;

l. explanation of grammar and its analysis is "rigorously subordinated to the formation of habits" through the use of pattern drills.

To these 12 characteristics of the *ideal* FLES program may be added two further statements on the *ideal* FLSS (Foreign Languages in the Secondary School) program taken from the conclusions of Working Committee II of the 1964 Northeast Conference and also reprinted in Michel (1967):

a. The "primary all-important goal of a secondary school modern foreign language program in the second half of the twentieth century . . . should be to teach as much *language* as possible." By "language" is meant "the four skills of communication: listening comprehension, speaking, reading, and writing." Other goals such as the "development of cultural sensitivity and awareness of humanistic values" are "eminently desirable objectives" but remain nevertheless secondary in importance.

b. Reading skills are important to develop, but "premature preoccupation with [literary studies, such as literary history, analysis, and criticism] constitutes the most discouraging obstacle to the successful teaching of the language skills in high school; . . . reading, in the sense of translation, is not an objective at all. Translation is a special skill which requires special training. It has no place in a secondary-school program. . . . A prerequisite for the *genuine* study of literature is, or ought to be, language proficiency" and since available time for study is so limited, a preoccupation with literature detracts from the development of the oral-aural skills."

2.1.8 Commentary

The statements summarized in the last three subsections represent the distilled knowledge of the *state of the art* in FL teaching today.

To ask whether these recommendations are valid or not is essentially not a meaningful question. There are two reasons for this. The first is that behind most of the recommendations lie implicit certain assumptions about the value and goals of FL study and these assumptions stem from larger social and educational premises which are not reducible to true-false considerations. The second reason is that, as pointed out in Section 2.1.1, research methodology in education and psychology is too weak to assess unequivocally the truth value of most of the generalizations and recommendations that have been offered. About the only reasonable thing that can be done at this juncture is to point out the fact that there are individuals engaged in research and teaching who disagree with many of the recommendations that have been outlined. For example, Monot-Cassidy argues that "the method advocated in perfecting oral learning goes against the main educational trends of the last two hundred years and more specifically against the learning patterns instilled in the American child from birth onward. It fails in one fundamental: it does not teach the student to respect the subject matter of the course. . . . If we want to keep alive the wonderful renewal of interest in foreign languages, we must cease to treat a fifteen-year-old boy as if he were a bright three" (1966, pp. 16-17). A similar motive, that of introducing adult (rather than childish) content and syntax right from the beginning of FL study, prompted Burling (1968) to make what he calls some "outlandish" proposals whereby reading materials are mutilated in successive steps starting from a mixed English-FL version and gradually replacing the English words and morphemes until at the final step the text appears in the original FL version. Others, like Belasco (1967), while not subscribing to quite such an extreme method, nevertheless maintain that translation can be useful to convey the meaning of the original and do not hesitate to use it whenever they deem it desirable.

2.2 WHAT IS IT "TO KNOW A LANGUAGE"?

It has been pointed out earlier in this chapter that disagreements about how best to teach a FL cannot be unequivocally resolved by experimental research methods. But the inability of research to solve these practical problems is not the only difficulty to be contended with. There are fundamental differences in what language teachers perceive to be the goals of a specific FL course. Some of the differences pertain to esthetic considerations, such as for example whether or not to insist on *correct* speech, both in the grammatical and phonological areas. This is clearly an esthetic rather than a functional criterion as indicated by the fact that first, effective communication is possible without a high degree of accuracy in phonology and syntax, and second, native speakers of a language do not typically produce grammatical sentences in everyday speech (as a literal transcription of a tape recorded conversation would show). Other differences pertain to conceptions about the *correct* order of development of language skills; thus, listening comprehension and speaking are considered to be *primary* skills and reading and writing *secondary* skills; paralinguistic features of speech and knowledge about the foreign culture are usually taught after the *basic* linguistic skills are already at a fairly advanced level, the assumption being that these constitute parallel knowledge rather than linguistic knowledge per se.

These various issues constitute basic and unresolved differences about the fundamental question of what it is to "know a language." Language tests that researchers devise and teachers use are interesting in this connection because they reflect the conceptions one has about what it is to know a language. And what are the constituent elements of most language tests currently used? Vocabulary knowledge, recognition of correct grammatical structure, reading comprehension, dictation, translation, and so on: these may be termed knowledge about the mechanics of language and reflect what some linguists currently call linguistic competence. Linguists like Chomsky (cf., 1965) argue that the fact that native speakers do not typically speak grammatically is not an indication that their linguistic competence is wanting; he insists on a distinction to be made between linguistic competence and linguistic performance. The latter is influenced by presumably nonlinguistic factors such as inattention, limited memory, time pressure, emotional involvement, and so on, which interfere with the act of speaking and cause disfluencies, false starts, unfinished sentences, lack of grammatical accord, etc. He points out that when native speakers are presented with a written transcription of such sentences or an oral version presented piecemeal, they can recognize the ungrammatical elements and correct them, thereby showing that linguistic performance is not a good measure of linguistic competence.

This argument is quite convincing and seems essentially correct as far as it goes. But it neglects certain crucial facts about how language is used for communicative purposes. An individual who has mastered the mechanics of a language, in short knows the meaning of so many words, knows the syntactic and phonological structure of the language, and nothing else, would be quite incapable of communicating in that language. Language teachers are well aware of this fact and have sometimes expressed it in no uncertain terms, as the following blunt quotation indicates: "The pedagogues supply ample anecdotal evidence not only that there are students who can perform beautifully on substitution drills, transformation drills, etc., yet with whom communication is virtually impossible; but also that there are students who 'do miserably on your tests, but, hell, we can talk about anything together' " (Upshur, 1968, p. 5). Spolsky (1968) has documented the fact that non-native speakers who have attained a certain sufficiently high level of proficiency can perform at almost native level on certain language tests, but as soon as they are presented with artificially mutilated speech (e.g., with background noise on a tape recorded conversation) they perform much lower than natives–indicating that they have not internalized certain fundamental knowledge about the language. Spolsky refers to this type of knowledge as the "redundancy aspect of language" and includes such things as knowledge of sequential probabilities of phonemes, letters, and lexical items in strings, knowledge about how words are organized semantically in lexical fields, cultural facts (e.g., what is appropriate to say under given situations) and psychological facts (e.g., what an individual is likely to say or think under given circumstances). As Upshur points out, this principle of redundancy "suggests that it will not be possible to demonstrate that any given language item is essential to successful communication, nor to establish the functional load of any given item in communication. Consider the ease with which speakers of different dialects, dialects even with different number of phonemes, manage to converse, or the ways in which speakers constantly handle their forgetting a specific word. All of this suggests then that while a testing of specific linguistic items is likely to be valuable in the control of instruction, the assessment of proficiency in a language must rather be based on functioning in a much more linguistically complex situation than is provided by the one element test" (Upshur, 1968, p. 11; for a similar view, see Chapter 4, Section 4.1).

Belasco's (1967) call for the "total language experience" is motivated by a similar recognition of the independence of various aspects of knowing a language. He points out the following facts: "A student often has difficulty understanding a spoken sentence that he understands quite easily in print" (1967, p. 86); "We have shown elsewhere [Belasco, 1965] that it is possible to develop acceptable speaking ability without a concomitant development in listening comprehension" (1967, p. 86); "A student might control every structure and know the meaning of every word in a reading selection without understanding the selection" (1967, p. 86).

None of the foregoing remarks are likely to contain any elements of surprise to the experienced language teacher. Yet many of them would insist that mechanical skills are *logically* to be taught separately and prior to communicative skills. But is this truly a logical requirement or an esthetic preference for which too high a price is being paid when students bored with practicing mechanics end by giving up any real interest and motivation in FL study? And are teachers not placing such an emphasis on the acquisition of mechanical skills partly because currently used proficiency tests measure mechanical rather than communicative skills–thus allowing the curriculum to be guided by available tests rather than the reverse?

There is evidence that there is developing increasing awareness in the FL field of the importance of teaching communicative competence. Hayes (1964), being concerned with teaching "cross-cultural communication," has reviewed the pedagogical perspectives of *paralinguistics* and *kinesics,* these terms being defined as "the study of patterned tone-of-voice and body motion aspects of human communication, respectively" (1964, p. 152). "Pedagogically," he asserts, "we can expect the paralinguistic frame of reference to broaden considerably the scope of the descriptive component which underlies teaching materials" (Hayes, 1964, p. 155; see also Nostrand, 1966).

As soon as we raise the question of communicative, rather than linguistic, competence, it becomes clear that the traditional four-fold division of levels of skills–listening, speaking, reading, writing–becomes totally inadequate. Fishman has repeatedly emphasized that the FL teacher must make decisions about which communicative skills to teach within a much more complex framework. For example, in a recent article (Fishman, 1966b) he reviews the "bilingual dominance configuration" in terms of the following factors: (a) What is the desirable level of proficiency in the second language to be encouraged in the various *media* such as listening, speaking, reading, writing? (b) What are the priorities the teacher wants to establish concerning the degree of proficiency to be encouraged in various *roles* such as comprehension, production, and inner speech (talking to oneself, thinking out loud)? (c) Which *formality levels* ought to be emphasized: intimate, casual, formal? "Each level of formality requires a vocabulary, a sentence structure, and a set of attitudes toward oneself and one's interlocutors quite different from those required by the others" (p. 125). (d) How shall the teacher treat the various *domains* of interaction: art, music, government, religion, business, home, school? As he points out, these are contextual factors, and the teacher must arrive at simultaneous decisions concerning all of these. 'In doing so, he will have determined the bilingual dominance configuration that he is seeking to create in his pupils" (p. 126). This decision cannot be made by default by pretending to teach *general* language skills. "Foreign language teachers are producers of bilinguals" (Fishman, 1966b, p. 121) and the assessment of the success and relevance of the teaching process which creates "school-made bilinguals" must be made in no less complex and realistic terms than the description of "natural bilinguals" by such a communication framework as that suggested by Fishman (1966b) or Mackey (1966).

2.3 THE PHYSIOLOGY OF SECOND LANGUAGE LEARNING

Educators in this country and throughout the world have been concerned with the question of "What is the optimum age of beginning the study of a FL?" (e.g., Anderson, 1960, Kirsch, 1956, Larew, 1961). There has been in recent years a definite bias towards the view that FL's should be taught early in childhood, at least before puberty. This view is based on the observation that when children are exposed in a natural setting to two languages during their early childhood they achieve a mastery of both languages (sometimes even three or four languages) that is native-like in fluency and pronunciation and do so with natural ease and apparently without any special effort. In fact, many people believe that *true* bilinguals are produced only under these conditions of childhood learning. This view was strongly reinforced by statements made by the eminent Canadian neurosurgeon, Dr. Wilder Penfield, who for many years has argued that the human brain loses "plasticity" after puberty and language learning after that age becomes increasingly difficult.

There are, however, opposing views to this argument. Many educators who have examined the effects of the early introduction of a second language in the elementary school curriculum caution against what has come to be known as *the balance effect.* This refers to the hypothesis that the more time is spent on the second language the less well one learns the first language, with consequent detrimental effects on the native language, on education, and on the intellectual development of the child.

The purpose of this section is to review the arguments for and against the early introduction of a FL in the school curriculum and to examine the physiological and educational implications that are involved in this topical and crucial question.

2.3.1 The Evidence from Neurophysiology

The views of Penfield on the physiology of language learning have appeared principally in two places: in a speech given at the 134th meeting of the American Academy of Arts and Sciences in Boston (Penfield, 1953) and in the Epilogue of *Speech and Brain Mechanisms* (Penfield and Roberts, 1959), a chapter that has been reprinted by the Modern Language Association and widely circulated (also reprinted in Michel, 1967, pp. 192-214). A summary of his views is given by the following quotations:

> "In 1939 I was asked to give an address at Lower Canada College. . . . 'I have long wondered,' my talk began, 'about secondary education from the safe distance of a neurological clinic. I have wondered why the curriculum was not adjusted to the evolution of functional capacity in the brain . . .
>
> Before the age of nine to twelve, a child is a specialist in learning to speak. At that age he can learn two or three languages as easily as one. It has been said that an Anglo-Saxon cannot learn other languages well. That is only because, as he grows up, he becomes a stiff and resistant individualist, like a tree—a sort of oak that cannot be bent in any graceful manner. But the Anglo-Saxon, if caught young enough, is as plastic and as good a linguist as the child of any other race. . . . when you enter [the teaching] profession, I beg you to arrange the curriculum according to the changing mental capacities of the boys and girls you have to teach. . . . Remember that for the purposes of learning languages the human brain becomes progressively stiff and rigid after the age of nine.
>
> Again in 1953 I was called upon to address a lay audience. It was at a meeting of the American Academy of Arts and Sciences in Boston. . . . I chose as my subject: 'A Consideration of the Neurophysiological Mechanisms of Speech and some Educational Consequences.'. . .
>
> This aroused far more interest than I could have anticipated. The officers of the Modern Language Association of America heard of it, and, probably because it coincided with their own views, they had it reprinted. It was distributed then to the far flung membership of that Association.
>
> . . . It may well be convenient, for those who must plan the curriculum, to postpone the teaching of secondary languages until the second decade of childhood. But if the plan does not succeed, as they would have it, let them consider whether they have consulted the timetable of the cerebral hemispheres. There is a biological clock of the brain as well as of the body glands of children.
>
> . . . The learning of language in the home takes place in familiar stages which are dependent upon the evolution of the child's brain. The mother helps, but initiative comes from the growing youngster. The learning of the mother tongue is normally an inevitable process. No

> parent could prevent it unless he placed his child in solitary confinement!
>
> The brain of the child is plastic. The brain of the adult, however effective it may be in other directions, is usually inferior to that of the child as far as language is concerned. This is borne out still further by the remarkable re-learning of a child after injury or disease destroys the speech areas in the dominant left cerebral hemisphere. Child and adult, alike, become speechless after such an injury, but the child will speak again, and does so, normally, after a period of months. The adult may or may not do so depending on the severity of the injury."(Penfield, in Penfield and Roberts, 1959, pp. 235-240).

It is clear from this extended quote, and from the rest of the article that Dr. Penfield does not claim any special expertise in FL teaching. One must therefore clearly separate what he says as an expert in neurophysiology from what he says as a concerned Canadian citizen interested in promoting bilingualism in that country. The FL teacher, not being an expert in neurophysiological matters may be quite justified to rely on the expertise of specialists such as Penfield and Roberts. The evidence and arguments they present on the neurophysiological bases of speech development in the infant appears convincing, at least to the nonspecialist (but see the critique by Milner, 1960). This confidence in their argument is strengthened even more now that it has received further extensive confirmation by the recent comprehensive review of the subject given by Lenneberg (1967) in his book on the *Biological Foundations of Language* and elsewhere (see Lenneberg, 1966).

However, the crucial question which the FL teacher must carefully examine is just what is the relevance of the neurophysiological evidence for *second* language learning and teaching. It is clear that the learning of language, that is, *first* language, is dependent upon the child's biological mechanisms, that these brain mechanisms develop at crucial time periods, and that unless the child is exposed to human speech before the age of puberty he will most likely never speak a human language. Lenneberg presents the argument succinctly:

> "*Primary language* cannot be acquired with equal facility within the period from childhood to senescence. At the same time that cerebral lateralization becomes firmly established (about puberty), the symptoms of acquired aphasia tend to become irreversible within about

three to six months after their onset. Prognosis for complete recovery rapidly deteriorates with advancing age after the early teens. Limitation to the acquisition of *primary language* around puberty is further demonstrated by the mentally retarded who can frequently make slow and modest beginnings in the acquisition of language until their early teens, at which time their speech and language status becomes permanently consolidated.

. . . Thus we may speak of a critical period for language acquisition. At the beginning it is limited by lack of maturation. Its close seems to be related to a loss of adaptability and inability for reorganization in the brain, particularly with respect to the topographical extent of neurophysiological processes. (Similar infantile plasticity with eventual irreversible topographical representation in the brain has been demonstrated for many higher mammals.) The limitations in man may well be connected with the peculiar phenomenon of cerebral lateralization of function, which only becomes irreversible after cerebral growth phenomena have come to a conclusion" (Lenneberg, 1966, pp. 246-247; emphases supplied).

Here again it is clear that the neurophysiological evidence is restricted to *primary* or *first* language acquisition. However, Lenneberg too sometimes tends to overgeneralize the applicability of his evidence and to make certain claims about second language acquisition which are questionable. For instance, he presents a table of the process of language development throughout the life history of the individual which confounds at one point primary and secondary language acquisition. The table is presented here in a slightly altered form: (Lenneberg, 1966, p. 248)

Age	*Usual Language Development*
Months 0 to 3	Emergency of cooing
Months 4 to 20	From babbling to words
Months 21 to 36	Acquisition of language
Years 3 to 10	Some grammatical refinement; expansion of vocabulary
Years 11 to 14	Foreign accents emerge
Mid teens to senium	Acquisition of second language becomes increasingly difficult (?)

The first four entries in the table concern primary language acquisition while the last two deal with second language acquisition. None of the evidence considered throughout his book on "biological foundations" is directly relevant to the learning of a second language. Furthermore, both generalizations are questionable, especially the last. For instance, a recent study was designed to "examine some aspects of the commonly held view that young children are better able to learn the phonology of a second language than adults" (Yeni-Komshian, Zubin, and Afendras, 1968). The study used only two subjects (ages 5 and 21, respectively) and limited itself to seven hours of training two Arabic phoneme discriminations, and thus the results obtained are to be considered merely suggestive. The authors concluded that their results "do not provide any evidence indicating that children are better than adults in acquiring novel speech sounds" (p. 276). Nevertheless, observation indicates that the children of immigrants who are exposed to a second language before their mid teens or thereabouts do seem to speak that language with closer native pronunciation than their parents or older siblings. But this difference cannot be unequivocally (or even probably) attributed to neurophysiological factors since (a), children learning a second language in a school setting do not always (or even often) develop native pronunciation, and (b), some adults are capable of acquiring native-like pronunciation of a FL. The biological time table that Lenneberg speaks of and the correlated developmental stages of first language acquisition typically follow rigid patterns and do not permit variations of this sort.

Finally, concerning the last generalization in the table, namely that the acquisition of a second language becomes increasingly difficult after the mid teens, there is no evidence to support it. A number of known facts actually contradict it. For instance, a college level FL course of one semester is typically considered to be the equivalent of a whole year of study at the high school level. Also, some intensive FL courses for adults are capable of imparting a conversational knowledge of the language with native-like pronunciation in about one thousand hours with an active vocabulary of up to three thousand lexical items (Mueller, 1967). This rate of acquisition appears to be at least as good as that of the much younger immigrant child who is immersed in a foreign culture, and is probably superior to it. Again, although these intensive courses are for "gifted" adults, the number of such people is sufficiently large (up to 33 per cent of the population according to one estimate, see Carroll, 1965) that a neurophysiological explanation must be excluded.

2.3.2 The Educational and Intellectual Evidence

The preceding section attempted to show that there is no neurophysiological evidence to the effect that children are more capable of learning a second language than adults. This section will briefly examine the evidence concerning the educational and intellectual consequences of the early teaching of a FL.

Macnamara's (1966) book on *Bilingualism and Primary Education* is the most extensive review on the subject to date. A large number of studies have been devoted to this question. Macnamara selected 77 of these for detailed analysis, those that seemed to him to have the most adequate experimental controls. The majority of these studies confirmed the balance effect indicating that on the whole children who were required to learn, use, or be educated in two languages had a weaker grasp of either language than monolingual children. Macnamara's own careful study of the "Irish experience" was consonant with this overall pattern. In his concluding chapter he states:

> "Yet despite the differences between Ireland and other countries in the conditions relating to the learning of languages the findings of our own study closely parallel those of the majority of papers which have been reviewed. Our own research adds to the already considerable evidence that there is a balance effect in language learning, at least where the time devoted to the second language is so extensive that the time available for the mother tongue is reduced. Native-speakers of English in Ireland who have spent 42 per cent of their school time learning Irish do not achieve the same standard in written English as British children who have not learned a second language (estimated difference in standard, 17 months of English age). Neither do they achieve the same standard in written Irish as native-speakers of Irish (estimated difference, 16 months of Irish age). Further the English attainments of native-speakers of Irish fall behind those of native-speakers of English born in Ireland (13 months of English age) and in Britain (30 months of English age).

> Comparisons among groups of Irish children yield results which are also for the most part similar to results obtained in the majority of earlier researches. Teaching arithmetic in Irish to native English-speakers is associated with retardation in problem, but not in mechanical, arithmetic. The retardation in problem arithmetic is estimated as about 11 months of arithmetic age. . . .
>
> . . . The Irish findings relating to the teaching of other subjects through the medium of the second language are particularly discouraging. For it seems that the teaching of mathematics, at least, through the medium of the second language does not benefit the second language, while it has a detrimental effect on children's progress in mathematics" (Macnamara, 1966, pp. 135-137).

It ought to be kept in mind that there are a number of studies which, even if they are in the minority, do nevertheless provide a counterargument to the balance effect and to the alleged detrimental educational consequences of the early use of a second language. One recent study in particular carried out under the direction of Dr. Wallace Lambert, an eminent colleague of Macnamara at McGill University in Canada, shows that French-Canadian children in one bilingual setting in Montreal who have developed a good grasp of English are superior in both verbal and non-verbal intelligence to their French-speaking monolingual peers (Peal and Lambert, 1962). These authors hypothesize that early bilingualism "might affect the very structure of intellect . . . : . . . a large proportion of an individual's intellectual ability is acquired through experience and its transfer from one situation to another." They argue that bilingual children are exposed to "wider experiences in two cultures" and these will give them "advantages which a monolingual does not enjoy": "Intellectually [the bilingual child's] experience with two language systems seems to have left him with a mental flexibility, a superiority in concept formation, and a more diversified set of mental abilities . . . "

The educator and the FL teacher are likely to experience some confusion and frustration at such seemingly opposing views which these researchers hold, each buttressing their views with hard experimental data. A conclusion stated earlier in this chapter (Sections 2.1.1 and 2.1.8) once again comes to mind, namely that research by itself is incapable of providing ready answers to complex and perplexing social and educational problems. It seems pointless to play the *data game* whereby an educator or a politician, having made up his mind in favor of bilingual education or the early teaching of a FL attempts to *justify scientifically* that his policy is a correct one by quoting those experimental reports which happen to agree with his bias. It would be too easy to find experimental reports that show just the opposite. The serious educator must recognize the fact that in complex social and educational settings experimental findings are not easily generalizable: the conditions that hold for any particular setting are likely to be quite different, and significantly so, from any other setting, and his decisions must be made within a complex matrix of interacting factors, educational, social, political, philosophical, etc. Such decisions are always uncertain from the scientific point of view and the latter by itself can never provide a strict and sufficient justification.

This conclusion is supported by a report on an "International Meeting of Experts" presented by H. H. Stern. The report was published in 1963 by the UNESCO Institute for Education and has as its topic "The Teaching of Foreign or Second Languages to Younger Children":

> "It is not necessary to justify the teaching of languages in the primary years on the grounds that it is *the* optimum period. What is needed is (1) to show that it is socially and educationally desirable. . . . (2) It must be shown that it is sound from the point of view of the development of children, that, in fact, there are no contradictions on psychological grounds for teaching a language at this stage. (3) If, in addition, it can be demonstrated that the learning of languages in the early years has certain special merits this would add further weight. In other words, instead of searching for the optimum-age-in-general, it should be sufficient to show that the primary years are a good period for beginning a second language, offering certain special advantages . . . (Stern, 1963, p. 22).
>
> . . . Where no immediate urgency dictates a very early start the age to begin language instruction can therefore be decided on grounds of educational expediency. . . . We conclude that the introduction of a language is not simply a matter of curriculum and method, nor one of correct psychological timing. It must also be viewed against the background of aspirations and social attitudes among the population served by the school system" (Stern, 1963, pp. 26 and 65).

Faced with the necessity of having to make a practical decision concerning the teaching of a second language, the educator must consider all the relevant aspects of the problem and weigh each of them according to the demands of the conditions that hold in his particular setting. In some countries and communities the decision will be dictated by political factors, as was the case with the "Irish experience" (see also Ferguson, 1966). In the United States there are powerful social forces in favor of language loyalty and maintenance (see Fishman, 1966a) by immigrant groups, significant political factors in favor of FL study as a means toward international cooperation and understanding, and there are also present traditional cultural views that favor the study of the major European languages. These various motivations are usually primary and take precedence over the more specialized scientific concerns such as the neurophysiological underpinnings and psychological consequences of early or late FL study. A useful role that the latter concerns can play is to help implement whatever decisions were made on the basis of the more general social concerns by discovering the advantages and disadvantages of the policy being followed and showing ways of maximizing the former and counteracting the latter by special or remedial training.

After reviewing the evidence on the relation between age and FL study, Stern (1963, p. 23) presents a summary table of the pros and cons of the early teaching of a second language. The table is presented below in slightly modified form:

(1) Age of acquisition: before adolescence (ages 3-10):
- (a) *Advantages*:
  - (i) Accords with the neurophysiology of the brain. (?)
  - (ii) Easiest and most effective. (?)
  - (iii) Natural good pronunciation.
  - (iv) Leaves richer linguistic memory traces for later expansion.
  - (v) Longer time for language can be allowed.
- (b) *Disadvantages:*
  - (i) Possible confusion with first language habits.
  - (ii) No conscious acquisition of language learning process.
  - (iii) Time spent not commensurate with results.

(2) Age of acquisition: at adolescence (ages 11 to school leaving):

(a) *Advantages:*
  (i) Increased capacity to appreciate many aspects of language and culture contacts.
  (ii) Still sufficient time to attain high standard.
  (iii) Improved memory and higher level of intellectual growth.
  (iv) First language skills well established, hence no confusion.

(b) *Disadvantages:*
  (i) More laborious than early learning.
  (ii) Success demands tenacity.
  (iii) Self-consciousness.
  (iv) Possible refusal to memorize.
  (v) Experience has shown poor results frequent.
  (vi) Already crowded curricula and specialization of studies.

(3) Age of acquisition: adulthood:

(a) *Advantages:*
  (i) Specificity of purpose.
  (ii) Good motivation added to reasons mentioned for adolescence.
  (iii) Greatest amount of learning in least amount of time.

(b) *Disadvantages:*
  (i) Not enough time.
  (ii) Other preoccupation.
  (iii) Irregularity of study.

Several of the listings above are either in error (e.g., 1.a.i.) or contradictory (e.g., 1.a.ii. with 3.a.iii.); others are at best highly controversial. No mention is made of the potential balance effect. Despite these shortcomings, however, the table is useful because it poses the problem of early FL teaching in terms of relative advantages and disadvantages rather than in terms of the pseudoquestion of which is *the* best time. (Note: the agruments listed above do not necessarily represent Dr. Stern's own views on the subject [Stern, 1970, personal communication]).

2.4 MOTIVATIONAL ASPECTS OF FL STUDY

Bilingualism and multilingualism represent today a major problem in the world, as they have in the past and undoubtedly will remain to be in the foreseeable future. In the history of this planet there have been periods and situations where people have stood ready to die for maintaining the use of their language and resisting the attempt to impose upon them the use of a FL. In this decade of the 1960's there were times we could read in the daily newspaper of bloody riots and deaths, of terrorisms and civil strife associated with language conflicts in India, in Belgium, in Canada, and elsewhere. In all these situations much more was involved than the language question per se, questions of national identity, of cultural self-assertion, of social and economic competition, but the language question stood as a symbol for all these and was inextricably tied to them. The language of a people is a living, growing, changing reflection of that people's heart and mind. When we learn a FL we intermingle with a foreign people: language contact is inseparable from culture contact. In a real sense becoming bilingual entails becoming bicultural. When a person exposes himself to a FL he also exposes himself to a foreign culture. The latter kind of exposure can become for some individuals, we do not know for how many, a threatening experience. Professor Wallace Lambert of McGill University in Canada has for the last ten years explored the implications of such a threat. In one article he introduces the issue as follows:

> "This theory, in brief, holds that an individual successfully acquiring a second language gradually adopts various aspects of behavior which characterize members of another linguistic-cultural group. The learner's ethnocentric tendencies and his attitudes toward the other group are believed to determine his success in learning the new language. His motivation to learn is thought to be determined by his attitudes and by his orientation toward learning a second language. The orientation is 'instrumental' in form if the purposes of language study reflect the more utilitarian value of linguistic achievement, such as getting ahead in one's occupation, and is 'integrative' if the student is oriented to learn more about the other cultural community as if he desired to become a potential member of the other group. It is also argued that some may be anxious to learn another language as a means of being accepted in another cultural group because of dissatisfactions experienced in their own culture while other individuals may be equally as interested in another culture as they are in their own. However, the more proficient one becomes in a second language the more he may find that his place in his original membership group is modified at the same time as the other linguistic-cultural group becomes something more than a

reference group for him. It may in fact become a second membership group for him. Depending upon the compatibility of the two cultures, he may experience feelings of chagrin or regret as he loses ties in one group, mixed with the fearful anticipation of entering a relatively new group. The concept of 'anomie' . . . refers to the feelings of social uncertainty which sometimes characterize not only the bilingual but also the serious student of a second language." (Lambert, 1963, p. 114).

It is not known to what extent ethnocentrism and anomie might represent interfering factors in the study of FL's in the three school systems in the United States today. It is possible, however, that the change in instruction from reading and translation courses to audio-lingual speaking courses may have increased the importance and effects of these social psychological factors. Some of Lambert's findings tend to show that students who are integratively oriented towards language study and those who show evidence of anomie are ultimately more successful than the instrumentally oriented students and the psychologically more detached learners, suggesting that the conflicts of anomie may serve as an internal drive and motivating factor. However, our knowledge on this is still very sketchy. Much may depend on how capable the individual is in handling and successfully resolving the conflicts of anomie. If these conflicts become unmanageable and psychologically too threatening a convenient defense reaction which serves as a protective device might be to slow down progress in the language or eliminate language study altogether (see Chapter 4, Section 4.6). According to one estimate, up to 20 per cent of the student population in high schools and colleges are "beset by a frustrating lack of ability" in FL study (Pimsleur, Sundland, and McIntyre, 1964). These students have been labelled "underachievers" in FL study in view of the fact that their grades in FL courses are "*at least* one grade-point lower than [their] average grade in other major subjects." To what extent is this "lack of ability" attributable to motivational problems and conflicts involved specifically with FL study? It is significant for this question that two of the seven subparts of the FL Aptitude Battery developed by Pimsleur and his associates as a means of measuring ability to learn FL's consist of "Interest Tests" designed to assess the student's attitudes towards FL study. The FL teacher and the learner himself ought to be made more aware of the complex psychological issues that may be involved in the study of FL's. The teacher and the student may be aware of a lack of genuine interest in FL study, but to what extent are they aware of the *reasons* behind such a lack of interest? Teachers, educators, parents often ask the question "How can we infuse more motivation for FL study?" Part of the answer may lie in a recognition of the problems discussed in this section and in finding ways of helping the student manage feelings of anomie and transform it from a conflictual stumbling block into a positive driving force.

The management of anomie may be an important factor in the motivational problem of FL study, but there are undoubtedly additional factors that must be considered. Two of these will be discussed in this and the following section: the development of realistic self-evaluation criteria and the perceived relevance of specific instructional activities.

2.4.1 Self-Evaluation Criteria

It is an interesting psychological observation, whose causes are not obvious, that the individual engaged in the study of a FL has some very definite ideas about the progress he believes he is making. Perhaps this pertains to the area of "folk linguistics" which Hoeningswald (1966) brought to our attention in a most interesting and perceptive article. People appear to have strong feelings about what constitutes *knowing* a language and who is or is not a *bilingual.* A person who is capable of uttering a few mechanical and superficial sentences in a FL with good pronunciation and accurate syntax is a "good bilingual" and "knows the language well" while a person who is quite fluent and is capable of communicating over a wide range of situations, but whose pronunciation is foreign and whose syntax is inaccurate, but perhaps not more so than the conversational speech of the average native, is nevertheless not considered to be a "good bilingual." A student capable of reading advanced materials in a FL but who cannot understand the spoken language may minimize his actual achievement and knowledge of that FL. A student who speaks a FL with halting hesitations and uses stylistic circumlocutions to make up for a lack of vocabulary richness may grossly underestimate his actual knowledge of the language by a tendency to compare this performance to the effortless and automatic expressiveness he experiences in his mother tongue.

It is not known to what extent these kinds of self-generated presumptions affect the student's maintenance of motivation in FL study but it is not unreasonable to suppose that they may sometimes be a source of discouragement and a cause of loss of interest. The FL teacher can help the student develop more objective and more realistic evaluation criteria for assessing progress and achievement. Students can be given some insight into just how complex a system language is by pointing out the amount of knowledge they must have in order to be able to speak their mother tongue as they do and not be misled by the apparent effortlessness with which they speak it. They may thus gain a greater understanding about why it is that learning a FL requires so much effort and perhaps view with greater respect the "modest" achievements they attain at various stages. The FL teacher could further carefully examine his own brand of "folk linguistics" to see whether he is rewarding meaningful achievement rather than superficialities. Does he insist on an inordinate degree of correct pronunciation and syntax too soon or even at any time? Does he appreciate the student's achievement in terms that are relevant to the latter's ability and effort rather than in terms of some general standard that may be unrealistic or irrelevant for this particular student? Does he have realistic expectations about how much progress can be made under the conditions he is teaching? These are important questions because the teacher is a source of feedback for the student whether this process is made explicit or remains unconscious and unstated.

Finally, the student's parents and their version of "folk linguistics" may be an influential source of encouragement or discouragement to him. In a recent national poll that was publicized over the news wire services, the majority of parents were reported to have said that they consider FL courses the weakest part of the school curriculum and should be the first to go if anything had to be cut (see also Wagner, 1966). In view of the widespread social, cultural, and political forces in favor of FL study which has traditionally existed in this country, this mounting negativism is both paradoxical and alarming. Much of it can undoubtedly be attributed to a gap between what the parents define as progress in a FL and what their judgment is about how close or how far their children approximate it. Again, are their expectations realistic? Are their evaluation criteria accurate and relevant? These are questions which the FL teacher and the school administrator may find it profitable to discuss at PTA meetings.

2.4.2 The Student's Attitudes

To the student the purpose of the activities in the classroom and the laboratory or the assigned homework may often appear obscure and mysterious and sometimes even irrelevant and silly. Younger children and the more dull among the older children may not question these practices as much as the older and brighter students. But it is a sign of our times that students in our high schools and in our colleges are increasingly demanding that their studies be relevant to their goals and aspirations. The teacher and educator can view this age of the "New Student" with either alarm and worry or with excitement and confidence depending on whether he defines it as rebelliousness or maturity and involvement. Whatever the case may be, this new development in education is affecting the student's attitude toward and motivation for FL study. It must be dealt with.

What is the New Student's attitude toward FL study? A survey conducted at the University of Illinois (Urbana) in 1968 by a student committee of the Students Council of the College of Liberal Arts and Sciences provides some answers. The survey was planned, executed, and analyzed by the student government representatives entirely on their own initiative. Five thousand questionnaires were distributed to the student body of which 863 were returned. The questionnaire consisted of 21 questions. The distribution of answers for 13 of these is presented below: (see also Chapter 5, Section 5.2).

a. Were your grades in language lower than your grades in other courses outside your major field?

Yes (444) No (374) Blank (20)

b. Did you start with a language, then find that you had difficulty with it and then switch to another language?

Yes (53) No (785)

c. Do you prefer a language course oriented toward understanding of grammar and reading comprehension rather than a course oriented toward oral-aural comprehension?

Yes (414) No (392) Blank (28)

d. Has the time spent in the language laboratory been beneficial to your study of a language?

Yes (160) No (650) Blank (28)

e. Do you feel that you have to study more for a language course (per credit hour) than for other courses?

Yes (676) No (137) Blank (25)

e.1 If so, do you feel that this is unfair?

Yes (536) No or Blank (140)

f. Do you read any material voluntarily in the language you are taking or have taken?

Yes (233) No (598) Blank (7)

g. Has the language requirement [for graduation in LAS at the University of Illinois] prevented you from taking other courses in which you were very interested?

Yes (514) No (312) Blank (12)

h. Do you plan to be able to use the foreign language which you studied to meet graduate school requirements?

Yes (373) No (446) Blank (19)

i. Has foreign language helped you to develop discipline or learn better study habits?

Yes (145) No (679) Blank (14)

j. Do you approve of the present foreign language requirement in LAS?

Yes (199) No (634) Blank (5)

k. Do you think more language should be required, or less?

More (53) Less (674) Blank (111)

l. What is your attitude toward foreign language study?

Interested	(306)
Study primarily for the grade	(521)
Blank	(11)

m. Would you prefer the alternative of taking a two-semester sequence on the literature (in English translation) of the language rather than 103 and 104 of that language? [Note: 103 and 104 are primarily audio-lingual courses.]

Yes (561) No (261) Blank (16)

n. Overall do you think that your study of foreign language here has been beneficial or detrimental to you?

Beneficial (427) Detrimental (339) Blank (72)

If the opinions of students at the University of Illinois can be taken to be fairly representative of the national college population, then this survey shows that all is not well with the college FL curriculum. Several of the answers are in fact quite disturbing. While the LAS college curriculum forces everyone to take audiolingual courses, only 47 per cent of the students are actually interested in "oral-aural comprehension" and 50 per cent would prefer "grammar and reading comprehension." The evidence for a lack of an intrinsic interest in FL study is clear: only 28 per cent read any material voluntarily in the language they are taking, 80 per cent feel that they have to work harder in FL courses–a situation which they consider unfair, and for 61 per cent of the students this extra work prevents them from taking other courses in which they are interested. Furthermore, 53 per cent don't even feel that they would be able to use the FL they studied for meeting graduate school requirements, and 80 per cent doubt that FL study is helpful in developing "discipline" or "better study habits." Finally, 76 per cent disapprove of the FL requirement and 40 per cent feel that FL study in college has actually been detrimental to them.

In considering the significance of these results two important questions pose themselves: Should the school curriculum be determined by a majority opinion of students or by the considered professional judgment of educators? and: Given a lack of intrinsic interest in FL study on the part of many students what should be done about it? Let us examine the implications of both questions.

Given the pedagogical philosophy that is prevalent in our society today very few educators would allow the school curriculum to be dictated by a student body vote, and in any event, the students themselves would be just as opposed to such a process. The real issue is not so much as who makes the specific decisions as whether the decisions made allow for sufficient flexibility to accommodate individual needs and interests. For instance, it would seem that the insistence on a single goal for FL study is open to question on both educational and philosophical grounds. If roughly half of the college student body is interested in a reading knowledge of a FL is it good educational policy to insist on everyone taking an audiolingual course? Given the low degree of success attained by some students in speaking and reading a FL, would it not be more educationally profitable to allow these particular students to study a foreign culture through the medium of their mother tongue and thus still gain some, if not a completely adequate, knowledge of other peoples in the world? Just how useful is it to develop speaking and reading skills in a FL when the educational system fails to provide meaningful opportunities for the use of these skills? It would seem that to make FL study more meaningful to the student it would be desirable to integrate the FL study with the rest of the educational curriculum. For instance, the student could be encouraged to use his FL skills in pursuing projects in other courses in the sciences and the humanities by reading relevant materials in a FL. Travel and study abroad, foreign films and plays, games and play-acting (Lee, 1965, Morgan, 1967), "The French Club" (see Kansas State Teachers College, 1967), summer "language camps" (Haukebo, 1967), interaction with aliens in this country, are all activities which are encouraged and made increasingly available to the students in recognition of this principle, and the more we move in these directions the less we will encounter a "motivational problem" in FL study.

Recent advances in self-instructional FL courses (see for example, Valdman, 1966b) represent another promising development not only because of the efficiency associated with programed instruction but also because these types of courses succeed in eliminating some of the motivational problems discussed in this section. Carroll (1966b) reports certain cases in which "well-developed programs of instruction, particularly of the 'programed' variety, yielded low correlations between [FL] aptitude and performance suggesting that the obstacle of low aptitude may sometimes be surmounted by the use of small-step increment materials that do not challenge language aptitudes" (p. 29). For instance, Mueller and Harris (1966) attempted to reduce the high drop-out rate in an audiolingual French course in college which a previous survey (Mueller and Leutenegger, 1964) had suggested is attributable to the students' disturbance over having to talk too soon and their feeling that too much emphasis was being put on sounds. A reduction in drop-out rate was achieved when a special French course called "Audio-Lingual Language Program (ALLP)" was developed. The course uses programed instruction techniques and states its terminal goal as the "native-like pronunciation and facility in speaking the language equivalent to that of a seven-year old." The sounds of French are taught with "very little visual support" and sound drills are carried out sometimes without knowledge of the meaning of what is being said. These authors believe that the aversion to the sound emphasis which students often feel is overcome under conditions of programed instruction where the students aren't being overwhelmed thanks to the step by step progression and immediate feedback.

The experienced FL teacher is well aware of the fact that the problem of student motivation is complex and multidimensional and cannot be solved by any one "trick." The solution attempted by Mueller and Harris just discussed seemed to work for them (drop-out rate was reduced by 20 per cent at the end of the first year of study) but may not be equally successful in other situations and with different students. Its interesting feature was that it first determined what the students found objectionable then attempted to solve the problem by eliminating the source of dissatisfaction *without changing the original goals of the course*. The FL teacher ought to be aware of the possibility that the explicitly stated objections which students formulate merely represent their personal hypotheses about the dissatisfactions they feel and in these they may in fact be in error. Thus when students state a preference for reading comprehension courses it may reflect either a genuine interest in reading over speaking or a reaction against boring drills in the laboratory or a demand for more "content" or a discouragement with a perceived (real or imagined) lack of progress, or several other possibilities. The solution is not necessarily to change the goals of the course, although that too ought to be considered, but to locate the real source of dissatisfaction and change it. The numerous studies that have been carried out with the purpose of determining which method of instruction is most effective have in general led to disappointing results. It is clear that an important reason for this failure is that the concept of "a method of instruction" actually subsumes a very large number of separate and variable instructional activities in the classroom and laboratory. A much more realistic objective for comparison studies would be to examine the effects of such specific and limited instructional activities. Hayes, Lambert, and Tucker (1968) have recently published a check list of several hundred of such specific activities associated with FL instruction and efforts of this kind are more likely to yield real progress than the more traditional monolithic studies on "overall methods."

2.5 SUMMARY AND CONCLUSIONS

The major theme of this chapter has been the exposition of two curious paradoxes that beset the FL teaching field today. The first paradox consists of the widespread tendency on the part of FL teachers to seek justification for their practices in the classroom in originally weak and currently outdated *scientific* theories despite the fact that few experimentalists ever claim for their theories this kind of infallible generalizability to situations outside the laboratory. The most unfortunate consequence of such an outlook has been that classroom practices have tended to become rigidified in the attempt to follow closely the dictates and prescriptions of so-called scientific principles. Thus, the New Key to FL instruction has turned into a mechanistic exercise of rote habit drills in which the original goal of liberated and sustained expression–that of communicative competence–has been in practice lost sight of and relegated to a supposedly utopian and unattainable status for the majority of students.

The second paradox lies in the fact that although we have achieved in the last twenty years a major breakthrough in the technology of teaching FL's the success of the FL curriculum in our schools has remained extremely limited. Serious dissatisfaction with it is being expressed at all levels by teachers, students, and parents despite the fact that strong social forces remain in this country for the maintenance of an interest in FL's and foreign cultures. Being bombarded by criticisms from both external and internal sources, the FL teaching field now finds itself on the defensive after enjoying two decades of unparalleled expansion and support.

This then is the sobering assessment with which the field is confronted today and the situation from which it must recover Corrective measures are clearly in order, but what are they to be and which direction are they to take? There is a danger here which must be avoided and which lies in the fact that redressive activities that stem from a reaction to the inadequacies of existing conditions tend to overshoot the mark whether it be in the area of politics, legislation, or education. The present shortcomings of the not-so-new audiolingualism may be viewed in part as attributable to the unchecked swing of the pendulum away from the earlier traditionalist emphasis on prescriptive grammar, translation, and the reading of belletristic literature. The danger, now that audiolingualism is on the defensive and students are increasingly demanding "reading" courses, is that the pendulum might be allowed to swing back too far so that we lose sight of the vastly superior instructional technology which we now have at our disposal but was nonexistent in the earlier dark ages of FL teaching. We must strive to reach a correct balance between what our educational technology gives us the potential to achieve and what the students are interested in attaining. The key to this balance (the *Newer Key*, one might say in jest), lies in individuated FL instruction that is sufficiently flexible to adjust to the particularized characteristics of the individual learner and the learning context. Let us review here the arguments that are presented in this chapter concerning the psychology of second language learning and teaching. These might perhaps serve as guidelines to the corrective measures that are needed.

a. There is no one single *proper* goal for FL study which can *logically* be demonstrated. There is no proof that speaking is necessarily primary or more desirable to reading and, of course, vice versa. Neither can one rationally justify the claim that proficiency in all four skills should be the ultimate goal of FL study. We must recognize that students have different interests, needs, and aptitudes and to refuse to accept this fact has the simple and devastating consequence that they shall learn nothing of significance.

b. The goals of a particular course in a FL program must be clearly defined in specific terms that specify the terminal knowledge and skills to be reached. To purport to teach general language skills is a retreat from reality in that it ignores the facts of the matter which are that under such conditions a substantial proportion of students fail to derive any demonstrable value out of their FL study. The extent of specificity of goals to be defined for any particular course would seem to depend on the conditions that hold for that situation: the specific needs, interests, and aptitude of the students involved, the time available for study, the age of the learners, the overall FL program and its cumulative effect, the wider conditions of social support and maintenance interests, the particular language and culture involved, and so on. Some examples of such specific goals may be, "to be able to read German literature on chemistry" or, "to be able to obtain information for travel purposes" or, "to be able to understand radio broadcasts" or, "to be able to write business letters," etc. The assessment of FL attainment for degree and requirement purposes should not be in terms of course grades or number of years of study but rather in terms of tests that evaluate such terminal behaviors. In that case, a variety of such terminal behaviors and combinations thereof may be defined for different degree and curricular requirements.

c. Not only must we recognize variable goals and interests in FL study but also variable abilities and FL aptitude. In the past differential aptitude was tacitly recognized by the expectation of a distribution of grades in standard FL courses as well as, more explicitly, by the placement of students in classes being taught at different rates. But what is needed is the recognition that different aptitudes permit the attainment of different terminal goals both in range and degree within the time requirements and opportunities to learn provided by the FL program. Students should be counseled with respect to the specific terminal goals they may reasonably be expected to achieve taking into account their aptitude, the time available for study, and the amount of effort it may require within the context of their motivation and their other educational aspirations and requirements.

d. The question of when FL's are to be taught within our educational system is a complex problem that involves political, social, philosophical, and psychological considerations and should not be reduced to a matter of neurophysiology—as it has become fashionable to do in recent years. Since the sociopolitical context varies from place to place, not only on the international plane but also within a particular country, including, of course, the United States, the decision must be considered by each school district in the light of the conditions that prevail within its geographic boundary. The knowledge that has accumulated on this matter indicates that there are both advantages and disadvantages to FL study *at any age* compared to any other age. Generalizations about the optimum age that fail to take context into account are almost certainly to be false.

e. More serious attention must be given to the social-psychological ramifications of FL study. The proposition that bilingualism entails biculturalism has serious implications for both the personal adjustment of the individual and the wider sociocultural character of a nation. There is evidence that it also relates to the type and degree of achievement in FL study, and thus, is an additional important variable which the FL teacher must contend with.

f. Global comparisons between methods of instruction are unrealistic. In general studies that have attempted such comparisons were unproductive. There are two principal reasons for this. One is that what is usually defined as a method actually consists of a large variety of instructional activities most of which remain undefined and unobserved. The other reason is that the learner makes his own contribution to the learning situation and these learner strategies are to a greater or lesser extent independent of the teacher's activities. What is needed is a more detailed and explicit description of the specific activities of both the teacher and the student in the instructional situation. Once adequate observation techniques are developed, evaluation criteria of effectiveness can then suggest specific changes in instructional activities.

g. It is necessary to take seriously the oft-quoted distinction between competence and performance, between knowledge and behavior. Experience has indicated that there are no mysterious transfer effects across various language skills and competencies. Not only is it true that ability to read does not insure ability to speak, and vice versa, but also, ability to function in one communicative context is not necessarily matched in other contexts, and this means that the instructional program that produces school-made bilinguals must take into account the full "dominance configuration" of the natural bilingual. The question of what it is *to know a language* is not yet well understood and consequently the language proficiency tests now available and universally used are inadequate because they attempt to measure something that has not been well defined. The tendency to gear the instructional program to enable the achievement of high scores on these tests is thus inappropriate, as is the evaluation of the success of the program in terms of these tests. No doubt due to considerations such as these, some specialists in the language testing field are attempting to develop new kinds of tests that are not based on the notion of sampling the surface manifestations of linguistic items and units but rather the underlying potentialities of functionally significant aspects of utterances. These newer efforts take seriously what every FL teacher knows but often neglects in his teaching, namely that learning a FL cannot be separated from learning about the culture for which it is a vehicle.

h. The instructional process involved in the teaching of a FL must take proper account of the existence of a "folk linguistics," a term used here to refer to assumptions which individuals hold about language and language acquisition. Students have definite ideas about what it is to "know" a language and use self-generated evaluation criteria to assess their progress. These notions are often unrealistic and tend to underestimate both the complexity of the knowledge to be acquired and the extent of their true achievement. The result is frequently discouragement and a consequent loss of motivation. Likewise parents may have inappropriate expectations about the rate of progress of their children, minimize their achievement and ultimately withdraw their support and encouragement for FL study. Teachers, too, may not sufficiently differentiate between essential and nonessential features of variations in their students' performance, may not be sufficiently aware of subcultural and idiolectal variations in codes in the language, and may use general standards of evaluating achievement neglecting in their demands to take account of individual capacities. To take proper account of the existence of folk linguistics would involve activities of the following sort: to determine what notions the student has about language and critically discuss their validity with him; to make the student aware of the true complexity of language so that he may appreciate the difficulty of the task he sets for himself; to justify *in terms that are meaningful to the student* the relevancy of the classroom activities and study assignments; to disabuse parents of their unrealistic expectations and make them aware of the cumulative long term impact of FL study; and finally, to make sure that the teacher himself is knowledgeable about recent sociolinguistic and ethnolinguistic advances.

It might be well to end this chapter by reminding the reader that teaching is an art and that there are no sure methods of extrapolating scientific knowledge to the classroom. This review represents the point of view of its author, which is one possible vantage point, and it is safe to say that for every argument presented here one can probably find one or more counterarguments. This is the nature of the beast. But some arguments are more convincing than others, not, hopefully, because of their authoritativeness, but because they may be more rational and their assumptions more likely correct in the light of existing knowledge. As long as decisions about educational matters must be made and ineffective practices corrected, it behooves us to be self-critical about our activities as teachers and researchers and to continually strive for the best possible solutions which available knowledge and logical reasoning can provide.

Chapter 3

COMPENSATORY FOREIGN LANGUAGE INSTRUCTION

This chapter has two objectives. The first is a critical examination of current psycholinguistic views on the nature of language and on the process of second language acquisition. The second objective is to propose a program of research designed to offer solutions to major problems in language didactics. The point of view adopted in this analysis is that of a psychologist interested in human communication. The qualification of the analysis as a *psycholinguistic* one is intended to indicate such a focus and to distinguish it from other possible and potentially useful perspectives, particularly linguistic, ethnographic, and sociological.

More often than not, a "critical analysis" ends up being a negative piece of work. Yet the meaning of "critical" is not solely "fault-finding or carping"; it also means "disposed to judge with care and precision." This review will find many things at fault, but it will spend more time in analyzing issues and suggesting constructive alternatives than in carping. I am also aware of a third meaning of "critical," namely, that which is "of doubtful result," even "risky" and "perilous." The extent to which this review avoids this latter characteristic, it is for the reader to judge.

Section 1 considers the complexities involved in the answers to three basic questions. What does it mean "to know how to use a language"? What does it mean "to be a bilingual"? What does it mean "to teach a second language"?

Section 2 presents an outline for the analysis of language teaching and specifies the factors to be considered from three points of view: the learner, the instructional process, and the sociocultural environment.

Section 3 is a critical examination of the role research can play in increasing our understanding of language teaching and language learning processes.

Section 4 outlines a major research program which is guided by the problems and principles discussed in the first three sections.

3.1 SOME QUESTIONS ABOUT DEFINITIONS

3.1.1 What Does It Mean "to Know How to Use a Language"?

The changes which have occurred during the past decade in the field of linguistics are familiar to anyone who possesses a professional interest in the study of language and there is no advantage in reviewing these developments here. The question which is posed here requires an answer not from the field of linguistics but rather from its sister discipline known as "psycholinguistics." It is a question that pertains to language performance rather than language competence; or, more accurately perhaps, it is a question about communicative competence and performance.

One possible answer to this question is provided by an examination of language tests for they are designed and used for the explicit purpose of assessing an individual's knowledge of a particular language. The most common and widely used language tests are composed of items which attempt to sample the significant units in specific linguistic fields such as vocabulary, phonetic contrasts, and grammatical relations. The rationale behind these attempts has been that in order to know how to use a language one must know a minimum number of discrete facts about that language and the major problem in test construction consists of making up an adequate sample of discrete units which would be representative of the minimum number that defined "knowing" the facts of that language.

The discrete-point approach is still the major one in the language testing and teaching fields today; it can be shown to be seriously inadequate on both theoretical and practical grounds. From the practical point of view, its inadequacy is clearly demonstrated by the fact, well known to all teachers, that students who obtain relatively high scores on such language performance tests (also: achievement tests) do not necessarily at the same time also have the capacity of using the language in a communicative setting such as carrying out a free conversation with a native speaker. Similarly, individuals who are quite capable of communicating with natives in a variety of settings do not necessarily obtain high scores on such performance or achievement tests. Thus, performance on these language tests and the ability to make use of the language for communicative purposes are not necessarily related, indicating that the former is not a good measure of the latter.

This lack of intrinsic relationship is clearly accounted for by the conceptions currently in vogue in linguistics, thus also demonstrating the theoretical inadequacy of the approach under consideration. According to these views, knowledge about a language does not consist of a finite set of facts that pertain to the surface structure of a language (which these tests attempt to sample). Current linguistic theory has clearly shown that a significant (if not major) portion which constitutes knowledge about a language is not even expressed at the surface level but lies hidden in its deep or underlying structure, and thus far no standard tests have been developed which measure this knowledge.

One does not need a great deal of formal linguistic sophistication to convince oneself of the superficiality of surface features for an understanding of sentences. Consider just a few examples (based on Rutherford, 1968). The difference between the following two sentences

(1) It's a shame he never wins
(2) It's a game he never wins

is felt to be much deeper than what is indicated by the surface difference between "shame" and "game." Sentence (1) is obviously related to "That he never wins is a shame" in a way that (2) is not, and sentence (2) is related to "He never wins the game" in a way that (1) is not. The surface "it" in the two sentences are furthermore quite different as shown by the fact that one can say "Tennis is a game he never wins" but not "Tennis is a shame he never wins"; in (1) "it" is the extraposed "it," whereas in (2) it is the pronominal "it."

To take another example, contrast the following two phrases:

(3) the keys to the house that he bought
(4) the keys to the house that he brought

No information in the surface structure of these two phrases allows the correct deduction that the buyer did not bring the house and, most likely, did not buy the keys. Finally, consider the case where a "syntactophonemic" fact is realized by nothing more profound than a slight phonological contrast as in

(5) They're going to battle with their allies. /gówintə/
(6) They're going to battle with their allies. /gónə/

In (5), "battle" is a noun, part of "go to battle," and "with" is the *comitative* "with"; in (6) "battle with" is verb + preposition. The result, semantically, nowhere to be found in the surface structure, is that in (5) the "allies" are truly comrades-in-arms, while in (6) the "allies" become the enemies to be defeated.

The linguistic facts illustrated in these examples are explainable by generative transformational grammar, but many more facts about English are not. There is no guarantee that generative transformational grammar, or for that matter any other linguistic theory, will be able to account for all the facts about language which native speakers possess. This consideration, coupled with the reasonable assumption that what is not known cannot be explicitly taught, leads to the sobering conclusion that language teaching may never become an exact science, and of course, it is not now, or likely to become one in the foreseeable future. Similarly, and for the same reasons, it is not now possible to test adequately a person's knowledge about a language.

It is quite a different matter, however, to ask the more specific question of the extent to which an individual is capable of using a language for this or that purpose. Can he carry out a conversation on the weather and on sports with a monolingual native speaker of language X? Can he write a scientific article in language Y about the biochemical synthesis of amino acids? Can he serve as an interpreter to a military officer engaged in the pacification program of villagers in country Z? And so on. Note that it would be a straightforward matter to assess an individual's performance on such specific tasks. Note, too, that such tests would reflect much more than the strictly linguistic component of the person's competence. It would include, to an unknown but not necessarily unknowable extent (this remains to be determined) his knowledge about the foreign culture, his ability to reason in communicative settings, and other things as well.

The various considerations just discussed clearly show that the original question posed at the beginning, namely what is it to know how to use a language, is indeed a very complicated one for which no clear answer is possible at this time, if ever. The most reasonable strategy as a matter of practical business would seem to be that of defining specific communicative goals and of assessing the extent to which an individual is capable of meeting these goals. Clearly, these communicative goals will need to be specified in sufficiently detailed manner, since there is no guarantee of transfer effects across modes, settings, and topics.

The implications of these arguments for the strategy of language teaching and language testing are profound and need to be spelled out. First, what is the function of present-day language tests, i.e. tests that are designed to sample knowledge about discrete units? From one point of view, these tests accomplish fairly well what they are designed to do: as long as FL courses restrict themselves to imparting a given amount of discrete surface facts about a language, these tests meet reasonably well the purpose of assessing how many of these facts an individual has acquired. One may take the point of view that at the beginning stages of FL study, this is a reasonable goal and, thus the available tests are adequate from that standpoint. Then, at more advanced stages of study, communicative competence and performance become the goals, at which time one can develop and use behavioral tests of the type discussed above. Of course, the content of these later courses would have to change in accordance with these different goals and presumably they would lay emphasis on cultural facts and on paralinguistic and kinesic features within sociolinguistically relevant settings. This kind of over-all strategy may be said to be representative of current ideas and practices in the FL teaching field. There are grounds to question the correctness and wisdom of this policy and we shall now turn to an examination of such criticisms.

The first and perhaps most damaging counterargument is the notable lack of success that such an approach has had thus far. By the early 1940's the language teaching field had achieved two highly significant goals which amount to no less than technological breakthroughs. One was an advanced state of knowledge of the surface facts of language made possible by structuralist linguistics, which yielded among other things highly efficient methods of contrastive analyses between the native and the target languages as well as the ability of breaking up the known facts into small units for their ordered and preprogrammed sequencing. The other breakthrough came with the availability of tape recorders, visual displays, and mechanical devices for presenting the surface facts of language in an efficient manner. If these two advances had represented the "correct" method of teaching a FL, then the didactic problem would have been solved. Nothing further of great significance remained to be solved, and indeed, the twenty years since that time have brought only improvements of a minor sort chiefly consisting of cheaper and faster machines. What has been the result?

Although an over-all assessment of the FL teaching program is not an easy business, its lack of success in imparting meaningful knowledge in sufficient proportions to generations of school children and college students is quite well known and hardly needs documentation (but see Carroll, 1968). Faced with this obvious failure, the FL teaching profession has been searching for an explanation. It has apparently found one in the "lack of student motivation" for learning FL, a topic which has become increasingly fashionable at conferences and in the literature. The cry of "how to motivate" a reluctant student body is now pervasive. But is this the answer to the problem?

It may be instructive to reflect upon the fact that the one instructional setting where FL teaching has had a considerable amount of success is the "intensive" course as developed by the Army Language Schools in Monterey, California and still used there today as well as in the U.S. Foreign Service Institute run by the State Department and in the Berlitz Schools throughout the world. The intensive language course differs from the school-type course in three important respects. One is the amount of concentrated daily individual instruction, which for intensive courses may run up to the limit of ten to twelve hours a day (but no less than four hours); another is the emphasis placed on the communicative use of the language which is begun immediately upon beginning study. The third factor is that intensive courses are typically taught to individuals who have been preselected for relatively high FL aptitude. Let us consider each of these differences, taking the last one first.

FL aptitude as measured by a short (two to four weeks) trial course or by the Modern Language Aptitude Test (MLAT, see Carroll, 1965) is indeed an important factor affecting success, but its chief influence appears to be in determining the time required for attaining a given level of achievement. For instance, according to the tables developed by the Foreign Service Institute (see Cleveland, Mangone, and Adams, 1960, 250-251), it takes an individual with "average aptitude" 50 per cent more time to attain "sufficient proficiency in speaking a FL [French, Spanish, Swedish, German, etc.] to satisfy routine travel requirements" as compared to an individual with "high aptitude"; it takes him 33 per cent more time to attain "fluency" in a "difficult" FL such as Arabic, Vietnamese, or Thai. In general, given more time (in weeks or months) with some minimum sufficient daily instruction, the person with lower aptitude can attain the same level of achievement as the person with higher aptitude. Thus, the fact that FL courses in the schools do not preselect the students for high aptitude is not a sufficient factor by itself to account for the difference in success between that setting and the intensive course. Furthermore, even where such preselection for aptitude (and high motivation) likely takes place, and in addition a considerable amount of cumulative time is spent in language study, as is the case for FL majors in colleges, the success achieved in communicative ability is considerably less than in the intensive course setting (see Carroll, 1968). Nor is the total cumulative study time sufficient to account for the difference: the typical college graduate majoring in a nonexotic language has accumulated in the order of 1,000 hours of study throughout his career as a student, as compared to 700 hours for the high aptitude student in an intensive course.

Thus neither aptitude nor total accumulated study time can account for the superiority of the intensive-type course over the school-type course.[1] There remains the matter of the differential emphasis placed upon communicative skills, and it is here that the significant difference likely resides. Carroll (1963a, p. 1069) has stated what he terms a "rather commonplace conclusion" that "by and large, students learn (if anything) precisely what they are taught" and this is precisely the point. Time spent in learning the discrete surface facts about language, in habit drills, in "automatization" of mechanical skills, in reading classical literature, etc., is time lost in learning and developing the communicative use of language. The irony of the matter lies in the fact that the "New Key" approach, unlike the traditional methods in which reading classical literature was considered a worthwhile activity in itself, does not attach an intrinsic value to grammatical knowledge per se, but views habit drills as a means toward achieving communicative skills, yet it seems that these very activities are the chief roadblocks to attaining meaningful skills ("liberated expression" as it has been called).

There may indeed be a problem in "student motivation," but to what extent is this problem caused by the method of teaching itself? Today is the generation of the "New Student" (see Chapter 2) who demands that his studies be "relevant" to his educational goals and aspirations. Habit drills do not apparently fall in the "relevant" category and the FL teaching profession must meet this new challenge if it is going to survive. Fortunately, the ultimate interests of teacher and student coincide. The question is a matter of change for the better. In subsequent sections we shall examine the possibilities for such an adjustment and the form it ought to take.

[1] An additional possibility not considered in the text lies in the difference between "massed" versus "distributed" practice. In general, the latter is more advantageous than the former, thus favoring the school-type situation, but this is by no means a simple matter since some type of massed practice may be superior to some type of distributed practice and there is the further complication of summer breaks during which considerable forgetting may take place. It should also be noted that intensive courses typically involve individuals that are more advanced in age than students in school, but this difference is not considered decisive; see Chapter 2.

3.1.2 What Does It Mean "to Be Bilingual"?

One of the facts of "folk bilingualism" is the following curious notion that native speakers have: a foreigner who is capable of uttering a few mechanical sentences with good pronunciation and accurate syntax impresses them as being "bilingual" whereas someone who speaks their language with a strong foreign accent and lacks fluency, does not, despite the fact that the latter's knowledge is considerably greater than the former's. Accent, pronunciation, and fluency are given a disproportionate degree of importance by the nonprofessional judge. So is accurate syntax, and a foreigner who speaks a "bookish" variety of speech, even where the native speaker would normally use a colloquial style, represents to them a more impressive accomplishment than the vastly more difficult achievement of the bilingual who can adapt his style to the sociolinguistic context of the communicative setting. The professionals–linguists, psychologists, teachers–have also their own version of "folk bilingualism." Some require equal facility in two languages ("balanceness") before they are willing to talk of "bilingualism"; others consider any occurrence of linguistic interference as evidence of bilingualism even if knowledge about the second language is minimal (cf. Mackey, 1956); still others prefer to talk of an intermediary stage as "incipient bilingualism" (see Diebold, 1961).

The question when is a person a bilingual is actually not a very interesting one and there seems to be no particular advantage in setting arbitrary limits for a definition. A more relevant concern is that of specifying the extent of an individual's knowledge about a second language. This specification, to be meaningful, would have to be in terms of the discussion in the previous section concerning what it is to know how to use a language. Such specification must include what Fishman (1966a) has called the "bilingual dominance configuration": that is, in terms of *media* (listening, speaking, reading, writing), *roles* (comprehension, production, inner speech), *formality levels* (intimate, casual, formal), and *domains* (art, government, home, business, etc.). Mackey (1962) has provided an even more complex description which includes *degree* at various *levels* (phonological, lexical, semantic, etc.) and in different *modes* (listening, speaking, etc.), *function* (external contacts: home, school, correspondence, mass media, etc.; internal: counting, praying, diary writing, etc.), *alternation* (rate and proportion over topics and interlocutors), and *interference* (type and locus).

It is clear that in view of such complex descriptions, two "bilingual" persons may possess quite different dominance configurations and what each of them knows about the second language may be quite different with conceivably little overlap. Statements about "over-all bilingual proficiency" are likely therefore to be quite misleading. This problem is particularly acute in situations where "bilingualism" is a prerequisite for employment. Hiring an individual on the basis of his performance on the usual language proficiency tests can be quite disappointing to the employer since performance on these tests may be irrelevant to the individual's capacity to function in the particular setting required by the job. Clearly what is needed here is a specification of the minimum functional skills demanded by the job requirements and an assessment of the bilingual's capacity to meet these needs in the second language.

Psychologists have expended considerable effort in developing so-called "indirect measures" of over-all bilingual proficiency (see the review by Macnamara, 1967a). This work, while of some theoretical interest, has not so far proved to be very useful for the problem that is being considered here. In general, these studies have not paid serious attention to the validation of the psycholinguistic measures that have been used, in some cases relying on their "face validity" (e.g., latency of giving translation-equivalent words), in others relating them to language-proficiency tests of the usual kind. Spolsky's (1968a) work is unusual in this respect in that he shows the proper awareness of the problem of validation. While he recognizes that discrete point proficiency tests may be useful in the control of instruction, whether for diagnostic purposes or as measures of achievement, he is clearly in agreement with the assessment given in the earlier section that such an approach is inadequate to characterize overall proficiency:

> "All of this suggests the impossibility of characterizing levels of knowing a language in linguistic terms, that is, as mastery of a criterion percentage of items in a grammar and lexicon. A more promising approach might be to work for a functional definition of levels: we should aim not to test how much of a language someone knows, but test his

ability to operate in a specified sociolinguistic situation with specified ease or effect. The preparation of proficiency tests like this would not start from a list of language items, but from a statement of language function; after all, it would not be expected to lead to statements like 'He knows sixty percent of English,' but 'He knows enough English to shop in a supermarket' " (Spolsky, 1968a, p. 93).

Selinker (1969) has recently focused on a most interesting characteristic of bilingual proficiency which he calls "fossilization." This refers to interference phenomena which permanently characterize the speech of bilinguals irrespective of the age at which the second language is acquired or the amount of instruction or practice in it. These bilinguals thus speak a kind of "interlanguage" which is different from the speech of native speakers of the target language:

"It is my contention that the most interesting phenomena in IL [interlanguage] performance are those items, rules, and subsystems which are fossilizable, and that investigators should concentrate on them, trying to relate them to the five processes listed above. [Also below.] If it can be experimentally demonstrated that fossilizable items, rules, and subsystems which occur in IL performance are a result of the NL [native language], then we are dealing with the process of 'language transfer'; if these fossilizable items, rules, and subsystems are a result of identifiable items in training procedures, then we are dealing with the process known as the 'transfer-of-training'; if they are a result of an identifiable approach by the learner to the material to be learned, then we are dealing with 'strategies of learning'; if they are the result of an identifiable approach by the learner to communicating with native speakers of the TL [target language], then we are dealing with 'strategies of communication'; and, finally, if they are the result of a clear overgeneralization of TL rules, then we are dealing with the 'reorganization of linguistic material.' I would like to hypothesize that these five processes are *central processes* to second-language learning, and that each process forces fossilizable material upon surface IL utterances, controlling to a very large extent the shape of these utterances" (Selinker, 1969, p. 8).

The suggestion that "interlanguage" is the relevant data for the study of bilingualism merits serious consideration even if one disagrees with Selinker's classification of established dialects as instances of it. I have proposed (see Chapter 4) a description of bilingual proficiency which is consonant with this suggestion. My "four-dimensional model of bilingual description" includes the following three-way relationship as one of the dimensions:

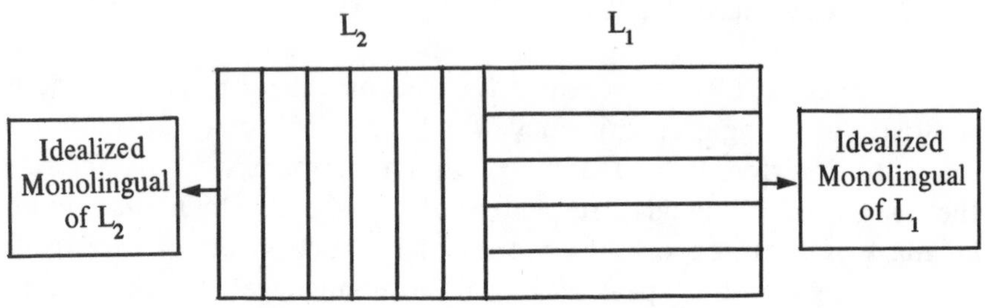

1. $R_A = f(X_{L_1} \rightarrow X_{L_2})$
2. $R_B = f(X_{L_2} \rightarrow \overline{X}_{L_2})$
3. $R_C = f(X_{L_1} \rightarrow \overline{X}_{L_1})$

Equation (1) refers to the *dominance relation* between the two languages (L_1 and L_2) and is given by a comparison of the bilingual dominance configuration, perhaps in such terms as discussed above. Equation (2) refers to the relation between the bilingual's skills in the second-language (X_{L_2}) relative to an idealized monolingual speaker of the target language ($\overline{X}_{L_2}$) and is coterminous with the concept of *interlanguage*. Equation (3) refers to *backlash interference* and focuses on the changes that may occur in the bilingual's native language as a result of his contact with the second language. The latter, when severe, may also develop into a kind of interlanguage so, perhaps, we should be speaking of an "interlanguage relative to the native language" as well as an "interlanguage relative to the target language."

Parallel to an interlanguage we must also consider the probability of an 'interculture' (again two kinds, relative to the native and to the target culture). Concerning the latter, Peal and Lambert (1962) and Kolers (1963) speculate on the existence of a conceptual suprastructure peculiar to the bilingual which enables him to draw upon experiences from two cultures. Peace Corps volunteers returning to the United States from overseas service have been reported to experience various degrees of feelings of estrangement as they found that "things back home just didn't seem the same any more."

The Peace Corps experience does not disentangle the bicultural from the bilingual experience as producers of the intercultural individual. However, there is other evidence to support the contention that bilingualism entails biculturalism. Lambert and his co-workers have for several years now gathered evidence which shows that as an individual becomes increasingly more proficient in a second language he experiences attitudinal changes involving his own as well as the culture of the target language, and that furthermore, these psychological factors may influence the individual's further progress in mastery of the language. I have suggested that an individual's attitudes towards the native and target cultures influence his bilingual proficiency in the manner shown in the figure below:

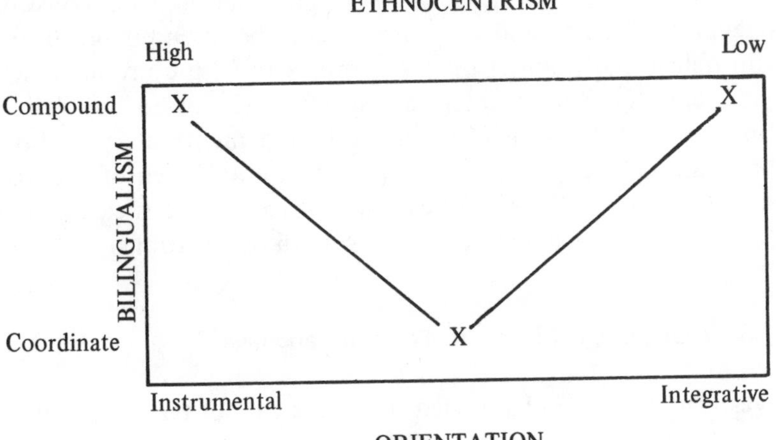

"Ethnocentrism" refers to the belief in the superiority in one's own culture. "Orientation" refers to the individual's stated purpose for studying the second language, and may be "instrumental" (e.g. usefulness in work or travel) or "integrative" (e.g. getting to know the people better). "Compound" and "coordinate" bilingualism refer to the dominance configuration in terms of the three-way distinction discussed above in relation to interlanguage and interculture. There are several hypothetical relationships depicted in the figure one of which is that very strong cultural attitudes (either "ethnocentric" [*High*] or foreign-culture oriented [*Low*] produce bilinguals with strong interlingual and intercultural characteristics (*Compound*). "Coordinate" bilingualism which more nearly corresponds to the linguistic and cultural features of the idealized monolingual within either language-culture community is attainable, according to the figure, only under conditions of moderately held attitudes. This type of individual can be said to be characterized by "bilingual schizophrenia" whereby he is virtually "two different persons in one." Ervin-Tripp (1967) has adduced evidence showing the personality changes such bilinguals undergo when switching from Japanese to English, and Howell (1968) has vividly described the interpersonal difficulties some bilinguals have in interacting in the "American way" while using Korean, and, of course, vice versa.

This discussion on the meaning of bilingualism, what constitutes bilingual proficiency and the interrelations between bilingualism and biculturalism has pointed up the complexity of the problem viewed psychologically (the sociological aspects as discussed by Weinreich (1968) or Lieberson (1969) were not even mentioned) and underscored the ludicrousness of a simple definition. Much of the discussion was based on "hypothetical" notions and there is clearly a critical need for empirical data based on careful observations.

3.1.3 What Does It Mean "to Teach a Language"?

Hayes (1964, p. 148) has stated that "one cannot teach what has not been described." Can we attribute the lack of success of the FL curriculum in our schools to the fact that as shown in Section 3.1.1, we have a long way to go before we understand in explicit terms what knowledge about a language consists of? Children learn their native language despite the fact that parents certainly do not know more about language than linguists or language teachers, but are children in fact being "taught" to speak? Our knowledge about the underlying structure of simple mathematics is quite explicit, certainly much more so than that of natural languages, yet school teachers often experience difficulty in teaching arithmetic, algebra, and geometry.

Thus it appears that one can learn without being taught and one may fail in trying to teach that which is well known and explicitly understood. The meaning of "teaching" as commonly understood can have associated with it two different claims, one of which is a strong one, the other weak. The strong version claims that the activity that is being acquired by the learner is contingent upon the specific environmental conditions arranged by the "teacher." Classical "conditioning" falls in this category, since the "response" of the subject is supposed to be directly elicited by the "unconditioned stimulus" provided by the experimental setting and the "conditioned stimulus" becomes attached to this response (or a slight variant of it) by virtue of its contiguous presentation within a highly restricted temporal span. "Operant conditioning" also falls within the strong claim category since it is asserted that a specific response (when it occurs) is strengthened by virtue of the presentation of a specific "reinforcing stimulus" presented in close temporal contiguity with the emitted response. Note that proponents of the strong claim prefer to use the term "conditioning" rather than "teaching" although it is usually asserted by them that the latter is to be understood by means of the former process.

When dealing with complex activities, the strong claim has been maintained with the help of the notion of "chaining" or of "shaping" whereby the complex activity is broken up into simple identifiable responses which are then said to be tied together by further conditioning in the case of "chaining" (e.g., programed instruction, or learning to play a piece on the piano) or by "successive approximation" in which the reinforcement is provided only with changes of the original activity that bring it increasingly closer to criterion until it is finally reached (e.g., mastery of articulation of the sounds of a foreign language). It is clear that in the strong sense of "teaching" one could not teach something unless one knew exactly what it was. In principle, it is not essential that one have an explicit understanding of the subcomponents of a complex activity; one need only wait until the desired activity is emitted (or a reasonable approximation of it) and then reinforce it. Thus, in principle, it is not essential to know explicitly the structure of a language in order to be able to teach it (in the strong sense), but only to recognize appropriate instances of it (e.g., well-formed sentences, meaningful sounds, etc.). Thus it is conceivable that parents could teach language (in the strong sense) to their children even though they are not applied linguists. Similarly, it is conceivable that language teachers could teach (in the strong sense) a second language despite the fact that their explicit understanding of its structure and subcomponents is inadequate or even inaccurate.

In practice, two highly crucial factors impose definite limitations on what is possible in principle, and in many situations these limitations reduce it to nil or close to nil. One of these is the fact that the desired activity is so complex and improbable that one may have to wait an indefinite length of time for it to be emitted spontaneously or solely through the efforts of the learner. Conditioning cannot therefore take place. The other factor is that when the structure of the activity is not well understood, and yet the activity is complex enough so that subgoals or approximations to it must be chosen for reinforcement, the subcomponents chosen to be reinforced may be either irrelevant or mutually contradictory, so that no significant progress will be made toward the ultimate goal. This may be the case in attempts at language teaching when the learner is provided with contradictory or erroneous rules or when irrelevant subgoals are chosen (e.g., translating skill, or knowing how to repeat learned sequences of questions and answers in the classroom). This is the sense in which the "good teacher," the "good textbook," the "good language program" are superior to their poorer equivalents, for they will avoid to a greater extent the pitfalls of irrelevancy and mutual contradiction. There is wisdom therefore in Mackey's (1965) insistence that effective language teaching must be based on accurate "language teaching analyses," for it is here that one must find the desired subcomponents that are to be reinforced positively, or negatively when the responses are erroneous such as incorrect hypotheses and generalizations which the student provides on his own. "Desired subcomponents" will have several characteristics: (a) they should be simple enough so that the learner can acquire them within a reasonable amount of time without frustration or loss of interest; (b) they must be explicitly defined so that the learner knows exactly what he is to acquire; (c) they must have demonstrated relevance to the criterion goal and this relevance must be perceived by the learner; (d) they ought to have as wide a range of applicability as possible and be practiced within a sufficiently variable setting; (e) they must be internally and externally consistent so that they do not involve contradictory principles and habits; and so on. Many language teaching procedures can be shown to violate principles of this kind. Let us mention a few: (a) some pattern drills are made up of sets of utterances that are superficially alike, but which because their underlying structure is very different, confuse the learner by suggesting similarities that aren't there; (b) some teachers avoid stating grammatical rules and relations explicitly on the assumption that it is better if the learner discovers them for himself. The assumption may be correct in some instances, but in others it does not seem to be, as in cases where the learner forms an erroneous hypothesis (which then must be unlearned), a weak hypothesis (does not cover many of the facts), or none at all (because it is too difficult for him); (c) many activities in the classroom that appear superficially similar to the criterion goal are in fact not so, such as the question-answer pattern which involves only minimally, if at all, the requirement to formulate one's free thoughts; (d) some teachers insist on subgoals that have no demonstrable relevance to the desired goal, as for instance the insistence on accuracy in pronunciation beyond the demands of comprehension, or the insistence on well-formed sentences in free speech (even natives do not meet this standard), or the use of particular dialectal or style forms that are unsuited for the learner's ultimate goals.

It is evident that there are aspects about the strong claim that appear reasonable and useful for rendering language teaching an effective process, even if, in practice, such a stage may not have been reached in any particular program. Particularly useful are the notions derived from the concept of "successive approximation" whereby subcomponents and subgoals are chosen that have characteristics which promote the ultimate goal in an effective manner, as discussed. But there are other aspects of the strong claim which are not viable and these are the notions associated with conditioning and reinforcement. Conditioning assumes that there occurs some identifiable response for reinforcement, but when we deal with "higher mental" or cognitive processes the relevant response is not identifiable, in large measure because it is not observable by the teacher. It would be a serious mistake, bordering on folly, to assume that the overt response the teacher can observe *is* the knowledge or principle the learner has acquired (see Chomsky, 1959). Furthermore, principles the learner acquires which underlie his overt activities do not seem to be very responsive to reinforcements doled out by the teacher, and certainly are not "controlled" by him in any real sense of "control." The truth of the matter is that "what goes on in the learner's head" proceeds in highly mysterious ways completely unknown and unknowable to the teacher, and yet it is certain that it is these mental processes and not the overt response that represent the significant aspects of what is being learned. Therefore the concepts of conditioning and reinforcement, in the sense in which they apply to classical stimulus-response analyses, become in these situations completely gratuitous and useless.

It is for these reasons that the strong claim, as presented, is untenable and a weaker one must be substituted for it. This concession should not be construed as a relinquishment of the belief in the ultimate effectiveness of the teaching process or even as a dilution of the teacher's role in teaching, for it will be seen that all the valid and useful aspects of the strong claim also apply to this weaker claim, and the only aspects which have been relinquished are those which in the strong claim were ineffective anyway (besides being invalid).

In order to understand the implications of what it means to "teach a language," in the present sense of "teaching," we must introduce a few additional terms and definitions. This analysis is specifically based on Carroll (1963b) and may be considered consonant with current views in educational psychology, even though these definitions are only approximate.

Learning: The acquisition of a task whose performance could not be previously accomplished; also: Arriving at the understanding of a concept, rule, or principle previously not understood or known about.

Transfer: The process whereby something learned in one situation manifests itself in another situation due to the inferred commonality between the two situations. "Transfer effects" are to be understood as "hypotheses about transfer," since in most situations the elements in common to two situations cannot be explicitly identified (see Chapter 4).

Learning time: Amount of time spent in the act of learning. This should not be confused with "elapsed time," which includes time spent on such activities as sitting at the desk dreaming, "wasting time," looking for a book or sharpening a pencil.

Aptitude: An inferred capacity which determines learning time under the most favorable conditions; the shorter the learning time, the higher the inferred aptitude. If the task is difficult and the learner's aptitude is sufficiently low, learning time may be indefinitely long. Aptitude is conceived to be specific to particular tasks and depends on possession of certain characteristics by the learner. These characteristics may be either innate (or genetically determined) or they may be dependent upon prior learning of a specific sort or prior exposure to certain situations.

Ability to understand instructions: This is conceived of as dependent upon two factors: general intelligence and verbal ability. The first enters into the ability of the learner to infer the concepts and relationships needed for mastery of the task, especially when these are not explicitly spelled out for him (which, one might add, is the usual case in most complex learning situations). The second comes into play in the understanding of the language used in the instructions.

Quality of instruction: The extent to which it is made clear to the learner what it is that he is supposed to be learning. This is to be understood to refer to highly specific elements within the over-all learning task. Telling the learner that he is supposed to acquire say "a reading knowledge of this foreign language" says very little about just what he is supposed to be learning: does he learn the writing system first, then vocabulary items (which ones?), is phonology necessary (how is he to learn it?), which sentence patterns (from "simple" to "complex"?)? What contrasts is he supposed to be paying attention to? How does he know whether he has understood the correct principles? It is evident that "quality of instruction" deals with such highly complex (and unsolved) problems as the identification of relevant contrasts, sequencing and choice of materials, the amount and type of practice needed at each level, and so on. It should also be noted that quality of instruction interacts with learner characteristics so that it does not have an absolute criterion. The question is to what extent has the task been made clear to *a particular learner:* his aptitude, previous knowledge, ability to infer relationships and understand instructions, all will influence the specific requirements for making it clear what he is supposed to be learning. It follows that a "standard" method of instruction which does not adjust to the learner's characteristics cannot be of high quality.

Perseverance: The time the learner is willing to spend in learning. This definition is not adequate since it is not clear what is involved in "willing to." Thus, are factors such as distractability, frustration, anomie, disinterest, all of which may reduce perseverance, pertain to "willingness to spend time in learning" or are they beyond the control of the individual? What about the type of motivation for learning: is one kind of orientation (say "integrative" or "intrinsic") more conducive to perseverance than another kind (say "instrumental" or "extrinsic")? These are unresolved issues that need further study and elucidation.

Opportunity to learn: Learning time allowed by the method of instruction and the environmental conditions. (Applies to substeps as well as to the over-all task.)

Degree of learning can now be expressed as a function of the ratio of two time factors related to these definitions, as follows:

Degree of learning = *f* time actually spent/time needed

The numerator in this equation will be equal to whichever of the following terms is *smallest:* aptitude, perseverance, or opportunity to learn. The denominator will be a function of the ability to understand instructions and the quality of instruction. Let us explore some implications contained in this equation.

Situation X: Student motivation is adequate (perseverance), opportunity to learn extensive, and ability to understand instructions high (general intelligence and verbal ability): degree of learning will then be a function of aptitude/quality of instruction. Of two students placed in the same program, the one with the higher aptitude will learn more than the one with the lower aptitude. Or, alternately, the one with the lower aptitude will need more time to reach the same criterion.

Situation Y: Student motivation is adequate, aptitude high, and ability to understand instructions high: degree of learning will then be a function of opportunity to learn/quality of instruction. Of two students placed in the same classroom, using the same text, practicing the same exercises, the one that is given more time will learn more than his colleague. Or, alternately, given the same amount of time for learning, the student who has the better text will learn more.

Situation Z: Opportunity to learn is fixed and ability to understand instructions equal: degree of learning will be a function of perseverance-aptitude/quality of instruction. Two students placed in the same program may learn the same amount despite differences in aptitude since the less capable student may compensate by higher perseverance. The interaction between perseverance and aptitude on the one hand and quality of instruction on the other needs to be explored. For instance, which student is better able to cope with a poor quality of instruction, the one with high perseverance and lower aptitude, or the one with higher aptitude and lower perseverance? Or which of the several other factors is more effective in compensating for poor instruction: aptitude, ability to understand instructions, perseverance? Do students who are low in ability to understand instructions suffer more from poor quality of instruction than students with higher ability to understand instructions?

Quite apart from the problem of interdependence, can the factors be measured independently? What constitutes "opportunity to learn" for students with differential ability to understand instructions? Can one specify in sufficient detail the task to be acquired when transfer effects are not well understood? How is one to assess the extent to which it has been made clear to the student just what he is supposed to be learning? How do we weed out time spent in active learning from "listening without paying attention"?

There have been various attempts at predicting success in second-language learning. On the basis of these studies (Carroll, 1965; Carroll and Sapon, 1959; Flaugher, 1967; Gardner and Lambert, 1961; Pimsleur, Sundland, and McIntyre, 1964), we can draw up the following table that shows the variance contribution of the various factors involved:

Variable	*Percent of variance explained*
Aptitude	33
Intelligence	20
Perseverance or Motivation	33
Others	14
Total	100

Grade-point average which includes intelligence and perseverance contributes up to 40 per cent of the total variance. Multiple correlations between grade-point average and aptitude can account for up to 52 per cent of the variance (Pimsleur, Sundland, and McIntyre, 1964). It should be pointed out that this table does not represent exact data but is rather an approximation based on various studies reported in the literature. Furthermore, only student variables are considered here. These predictions do not assess the contribution of the quality of instruction; they allow the latter to vary randomly or assume that it is "constant." There are two reasons for this: one is that educators find it useful to be able to predict success on the basis of individual differences independently of the variations in instructional practices. The other is that assessing the quality of instruction has proved to be a refractory undertaking without notable success.

Some other aspects of the table need to be commented on. The results it reflects are not independent of the variance distribution of the variables themselves. They are restricted to the particular population of students tested (mostly, although not exclusively, high school and college students in the United States) and ought not to be interpreted in absolute terms. For instance, although perseverance accounts for one-third of the variance in these situations, one can imagine that in another situation where perseverance is uniformly very low or very high throughout the population it might account for almost no variance; or, if it were to be bimodal and highly leptokurtic, it might account for much more of the variance, depending also on the distribution of the other variables. Finally, the results are also highly dependent upon the criterion measures used for validating the predictions. In general, these studies have made use of either grades attained in foreign language courses or scores on standard achievement tests of the discrete-point variety. As has been discussed in Section 3.1.1, these measures can be quite inappropriate and unrelated to over-all language proficiency defined in terms of the ability to use language for communicative purposes.

Nevertheless, the table is useful in that it suggests that the variability attributable to quality and method of instruction in high schools and colleges in the United States is quite small. This state of affairs can come about as a result of either or both of two factors. One is that the quality of instruction throughout the country is uniformly good or uniformly bad. The other is that learner factors such as aptitude, intelligence, and perseverance are sufficiently adaptable so that they can compensate for variations in the quality of instruction in terms of the criterion measures used. The latter possibility has important implications for the teaching of languages which should be examined.

If the learning task to be acquired is set at a fairly low level, quality of instruction is not likely to be a crucial factor and learner variables can be expected to act as compensating factors. This may indeed be the case under consideration. However, if criterion is set at higher levels, the learner variables begin to act as limiting factors and quality of instruction assumes a position of greater importance. This is the reason why intensive FL courses whose achievement criterion is set at a high level in absolute terms must exclude from its program individuals with low aptitude and perseverance.

What are we to conclude from all this concerning our original question of what it means "to teach a second language"? Forgetting about conditioning and reinforcement, and faced with uncontrolled (but important) learner variables such as aptitude, intelligence, and perseverance, the teacher is left with three factors under his control: the learning task to be acquired (defined in terms of some criterion goal), the quality of instruction, and the opportunities provided for learning. Let us assess the degree of control the teacher has over these variables.

The opportunities provided for learning consist mostly of the amount of time available for study (in months, years, or total cumulative hours) and the availability of opportunities for learning outside the classroom such as laboratories, travel to a foreign country, contact with native speakers, etc. These conditions are determined by the over-all school curriculum, the FL program as a whole, and the sociocultural context. Thus, teaching English as a second language in the United States has associated with it very different conditions from teaching Spanish; teaching French as a second language in Montreal is quite a different matter from teaching French in Toronto or Calgary. Some colleges and high schools provide "a year abroad" programs, while others do not. Some students are willing to try out outside opportunities when they are available, others are not. And so on.

The definition of the criterion tasks, the goals of the second-language course, are dependent to some extent on educational, economic, philosophical, and political factors outside the direct control of the teacher. But here the teacher can increase his influence by pluralizing the goals of the curriculum and offering various courses which have different purposes. The unifunctional character of the "New Key" approach in FL teaching with its exclusive emphasis on audio-lingualism has contributed to a significant extent to the decline of support of the FL curriculum on the part of students and parents (see arguments in Chapters 2 and 5). In the first place, such a single-purpose outlook is unresponsive to the needs of students, many of whom are either unsuited to develop meaningful speaking skills within the school program (given low aptitude and insufficient opportunity to learn), or have interests of a different sort (such as reading scientific literature) whose neglect by the FL program (if not outright deprecation) not only demonstrates a certain snobbishness on the part of some FL teachers, but also makes them the unwitting accomplices of those who would reverse the present trend towards universal FL instruction in our schools (since they contribute to the general dissatisfaction with what the FL curriculum accomplishes or fails to accomplish). By organizing a multipurpose curriculum composed of specialized courses each with a specific and limited goal, the FL teacher would increase the effectiveness of his teaching by the fact that he will thereby be able to make adjustments for those factors over which he has no or little control: perseverance, intelligence, aptitude, and opportunity to learn. Rather than try to "motivate the student" within the "standard" course (a futile and impotent attempt in most cases), the teacher can offer a course which the student wants–in which case there will be no problem of perseverance. Rather than be frustrated with the lack of success of many students in present courses the teacher can take pride in accomplishing more limited or different goals in courses suited for given aptitudes, intelligence, and opportunity to learn as determined by the composition of his students and the educational environment. Some fundamental rethinking on the definition of goals of particular language courses needs to be effected. It may be that we should not be thinking about language skills per se (listening, reading, etc.) but rather about limited communicative skills. Thus we might develop courses designed to enable an individual to "converse with a native on travel and shopping," or "to understand foreign movies," or "to be able to read newspapers," or "to listen to radio broadcasts," etc. These courses on "how to do something in a FL" may be as short or as long as their complexity warrants and the aptitude of the students requires, and students can take as many of these as their interest, aptitude, and time allow. For purposes of educational (e.g., college entrance) or employment requirements relevant combinations of such skills can be specified in accordance with the rational and justified (rather than arbitrary) demands of the situation. Finally, the quality of instruction is the major factor under the control of the teacher and it is here that the meaning of "teaching a language" assumes its most relevant aspect. As discussed previously, the essence of quality lies in adjustment–the adjustment of the instructional activities to the student's aptitude, intelligence, and ability to understand instructions within the defined goal of the course and the available opportunity to learn. Clearly, such adjustment is most effective under individuated instruction. Self-instructional programs based on careful "language teaching analyses" approximate this feature, and their current development represents one of the most exciting prospects for the future of second-language teaching. Small classes with a high teacher-student ratio also permit individuated instruction, and this characteristic is no doubt a major contributor to the success of intensive courses. From the previous discussion it should be clear that quality of instruction by itself does not determine the success of the course or the over-all program. One may end up teaching in a highly effective way, but one may teach the wrong thing. One must distinguish *what* is being taught from *how* it is being taught. The latter deals with quality of instruction, the former with the definition of the criterion task. The success of the intensive courses *is made possible* by high quality of instruction, but *what determines it* is the choice of the criterion task which, as discussed in Section 3.1.1, is defined in these types of courses in terms of specific communicative skills rather than in terms of some nebulous references to "knowing the structure" or "speaking ability."

We started out this chapter by referring to Hayes's statement that one cannot teach what has not been described. To this limitation we must add still another restriction, which is that one cannot teach without understanding the factors involved in the learning process. Our sketchy knowledge of what language is and our lack of understanding of how people acquire complex cognitive processes therefore represent very serious limitations to our ability to teach language. Either limitation alone would be sufficient to defeat the teaching process. Thus although we understand in complete detail how a computer learns (since we build the components and write the programs), yet because we do not know what language is, we have completely failed to teach computers how to use language. Similarly, although we know what simple mathematics is, yet because we do not understand how the brain functions, we sometimes fail to teach arithmetic or algebra. When it comes to teaching a second language we are working under a double handicap. And yet people do learn (second languages and mathematics and culture and other highly complex things), and although the amount and rate of learning are not always determined by the teacher, they nevertheless often are.

Compared to lower animals or to man-made automata, the human brain is an amazingly versatile and efficient learning device. Its ultimate limit is not known, or even that it has limits. The exact contribution of teaching to learning is not known. The capacity of the brain to learn—to extract knowledge from the environment and organize it—by far outstrips our capacity to teach. It is only when conditions to acquire knowledge are unfavorable (because of inadequate access to facts or lower intelligence or the presence of distractors) that the teaching process assumes significant importance. This importance stems from the fact that under such conditions the function of teaching is to counteract the disturbing factors by improving the accessibility of the facts (e.g., grammatical principles, useful vocabulary, contrastive presentations), by circumventing lower intelligence (e.g., clarifying instructions, giving more opportunity to learn), or by eliminating some of the distractors (e.g., identifying erroneous generalizations, rewarding the desired goals, changing attitudes). Thus, in the last analysis, teaching is a remedial or compensatory process, nothing more nor less.

3.2 LANGUAGE TEACHING ANALYSIS

This section bears the title of Professor William Mackey's book (1965), which is a careful and detailed analysis of the language teaching process. In the Introduction, Mackey describes his views on the problem as follows:

> "Here we are chiefly concerned with the factors involved in language teaching, and only with language learning to the extent that it is a factor in theories of language teaching and language analysis. Good teaching must take the learning process into account since its very purpose is to promote good learning; but the one can and does exist without the other. They must therefore first be analysed separately, for each contains its own complex of factors.
>
> "In the analysis of language teaching, it is essential to maintain a distinction between the method and the teaching of it, without forgetting the obvious relationship between them—since one of the purposes of a language teaching method is to direct the teaching of the language.

"A second distinction has to be made between the language and the method, between the description of the language as presented in grammars and dictionaries and the way this material is used in a particular language teaching method. Again it is important not to forget the relationship between both. All language teaching methods must be based on some knowledge of and about the language to be taught. The more that is known about the language, the more complete the method may become. But there are different ways of finding out about a language and of describing what it is made of; many of the differences rest on different ideas of what a language is.

"We therefore have three distinct but related fields of inquiry: I Language, II Method, and III Teaching" (Mackey, 1965, Introduction).

The notions that were discussed in Section 1 are entirely consonant with Professor Mackey's thesis. For language teaching to be effective, in the compensatory sense in which the concept of teaching was defined, the teacher must have knowledge about what language is (linguistic description), about what it means to know how to use a language and to be bilingual (criterion measures and goals), and about the factors that affect the learning process. Mackey devotes a third of his book to language analysis, but here we shall not be concerned with that aspect of the problem. The purpose of this chapter is to introduce in outline form an interaction model between three sets of factors with which the language teacher must concern himself in order to be an effective teacher. This will set the stage for the discussion in the last chapter, which will propose a program of research designed to increase our knowledge of the language teaching process. The three-way interaction model is outlined below:

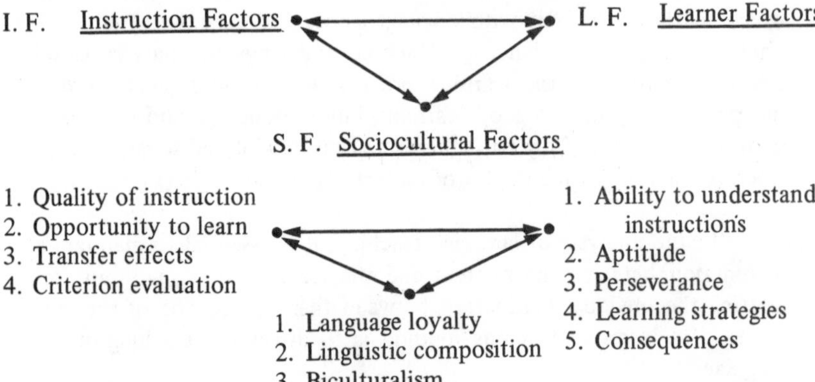

Let us specify, still in outline form, some further notions that must be considered under each of these headings:

LF. *Learner factors*

1. Ability to understand instructions
   1.1 General intelligence
   1.2 Verbal ability
2. Aptitude
   2.1 Components of FL aptitude
   2.2 Factors that determine aptitude
3. Perseverance
   3.1 Need achievement
   3.2 Attitude toward teacher
   3.3 Interest in second-language study
   3.4 Attitude toward foreign culture
   3.5 Ethnocentrism
   3.6 Anomie and its resolution
4. Learning strategies
   4.1 Tendency to assimilate new knowledge
   4.2 Resistance to transfer effects
      A.4.2.1 Structural
      A.4.2.2 Attitudinal
   4.3 Study habits
   4.4 Self-evaluation criteria
5. Consequences
   5.1 Intellectual functioning
   5.2 Educational achievement
   5.3 Personality

IF. *Instruction factors*

1. Quality of instruction
   1.1 Adequacy of linguistic description
   1.2 Adequacy of cross-cultural description
   1.3 Adequacy of paralinguistic and kinesic description
   1.4 Strategies of presentation of facts
   1.5 Teaching aids
   1.6 Degree of individuated instruction and responsiveness to learner factors

1.6.1 Aptitude
1.6.2 Motivation and interest
1.6.3 Feedback
1.6.4 Ability to understand instructions
1.7 Teacher observation and evaluation

2. Opportunity to learn
2.1 Time available for study
2.1.1 Number and distribution of hours for the course
2.1.2 Cumulative total amount of time
2.2 Opportunities outside the regular classroom activities
2.2.1 Use of the language for specific purposes
2.2.2 Direct contact with natives

3. Transfer effects
3.1 Structural
3.1.1. Areas of transfer
3.1.2 Level of operation
3.2 Environmental
3.2.1 Decoding aspects
3.2.2 Encoding aspects

4. Criterion evaluation
4.1 Achievement tests
4.1.1 Linguistic competence
4.1.2 Communicative competence
4.2 Definition of goals
4.2.1 Degree of competence
4.2.2 Area of competence
4.2.3 Nature of competence
4.2.3.1 Dialectal variations
4.2.3.2 Code switching
4.3 Strategies of gradation

SF. *Sociocultural factors*
1. Language loyalty
2. Linguistic composition
3. Biculturalism
4. Consequences

Let us now turn to a brief examination of these various topics.

3.2.1 Learner Factors

Psychologists and educators have known for a long time that "active learning" is by far superior to "passive learning" and in the discussion in Section 3.1.3 we have rejected the notion of teaching language through some automatic conditioning process. Both of these considerations point to the crucial role of "learner factors" in language acquisition and to the importance of knowing just what the learner contributes to the learning process so that it can be taken into account in the teaching process.

Intelligence is usually conceived of as the ability to learn and thus it is to be expected that I.Q. will be related to second-language learning as well, and indeed the evidence we have corroborates this expectation (see earlier discussion). This relationship, under conditions of school learning, appears to be in the order of 15 to 20 percent of the contributing variance. The importance of intelligence in second-language learning can be interpreted as stemming from the fact that the teaching process is incapable of making it completely clear just what the learner is to acquire. Thus the variance contribution of intelligence can be expected to increase under conditions where instructional procedures are weak and amorphous and decrease under conditions where they are effective and well integrated. In this sense, the correlation between intelligence and achievement can be viewed as an indication of the quality of instruction. The 20 percent variance contribution just referred to thus indicates that within the present conditions of language teaching in schools, given the criterion definitions and goals, and distribution of aptitude and perseverance factors that now prevail, the quality of instruction is quite high and the amount of possible improvement fairly limited (not more than one-fifth). This conclusion, if valid, is quite significant, since it suggests that in order to increase the success of the FL curriculum in schools the major changes and improvements will have to come in the area of criterion definition and implementation, i.e., a change in what is being taught under particular conditions. Note that quality of instruction can be high—that is, it is being made quite clear to the student just what he is supposed to learn—while the success of the over-all program can remain inadequate owing to lack of perseverance on the part of the student or to the choice of a criterion goal for the course that turns out to be not what was wanted (e.g., teaching a certain number of surface facts about language as opposed to some particular communicative skills). It should be realized that a change in criterion goal may affect the quality of instruction, since corresponding to a change in *what* is being taught there may have to be a change in *how* it is being taught. With these new goals, quality of instruction will have to be re-evaluated, since there is no guarantee that our present knowledge will be equally effective in teaching these newer skills.

Aptitude is another major factor and under present school conditions it appears to be more important than intelligence, contributing roughly one-third of the total variance. The two best known measures of FL aptitude for native speakers of English are the Modern Language Aptitude Test developed by Carroll and Sapon (1959; Carroll, 1965) and the Pimsleur Language Aptitude Battery (Harcourt Brace & World). According to Carroll, FL aptitude consists of at least the following four identifiable abilities: (a) *Phonetic coding,* which is "the ability to 'code' auditory phonetic material in such a way that this material can be recognized, identified, and remembered over something longer than a few seconds." Evidence shows that this is not a matter of auditory discrimination ability per se. "Most normal people apparently have enough phonetic discrimination ability to serve them in learning a FL, and in any case, it is more a matter of *learning* the discriminations over a period of time than any fundamental lack of auditory discrimination which can readily be tested in an aptitude battery" (Carroll, 1965, p. 96). Thus it appears that the popular notion of "having a good ear for languages" is an ability that does not depend so much on one's "ear" as on the brain's capacity to code and store for later recall auditory information of a phonetic type. (b) *Grammatical sensitivity,* which is "the ability to handle 'grammar,' i.e., the forms of language and their arrangements in natural utterances" and is measured by a subtest of the MLAT which requires the individual to recognize the grammatical function of words in various contexts using English sentences. (c) *Rote memorization ability,* which is measured by a "paired-associates test" that simulates vocabulary learning. (d) *Inductive language learning ability,* which is the ability "to infer linguistic forms, rules, and patterns from new linguistic contexts with a minimum of supervision and guidance." Unfortunately, this ability is not measured by the present commercial version of the MLAT.

The other commercially available aptitude test is the Pimsleur Language Aptitude Battery (Pimsleur, Sundland, and McIntyre, 1964), which differs from the MLAT chiefly in that it includes "interest" tests designed to index how eager the student is in studying a FL and the value he sees in such study.

The factors that determine FL aptitude are not known. Apparently, however, it stabilizes around puberty and continues without much change throughout adult life. There have been few attempts at improving foreign language aptitude through coaching, but in at least one area, that of phonetic coding, they have been unsuccessful so far (Yeni-Komshian, 1962), although clearly this is an area that needs to be further investigated. Certain kinds of early language experience or innate capacity, or both, may be the determining factors, and in that case it is not expected that coaching later in life would have significant effects on aptitude. Nevertheless, if research can identify the kinds of early experiences that lead to the full development of innate potentialities, the educational system can better insure full exposure to such needed experiences.

Even if FL aptitude proves to be refractory to improvement through special training, knowing its components can be used to great advantage in the FL teaching enterprise. It will be recalled that aptitude was defined as the amount of time needed to learn under best learning conditions. The subcomponents of FL aptitude are to a large extent independent, as shown by the low correlations between the scores on the subtests of the MLAT. Thus, an individual may be high on phonetic coding ability but low on grammatical sensitivity or rote memorization ability. This means that he will need relatively more time understanding and internalizing grammatical rules or acquiring vocabulary. The teacher who has information about the aptitude configuration of his students can adjust his instructional activities accordingly, speeding up the rate in one area, slowing down in another, or assigning remedial exercises as required. This type of "diagnostic" use of aptitude tests assumes the possibility of individuated instruction, but where this is not possible, selection procedures can be used where students with similar aptitude configurations can be placed in the same class. Furthermore, information about the aptitude configuration of students provides rational criteria for decisions about criterion goals: for instance, faced with a student who has low phonetic coding ability but adequate grammatical sensitivity, the teacher may decide to place him in a course that emphasizes reading skills unless quality of instruction and opportunity to learn are sufficiently high to compensate for the lack of aptitude in the audiolingual area.

Once more it appears quite clear that effective teaching consists of adequate compensatory activity on the part of the teacher. This principle applies equally to the area of perseverance. Anxiety about "how to motivate the student," which is a question that an increasing number of frustrated FL teachers ask the psychologist expert, is really not a well-motivated concern. It shows a lack of understanding of the factors that contribute to perseverance, i.e., the student's willingness to spend time in learning. What are these and are they under the control of the FL teacher? (a) *Need achievement:* the degree to which the student strives for accomplishing goals in life. This characteristic is deeply intertwined with the socialization process that is linked to parental attitudes and demands, their education, religion, and class, and has probably stabilized long before the student takes a FL course. (b) *Attitude toward teacher:* not much detailed knowledge is available here, but questionnaire surveys on student attitudes show that the student can and does make a differentiation between the instructional activity per se and the instructor: he may like one but not the other. In our current educational system, the old idea about the positive force of "emulating" the popular teacher sounds rather improbable. (c) *Interest in second-language study:* it was mentioned above that the Pimsleur Language Aptitude Battery includes "interest" tests and indeed, they have predictive value. But the relevant question here is, again, to what extent is this under the control of the FL teacher? A student who is not interested in developing audio-lingual skills, but might be in learning reading, is unlikely to have his mind changed by the teacher. In fact, the evidence available on this (Politzer, 1953-1954 and Chapter 5) shows the students' negative attitudes are actually strengthened, not weakened, by being forced to learn aspects of language in which they are originally disinterested. (d) *Attitude toward foreign culture:* these pertain to the larger socio-cultural context, the attitudes that prevail within the community. The study of German in the United States decreased markedly during the years of World War II and thereafter; Spanish has increased in importance with the influx of Mexican and Cuban immigrants; so has Russian in the post-Sputnik era, and when the figures are in, it would not be surprising if French has declined, or at least its ascendency checked, by what Americans perceived as the anti-Americanism of the DeGaulle era. Similar analyses would no doubt held up for bilingual countries such as Canada. (e) *Ethnocentrism and anomie:* the arguments indicating that these factors are influential in FL study have been discussed in Section 3.1.2. As indicated there, much research is needed to disentangle hypothesis from fact, but it is at least possible that the teacher might be able to influence the outcome of these feelings were he sufficiently aware of them.

It can be seen that the problem of how to handle the "unwilling" student is not one that the FL teacher is likely to solve by his own activities in the classroom. There is one important area where the teacher does have some influence on perseverance and that is the extent to which he is responsive to the factors just considered. The politician's time-tested adage "If you can't lick 'em, join 'em," admirably expresses the attitude of the FL teacher who is "aware" and "with it" in this age of the New Student.

The final set of "learner factors" to be considered deal with the various learning strategies that an individual uses in any learning task. Bugelski (1956), among others, has advanced the plausible argument that much of an adult's "learning" is really finding out for himself strategies of responding on the basis of what he already knows. "Child learning" is mostly concerned with building up "behavior elements," "reaction systems," or cognitive schemas; adult learning consists of setting up connections between these "building blocks." The process of generalization or transfer is the use of previously available strategies in new situations. In first-language learning the child uses strategies made available by innate capacities and prelinguistic experiences to organize the linguistic facts to which his environment exposes him. In second-language learning the available strategies the individual can call upon to organize the new set of facts are even more numerous, but this is a sword with two edges: some of these strategies will prove helpful in organizing the facts about the second language but others, perhaps owing to superficial similarities, will be misleading and inapplicable. In the former case we can speak of "positive transfer," in the latter case, "negative transfer." Contrastive analyses between the native and target languages represent explicit attempts at identifying the points of positive and negative transfer, although it is not yet clear whether surface features or deep structure features are the more relevant comparisons for assessing the operation of transfer effects.

The problem of analyzing transfer effects in language learning, sometimes considered under the topic of "interference," is a very involved one and has been reviewed in detail elsewhere (Chapter 4). Some aspects of this problem relate to activities of the teacher, some to the environment, some to the relation between the two languages, some to the learner. With respect to the latter, individuals differ in the extent to which they tend to "assimilate" new knowledge and facts to what they already know, and thus they may exhibit different patterns of positive and negative transfer effects. In addition, there appear to be attitudinal factors specific to language learning and usage that affect the extent to which assimilative (as opposed to separative) strategies will be used. For instance, individuals with low tolerance for ambiguity would tend to resist linguistic interferences that might lead to errors of confusion in the target language (e.g., failing to render an articulatory feature which might confuse two phonemes in the target language). Similarly, loyalty to the recipient language and an intolerance adopted from the community for linguistic importations ("linguistic purism") may increase the individual's resistance to certain interferences.

Another learning strategy that varies among learners relates to the pattern of their learning activities outside the immediate supervision of the teacher. This is sometimes considered under the topic of "study habits" and includes such things as regularity, "cramming" order of carrying out exercises, note taking, etc.

Finally, the question of self-evaluation criteria can be viewed as falling within the topic of learning strategies. Experience has shown that students have definite ideas about how well they are progressing in a course and when asked to give themselves a grade their estimate correlates reasonably well with the teacher's grade. In language courses, however, students appear to have certain misconceptions about what it is to know a language (misconceptions often shared by the teacher!) and these erroneous beliefs may lead to some difficulties. We have already discussed a few of these misconceptions in Sections 3.1.1 and 3.1.2, some of which were referred to as "folk linguistics" or "folk bilingualism." An individual who is used to the facile and apparently effortless flow of speech in his native language may underestimate the tremendous complexity of knowledge that underlies speaking and view with great frustration the halting and excruciatingly difficult productions in the target language. Once he gains a proper appreciation of the complexity of the knowledge he is being asked to acquire, he is more likely to accept the difficulty he is experiencing in the learning task.

3.2.2 Instruction Factors

We have already discussed in Section 1.3 and elsewhere many of the variables listed in the outline under this heading and only a few additional comments will be made here. It is important to realize that the quality of instruction in any course is not under the full control of the teacher, and in language courses the contribution which the teacher makes towards quality might be negative rather than positive. This may seem a rather harsh statement but consider the argument: the primary determinant of quality of instruction—the extent to which the learning task is made clear to the learner—is the adequacy of description of the criterion task and its subcomponents; for this, the language teacher is almost totally dependent on the available texts and teaching materials, and these in turn reflect the state of scientific knowledge in that discipline. Even if we had available today—which we have not—adequate descriptions of grammars, of semantics, of culture, etc., it would still be a long way from that point to knowing how to teach these facts to students. At any rate, the quality of instruction (as defined on p. 95) can never be higher than the state of knowledge as contained in the best texts available at any one time. The probability of improving on these texts on the part of the classroom teacher is slight indeed. His contribution to quality, therefore, is problematic: at his best he faithfully reflects what is in the best texts; at any other time, he simply detracts from quality by departing from the text or by supplying his own description of the facts. It is true that there is a time-lag factor also to be considered and the best available texts may not reflect the latest advances in a scientific discipline; in that case, the knowledgeable teacher has the opportunity of making a positive contribution to quality. Nevertheless, the argument presented here remains essentially correct for the majority of cases. (See 3.4.3.5).

There is an indirect contribution to quality which the teacher can make and which will now be considered. This has already been expressed earlier when it was argued that teaching is essentially a compensatory activity. To be at his best and to reach the quality contained in the best available texts, the teacher must be responsive to the learner factors considered in the previous section. This is clearly the function of the individual teacher, since textbooks and teaching materials are geared to the "ideal" or "average" student, and except for self-instructional texts or programs, they do not take into account individual variability. What is involved in "being responsive to learner factors" has already been discussed in the previous section.

There are a number of additional variables that are included under the heading of "instruction factors" in the outline; some of these have already received attention throughout this and the previous chapter, others will be considered further in Section 3.4.

3.2.3 Sociocultural Factors

The focus of the present analysis is not sociological or sociolinguistic. There are excellent treatments of the problem from that point of view in Weinreich (1968), Fishman (1966b), and Lieberson (1969) among others. Nevertheless it behooves us to consider the implications of the sociocultural environment for learner and instruction factors.

Language loyalty and maintenance activities of a community can have important effects on a number of variables: early exposure to certain language experiences that might affect FL aptitude; interest in second-language study, attitude toward the target culture, ethnocentrism, and anomie, all of which may affect perseverance; attitudes toward language "purity" which influence learning strategies such as resistance to interference, interlanguage, and interculture; ideas pertaining to "folk linguistics" and "folk bilingualism" which affect self-evaluation criteria and criterion goals; pressures towards bilingual education and bilingual requirements for employment; available opportunities to learn; environmental conditions that affect the nature of attained bilingualism (e.g., along the compound-coordinate continuum); the nature of the communicative competence that is set as a goal and which includes dialectal variations, code switching, and the bilingual dominance configuration; and perhaps still others. All of these were discussed in one form or another in the preceding pages, and although each of them merits further consideration, this is not possible within the limited confines of the present analysis.

3.3 STRATEGIES OF RESEARCH

An important purpose of the present analysis is to outline a program of research designed to increase our understanding of the language acquisition process and of the phenomenon of bilingualism. Such an understanding is a prerequisite to effective teaching. But because it seems that the nature and function of research in the social and behavioral sciences have been widely misunderstood, there is need for a critical examination especially in the light of recent developments in the philosophy of science.

3.3.1 The Functions and Limits of Research

The revolution in linguistics that was sparked by Chomsky's publication of *Syntactic Structures* in 1957 is now a dozen years old and in the modern scientific world this represents a substantial amount of time. (It is said that scientific knowledge doubles every decade!) We can now view this revolution with some historical perspective. In the field of linguistics proper, almost all of Chomsky's original proposals have now been challenged by his students and colleagues. "Generative transformational linguistics," the name by which the new field is known, offers today a picture of fantastic confusion, marked by "in-groupishness" and highly esoteric debates in which only a handful of people are the active participants, while an army of devotees sit by the side line waiting for the newest pronouncements from half a dozen centers that come almost on a monthly basis in hard-to-get preprints and dittoed papers. The ultimate outcome of these activities cannot be predicted at the moment, but there is no question whatsoever that they amount to a scientific revolution of major historical importance that has reverberated throughout the "social sciences" and continues to do so unabated.

It is now clear that it is not the detailed proposals advanced by Chomsky and his followers to which this revolution must be attributed, but to the philosophical implications of those proposals for the conduct of scientific research in the social and behavioral disciplines. Historians of science will no doubt refer to this period as the waning of "The Age of Behaviorism" and the waxing of "The Age of Rationalism." Scientists outside the United States (and perhaps the Soviet Union) may be much less impressed by this "revolution" since the rationalist position has continued to permeate their philosophical outlook and it is chiefly in the United States that behaviorism has had such staunch and rigid advocates.

A major distinction between the behavioristic and rationalist schools lies in the status of the primary explanatory concepts. In psychology, behaviorism is based on the notion that all behavior is analyzable into small units called "responses" and all of the brain's environment (external and internal) into "stimuli." Responses are allegedly built up into larger behavior repertoires by a process of conditioning whereby they become associated with stimuli (or reinforcing stimulus conditions). Various subschools within behaviorism exist and there is disagreement among them on many points: how associations are formed and forgotten, the nature of the reinforcing stimuli, the degree of willingness to speculate on higher order conditioning and inferred mediation processes, the role of neurophysiological explanations, and so on. These differences, however, do not affect the basic empiricist position to which all behaviorists subscribe, that all that the organism knows is viewed as (a) stemming from its interaction with the environment and the stimulus-response contingencies therein and (b) describable in terms of responses either observable or inferred.

It is a most curious fact, one which will no doubt puzzle future historians of science, that the weakest aspects of behaviorism lie precisely at the most obvious places. Any general theory of human behavior, if it is to be taken seriously, must attempt to explain the most widespread and obvious of human activities: speaking and thinking in all their commonplace manifestations: describing, reporting, joking, lying, planning, conceiving, realizing, willing, refusing, and so on. The most typical fact about human behavior is that it is *not* controlled (in any true sense of "control") by external stimuli but follows rather from highly mysterious and unobservable processes in the mind (or brain, if you prefer). Behavioristic speculations whereby these mental processes are redefined in terms of stimulus-response contingencies within the brain have been not only totally *ad hoc* and gratuitously designed to retain "consistency" of explanations for overt and covert behavior, but have also totally failed. None of these attempts had any measure of success, as has been demonstrated by a number of reviews (e.g., Chomsky, 1959; Katz, 1966; Fodor, 1968; Jenkins, 1968; Deese, 1968).

Despite the obvious theoretical shortcomings of behaviorism it has occupied a position of dominance in American psychology since the second decade of this century. This is puzzling enough; but even more amazing is the fact that it continues in this position of dominance now that its limitations are understood. One would have expected a collapse of the total enterprise, nothing short of a debacle; but, aside from a few defections from some noted Behaviorists (Jenkins, 1968, Deese, 1968) and some spirited polemical exchanges (Fodor, 1965, Osgood, 1966, Berlyne, 1966, Bever, Fodor, and Garrett, 1968), the position of behaviorism has not changed either in theoretical outlook or in disciplinary influence. How can that be?

Some ready explanations immediately come to mind, but none

of these are really profound and convincing. It is said, for instance, that American Behaviorists are too rigid and entrenched in their views to change their position, or that no competitive theories are available to replace the vacuum that would be created if behaviorism were abandoned. The first hypothesis, besides being offensively condescending, is quite contrary to fact: the history of American psychology, is characterized by functional eclecticism, which is in harmony with the larger American ethos of placing value on change and eschewing traditionalism. The second hypothesis is also contrary to fact for although behaviorism has been the dominant school, it has not been the only one and the existence of these other approaches, both American and European, have been known.

There is another sort of explanation, one which is more profound and goes deep into the nature of the social sciences, and which if valid, has very serious consequences not only for Behaviorism as a school within one discipline but for the totality of the scientific enterprise itself. According to this view the continued strength of behaviorism is attributable to its practical success, the power it has given to the manipulators of behavior: the educator, the animal trainer, the psychotherapist, the advertiser, the propagandist. The achievement of behaviorists in these areas is undeniable: programed instruction, the Skinner box, behavioral modification based on operant conditioning principles, attitude change, to name those that are best known and most significant. How can a school of thought which appears on theoretical grounds naïve, simplistic, and inadequate in the extreme lead to practical accomplishments in the area of human behavior that are so powerful and effective?

We are faced here with a tremendous paradox wherein might lie the bankruptcy of the modern social scientific enterprise: what seems to work best on practical grounds, should not, it seems, on theoretical grounds, while the more sophisticated and "powerful" theories do not enable us to develop effective practical approaches. There is obviously something very wrong with our notions of "theory," "science," and "research."

Careful analyses of the specific claims of one subschool of behaviorism, that of operant conditioning, has shown that they are not applicable to precisely those areas where that school has achieved its most notable practical achievements. In other words, "theory" seems to be an incidental adjunct to practice, and if the latter is effective it appears to be so despite the theory rather than because of it.[2] This argument is strengthened by a parallel observation in another area, that of FL teaching. The development of highly successful techniques for teaching audiolingual skills in the intensive wartime courses of the U.S. Army Language Schools was achieved, as far as is known, without the theoretical precepts of any school in psychology. Subsequently, a term, the "New Key Approach," was invented as these practices were adopted in our FL curriculum and the "theorists" went to work to justify these practices from the behavioristic perspective. Now the behaviorists view these practices as an offshoot (and proof) of their theoretical claims. Similar arguments can be offered for the successful practices of the advertiser and the politician.

What all this amounts to is this: human beings are tremendously more clever in doing things than in explaining how they do them. Scientific research is the organized and culturally sanctioned method of arriving at explanations. Here we find a difference in quality, not quantity, between the natural sciences and the social or behavioral sciences. The scientific concepts and explanations in physics or chemistry have led to degrees of control over the physical environment which was by far superior to the degree of control afforded by man's ingenuity without the benefit of these theories. The "scientific" concepts and explanations in psychology (sociology, education, etc.) have led to far less control of the environment than the nonscientific intuitions of practical men. This difference leads one to question the equivalence of the scientific enterprise in the physical and social (or behavioral) sciences, with the resultant suspicion that the meaning of "research" in the two areas is fundamentally different.

The architect of the revolution in linguistics has this to say about the problem:

---

[2]Note that successful animal trainers have existed for centuries before Skinner ever invented the concept of "shaping by successive approximatation."

> "Modern linguistics shares the delusion—the accurate term, I believe—that the modern 'behavioral sciences' have in some essential respect achieved a transition from 'speculation' to 'science' and that earlier work can be safely consigned to the antiquarians. Obviously any rational person will favor rigorous analysis and careful experiment; but to a considerable degree, I feel, the 'behavioral sciences' are merely mimicking the surface features of the natural sciences; much of their scientific character has been achieved by a restriction of subject matter and a concentration on rather peripheral issues. Such narrowing of focus can be justified if it leads to achievements of real intellectual significance, but in this case, I think it would be very difficult to show that the narrowing of scope has led to deep and significant results. Furthermore, there has been a natural but unfortunate tendency to 'extrapolate,' from the thimbleful of knowledge that has been attained in careful experimental work and rigorous data-processing, to issues of much wider significance and of great social concern. This is a serious matter. The experts have the responsibility of making clear the actual limits of their understanding and of the results they have so far achieved, and a careful analysis of these limits will demonstrate, I believe, that in virtually every domain of the social and behavioral sciences the results achieved to date will not support such 'extrapolation' " (Chomsky, 1968, Preface).

Integrity dictates that we clearly recognize the inherent limitations of the social and behavioral sciences as we know them today and not claim for them more than is reasonable. Practitioners, such as teachers and therapists, need not feel that they must take sides in theoretical controversies and should desist from their attempts to justify their practices by appealing to particular theories. It is more relevant and important to have a functional attitude concerning the effects of their methods which leads them to developing and making constant use of evaluation criteria upon which they can base their decisions for maintaining or altering their activities in accord with the results they achieve. Researchers should not insist on the use of traditional experimental techniques in the analysis of real-life situations where the term "control group" assumes a totally different meaning. Neither is it wise to restrict the scope of the research in deference to the maintenance of experimental techniques, for then the necessary extrapolation procedure vitiates the rigorous technicalities of the laboratory.[3]

The program of research outlined in the next section will attempt to steer clear of these obvious pitfalls. Given the limitations inherent in research of this kind, these activities should perhaps be referred to as "observation techniques" rather than "research." At any rate, the proposals are justified by the belief that systematic observation is a better technique for the discovery of facts than more intuitive approaches. Even this may not be true in some situations and for some gifted individuals but it is, at the moment, a plausible assumption for the majority of cases.

3.3.2 The Tactics of Research

The figure on the following page outlines seven kinds of approaches in research which can usefully be differentiated.

The first major tactical decision relates to whether the researcher intends to assess the effects of an attempt to *manipulate* conditions or to *describe* the variability of particular factors under existing conditions. There are two ways in which manipulation may be attempted: *selection* of naturally occurring phenomena and conditions and *induction* of some change that ordinarily would not be expected to occur in particular settings. An example of manipulation by selection is the control of the composition of a class in terms of some factor such as aptitude (cf. selection of students in intensive language courses). An attempt to improve grammatical sensitivity (a subcomponent of FL aptitude) by teaching transformational grammar is an example of manipulation through induction of change.

There are three basic approaches to description: the use of *standardized tests, questionnaire techniques,* and *field observations.*

---

[3]Postman has stated that "thus far, there is little empirical evidence in support of [the] assumption [that] forgetting outside the laboratory is a function of the same variables and represents the same processes as are involved in formal studies of interserial interference" (1961, p. 166).

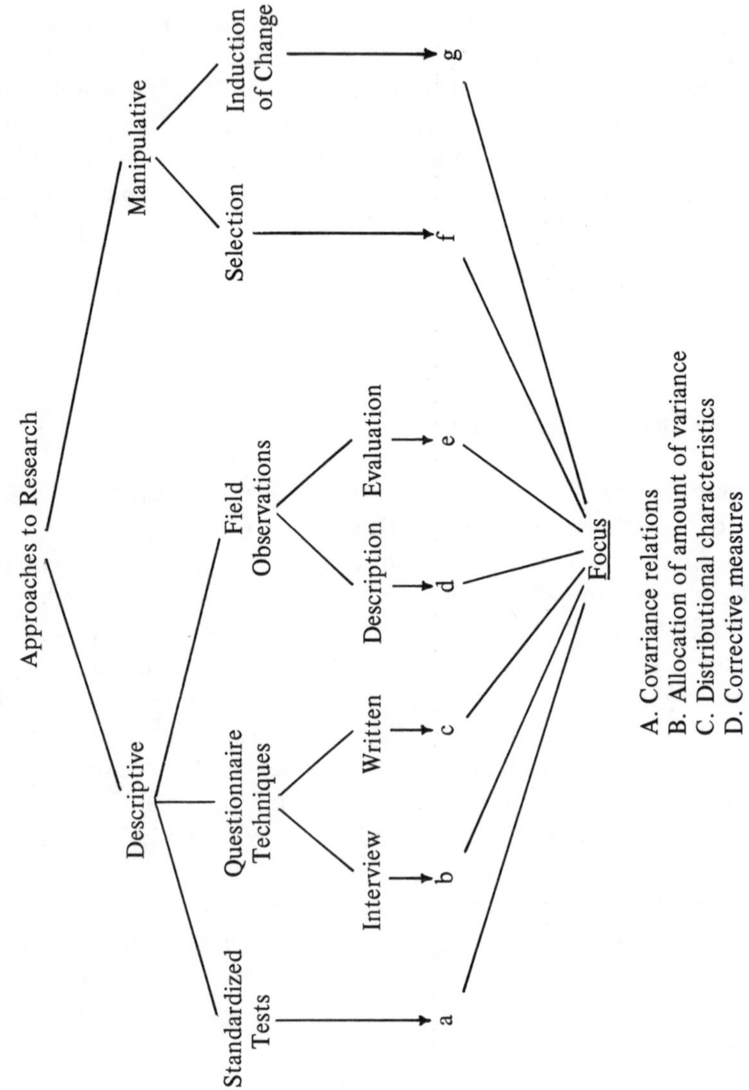
Approaches to Research
Descriptive
Manipulative
Standardized Tests
Questionnaire Techniques
Field Observations
Selection
Induction of Change
Interview
Written
Description
Evaluation
a
b
c
d
e
f
g
Focus
A. Covariance relations
B. Allocation of amount of variance
C. Distributional characteristics
D. Corrective measures

Standardized tests are as a rule commercially available, have known reliability, and the distribution of scores for defined populations (norms) allows transformation of scores attained by an individual into percentiles. The Modern Language Aptitude Test and the French Cooperative Tests are well known and widely used. Questionnaire techniques vary in structure and mode: the *oral interview* technique is usually not highly structured, although it may be, in which case it resembles *written questionnaire forms.* Both may vary in terms of "objectivity" which refers to the degree of bias that is likely to affect the scoring procedure. The nonobjective interview technique is useful in situations where the researcher does not have definite ideas about the information he is seeking and hopes that the unstructured interview will permit the spontaneous emergence of significant facts. On the basis of such information he may then proceed to the preparation of written questionnaires. If the variability of responses is limited and known, objective written questionnaire forms may then be prepared.

Field observations may be either *descriptive* or *evaluative.* The degree of systematization of the observation technique can vary widely. In general, the more systematic the observation technique is, the more it can be reliable, unbiased, and specific. Hayes, Lambert, and Tucker (1967) have recently developed a highly systematic check list technique for the description of FL curricula along several dimensions (teacher activity in the classroom, administrative support, etc.). The Absolute Language Proficiency Ratings described by Rice (1959) (see also Chapter 4) is an example of a systematic evaluation technique for rating oral proficiency along a six-point scale.

The *focus* of the observation refers to the primary goal the researcher has in mind and this will determine the kinds of statistical treatment imposed upon the data. The search for *covariance relations* most often occurs in situations where a large number of descriptive measures are obtained simultaneously. Usually, some suitable multivariate technique (e.g., factor analysis) is used to reduce the large number of correlations to a few clusters whose intercorrelations are interpretable by means of an underlying mediating factor common to a set of variables. The correlation approach is also used in attempts at prediction by means of regression techniques. Basically, a correlation coefficient is an expression of the degree of common variance between two variables. (The percentage covariance equals the square of the correlation coefficient multiplied by one hundred.)

The statistical technique known as "analysis of variance" enables the researcher to make statements about the *amount of variance to be allocated* to each of a number of variables that act simultaneously in a situation. Covariance information is also obtained.

The preparation of norms for standardized tests involves description of the *distributional characteristics* of scores within a defined population. Carroll's (1968) survey of foreign language proficiency levels attained by language majors near graduation from college is another example of a concern with the distributional characteristics of a variable, in this case proficiency level, in a given population.

A focus on *corrective measures* is unlike the previous three considered in that it represents a normative rather than a descriptive concern. Such a focus is particularly important in the light of our interpretation of teaching as a compensatory and remedial activity. The term "corrective measures" is intended to cover both perspectives in the teaching-learning situation: What adjustments can the teacher make in his instructional activities to take into account learner factors and teacher evaluation results?, as well as, What kind of direct manipulation on the part of the teacher can lead to changes in learner factors?

These are then the tactical features that make up the research strategy of the program outlined in the next section. It will be noticed that the problems that will be defined vary greatly on a number of dimensions: scope and range, specificity, objectivity and degree of systematicity, and the configuration of tactical features. It is obviously impossible to include all the problems that deserve the attention of the researcher, but an effort will be made to render the over-all program comprehensive in terms of the three-way model summarized in the outline on pages 105-106.

3.4 A PROGRAM OF RESEARCH

The discussion in the first three sections of this analysis forms the background for the program of research now to be outlined. Therefore there is no need to justify in detail the rationale for each problem. Rather, the reader will be referred to the relevant parts of the previous discussion whenever this is deemed useful. Questionaire forms marked by an asterisk can be found in Chapter 5.

3.4.1. Problem: To Assess the Learner Factors That Influence the Study of a Second Language

3.4.1.1 Reference

See discussion of "learner factors" in Section 3.2.1.

3.4.1.2 Tactics

3.4.1.2.1 Standardized Tests

(a) *Intelligence:* Stanford-Binet (verbal and quantitative parts), Primary Mental Abilities Test Battery (verbal, space, reasoning, number, word fluency), and others.

(b) *Aptitude:* Modern Language Aptitude Test and Pimsleur Language Aptitude Battery.

(c) *Perseverance:* Thematic Apperception Test (need achievement), California F-Scale* and E-Scale* (ethnocentrism).

(d) *Criterion Measures:* Most of these are of the discrete-point variety (e.g., the French Cooperative Test series) and are well known to language teachers.

(e) *Personality:* The MMPI is widely used, but there are many others well known to psychologists and there would be little advantage to name them here.

3.4.1.2.2 Interview Technique

(a) *Management of Anomie:* Lambert has developed and used a questionnaire for the measurement of anomie in second-language study (see 4.1.2.3.(a) below), but there is need for the development of questionnaire techniques to probe into the learner's attempts at handling anomie: When does it develop? Under what conditions? To what degree? How does the learner resolve it? etc. Frequent interviews in depth at different periods during language study can throw light on this phenomenon and would permit the development of written questionnaires. (See Section 5.8.2).

(b) *Learning Strategies:** Because tests are not available and, as an aid in their preparation, frequent interviews with the learner can help determine his typical mode of learning: Does he use an assimilatory or a separative strategy? Is he consistent in this in various areas (phonology, syntax, vocabulary)? Does he switch strategies as his proficiency increases? Is he a linguistic purist? Is he a perfectionist? etc. (See Section 5.8.11).

3.4.1.2.3 Written Questionnaires

(a) *Attitude and Anomie:** We know enough from surveys used in previous studies (see Chapter 5) to prepare questionnaires designed to assess the learner's attitudes toward FL study; see also forms used by Lambert and co-workers on "Francophilia," "orientation," and "anomie," as well as indirect measures of "evaluational reactions" reviewed in Lambert (1967). The semantic differential technique (Osgood, Suci, and Tannenbaum, 1957; Snider and Osgood, 1969) is also well suited as a measure of attitude.

(b) *Study Habits:** There may already be such questionnaires in "how to Study" books designed for students, but at any rate, their preparation should be a straightforward matter. (See Section 5.8.11).

(c) *Self-evaluation Criteria:* Interviews with students may need to precede the preparation of questionnaire forms to assess the learner's ideas pertaining to folk bilingualism.

3.4.1.2.4 Descriptive Field Observations

(a) *The School-type Setting:* This approach may be particularly useful as a check on learner reports obtained through the questionnaire techniques: How does the student conduct himself in the classroom? Does he ask questions when the task is not clear to him? Does he show shyness in using the language? To what extent does he make use of the various opportunities to learn?

(b) *The Natural Setting:* How does the individual get by with little knowledge of the language and culture? Does he seek out or avoid contact with natives? What developmental patterns in language use are evident? etc.

3.4.1.2.5 Field Evaluations

Because available tests of proficiency and achievement are mostly of the discrete-point variety, the development and use of field evaluations becomes highly crucial. The Absolute Language Proficiency Ratings (Rice, 1959) and the standards established by the Foreign Service Institute of the U.S. Department of State are examples of this type (see also Chapter 5, Section 1). But none of these are sufficient in themselves and a great deal of work remains to be done in this area (see suggestions in Chapter 4, Section 1; Spolsky, 1968b; and Upshur, 1968).

3.4.1.2.6 Manipulation by Selection

This approach can be useful when the researcher is interested in the effects of certain learner factors in special settings. Selection can be achieved statistically by separating out the data for those individuals possessing the desired characteristics or, naturalistically, by collecting data only in those settings where the desired features hold. For example, one may wish to assess the range of communicative abilities acquired by natural bilinguals as a function of the degree of anomie that develops in the early stages of immersion in a foreign culture. Or one may wish to assess educational achievement as a function of instruction in a second language in a cultural setting where the second language is not normally used–as was done by Macnamara (1966) in Ireland.

3.4.1.2.7 Manipulation by Induction of Change

This may be attempted whenever there is reason to believe that a learner factor can be changed through some action by the researcher, educator, or parent: coaching to improve aptitude, providing remedial practice exercises, using propaganda techniques to change attitudes, giving feedback information on learner progress, etc. The assessment of the effectiveness of the manipulatory attempt may be done in a number of ways: the "before-after" technique described in the attitude change literature, the use of control groups, the induction of opposite effects, etc.

3.4.1.3 Procedure

The implementation of the research on the present problem must proceed through a number of stages that will now be outlined.

3.4.1.3.1 Selection and Preparation of Observation Techniques

Where standardized tests are available, a decision will have to be made about selecting those that are best suited for the particular sample of subjects to be included in the study. The administration of some tests (e.g., TAT, MMPI) must be done by trained individuals having proper credentials. Appropriate steps must be taken for the recording of interview data, and questionnaire forms should be prepared, preferably after pilot versions have been tried out. The individuals that are involved in field observations should be properly trained and the reliability of their observations and evaluations assessed. Decisions about selection should be carefully considered and provisions made for including necessary comparison groups and conditions to determine the effectiveness of the induction manipulation.

3.4.1.3.2 Selection of Setting

There are many factors to be considered here: a sufficiently large sample of subjects with the desired characteristics, the representativeness of the sample vis-à-vis the population to which generalizations are to be made, the probability of getting good cooperation from the subjects, their parents, teachers, and school officials, and so on.

3.4.1.3.3 Analysis of Data

Decisions about this ought to be made prior to the start of the project and they will depend on the focus the investigator has in mind. Consultation with measurement experts and computer statisticians is of course highly desirable.

3.4.1.4 Overview

The over-all problem of this particular project concerns the identification of learner factors that influence the study of a second language. The strategy that has been described consists of obtaining a large number of diverse observations in a setting where individuals are engaged in the study of a second language. Some of the observations are restricted to naturally occurring circumstances, others are designed to record the effects of a manipulated change in these conditions. Statistical treatment of these data will yield information on a number of important problems, some of which are listed below.

3.4.1.4.1 Problems of Covariance Relations

How many learner factors should be kept track of in a second-language learning situation? Intercorrelations between the many variables recorded and subsequent factor analysis may show that there is no need in future studies to pay attention to all of them, since many variables may be highly intercorrelated and some can then be estimated on the basis of others. For example, high general intelligence, high need achievement, an assimilatory strategy in learning syntax, good study habits, and realistic self-evaluation criteria may all form a tightly intercorrelated cluster, and another cluster might be made up of a favorable attitude toward the teacher, low ethnocentrism, high phonetic coding ability, and high interest in FL study. These are pure speculations, but if the data were available hypothesis and fact could be separated.

The particular configuration of correlation clusters yields information about what might be the underlying factor that accounts for their intercorrelations. Thus, the first cluster in the example above suggests a general learning ability that also manifests itself in second-language learning, and the second cluster might suggest a general attitudinal component in FL study. These higher order mediating factors may subsequently be assessed by a single observational technique thus making for economy in both explanation and testing.

3.4.1.4.2 Problems of Allocation of Amount of Variance

Given the specific criterion measures that are included (proficiency tests, evaluation of communicative abilities, course grades), what amount of variance is contributed by each of the learner factors also measured (aptitude, intelligence, attitude, etc.)? Are some learner factors more important for some criterion measures? (e.g., intelligence may be more important for course grade, while attitude may be more important for acquired range of communicative abilities). Can learner factors compensate for each other? (e.g., whether positive attitudes could overcome the disadvantages of low aptitude). Are certain learner factors more crucial in the presence of certain others? (e.g., self-evaluation criteria may be important only under the assimilatory strategy; or aptitude may become more crucial with advanced age). And so on.

3.4.1.4.3 Problems of Distributional Characteristics

What is the distribution of attitudes toward FL study in a particular school district? Is the variance comparable across grades or does it become restricted in a particular direction after a year or more of study? Are there extremes in feelings of anomie and do these change with age or number of years of study? How do study habits vary, change? etc.

3.4.1.4.4 Problems Related to Corrective Measures

What learner factors can be manipulated? Which ones resist change more than others? How long does induction of change last? Is induction of change as important in variance contribution as the same characteristic that develops spontaneously?

These are then some of the problems for which this project would provide hard information. It may not be feasible to obtain all the measures suggested in any one study, but it should be realized that the more restrictions are imposed the less the "pay-off" value is likely to be.

3.4.2 Problem: To Assess the Instruction Factors That Have a Significant Effect in the Teaching of a Second Language

3.4.2.1 Reference

See discussion of "instruction factors" in Sections 3.1.3 and 3.2.2.

3.4.2.2 Tactics

3.4.2.2.1 Standardized Tests

There are no standardized tests for the assessment of instruction factors except those related to criterion evaluation (as in 3.4.1.2.1 (a) above). The development of standardized tests for the evaluation of communicative competence is a critical need in the language testing field today and this problem is examined in Section 3.4.3 below. The check-list form discussed under 3.4.2.2.4 below has the capability of developing into a standardized test for the evaluation of a FL program, but at the moment no norms are available for it.

3.4.2.2.2 Interview Technique

The area where this technique could be useful is that of "teacher observation and evaluation." If viewed in narrow terms, this approach would take the form of an interview between the instructor and his supervisor in which the latter would obtain information on a number of matters: the degree to which the instructor is aware of recent advances in language pedagogy, his satisfaction with the administrative support he feels he is getting, special problems with students on which he might need help, the degree to which he is responsive to learner factors, innovations in the instruction program that he might wish to bring about, his attitudes toward the native language and culture of the students when the latter have a different ethnic background, and so on. Defined in broader terms, the "interview technique" can be conceived in terms of "discussion groups" in which instructors and supervisors (and perhaps other "experts") examine jointly the problems they share and the solutions that might be available for them.

3.4.2.2.3 Written Questionnaires

The teaching inventory profile discussed below can be used as a questionnaire to obtain responses from teachers, supervisors, and students. This procedure yields information on what instructional activities are considered good or bad by each of these groups.

3.4.2.2.4 Descriptive Field Observations

Hayes, Lambert, and Tucker (1967) present a 324-item inventory that describes in fairly specific terms the principles and policies which language teachers consider relevant to the instructional setting. The inventory is grouped under six headings: (a) *Administration and policy;* (b) *Teachers and teacher competence;* (c) *Course design;* (d) *Testing;* (e) *Classroom and classes;* and (f) *Language laboratory.* The authors of the inventory propose that independent assessors visit schools and attend classrooms and make direct observations along each of the inventory items. This would yield a profile for each particular setting. Different profiles can be correlated with achievement measures on students matched on relevant factors (aptitude, intelligence, attitude, etc.) and statements can then be made about the effectiveness of specific instruction activities. Such results can be used in decisions about changes in practices and policies.

This approach is undoubtedly superior to previous attempts at comparing "*methods* of second-language teaching" in which a great deal of variability was subsumed under a single "method." However, there are two basic weaknesses with the proposal of Hayes et al. (1967) which ought to be remedied. The first relates to their suggestion to use matched groups of students. This would be practically impossible given the large number of learner factors that would have to be matched (see section I.F. of outline on page 105), and in any event, the sociocultural setting in each school is likely to be unique, and hence, would not be matched. The second weakness of their proposal lies in inadequate provisions being made for assessment of proficiency and achievement of communicative skills. This is extremely serious since the evaluation of the effectiveness of any instructional activity is dependent upon the availability of adequate criterion measures. It is important, therefore, that the teaching inventory be used in conjunction with a program of research that includes the identification of learner factors, as described in Problem 3.4.1 (above) and the development of adequate criterion measures, as discussed in Problem 3.4.3 (below). Statistical techniques can then be used to assess the interaction effects between specific learner and instruction factors as they affect particular criterion goals.

Some additional comments are in order. The inventory developed by Hayes et al., useful as it undoubtedly will be, neglects certain important instruction factors which ought to be incorporated in subsequent versions of it, or obtained by some other means. The most important of these is the degree to which the instructional program is responsive to learner factors as discussed in Sections 3.1.3, 3.2.1, and 3.2.2. What provisions exist for adjusting criterion goals to aptitude and interest? What corrective measures are being taken against inappropriate student self-evaluation criteria, learning strategies, and study habits? and so on. In other words, what is needed is not only a description of the "statics" of the instruction program, but its "dynamics" as well, viz., the built-in measures for change (direction and rate) as required by the existing demands.

3.4.2.2.5 Field Evaluations

The descriptive measures just discussed can serve as input to statements of evaluation about specific practices, policies, and characteristics, or about the overall program. Teachers can be rated on competence in terms of the degree to which they display desired characteristics. Such evaluations can serve a diagnostic function and suggest areas where they need remedial training. Schools can be given ratings for the effectiveness of their foreign language program which can serve the basis for administrative changes and a guide to be used by teachers and students in deciding about employment and attendance. Ultimately, national standards can be adopted which can have significant sociopolitical and cultural implications.

3.4.2.2.6 Manipulation by Selection

In the context of the problem under discussion, there are many occasions for using this technique to assess instruction factors in special settings. The sociocultural setting may result in certain peculiarities unique to that situation (e.g., schools in New York with a heavy proportion of Puerto Ricans, or schools in Montreal vs. Toronto, etc.) and this kind of "natural selection" allows for interesting comparisons. Intentional selection may be desirable in assessing experimental programs where the selection may occur at the level of teacher, student, or policy.

3.4.2.2.7 Manipulation by Induction

Teacher training programs combined with pre- and post-observations of effectiveness represents an example of this approach. Others include special programs such as "a year abroad," summer language camps and the "French House," and varieties of special techniques which the teacher might want to try out (e.g., language games) in combination with comparison groups or pre- post-designs.

3.4.2.3 Procedure

The same kind of considerations as discussed in Section 3.4.1.3 apply here as well with respect to selection and preparation of observation techniques, choice of setting, and analysis of data.

3.4.2.4 Overview

The problem reviewed in this section concerns the description and identification of instruction factors that have a significant effect in the teaching of a second language. The principal tactical approach here rests on field observation techniques that allow for sufficiently detailed description of the various practices, policies, and characteristics of a school setting. Evaluation of their significance is dependent upon the availability and use of adequate criteria of success (a problem to be taken up next) as well as assessment procedures of the degree of responsiveness of the instruction program to learner factors. Let us now examine the various focal points of interest in such an analysis.

3.4.2.4.1 Problems of Covariance Relations

The teaching inventory profile developed by Hayes, Lambert, and Tucker (1967) contains 324 items. Are they all necessary? What is their intercorrelation in different settings? Are the six groupings independent of each other or do some characteristics tend to go together (e.g., teacher competence and adequacy of language laboratories)? Regression techniques can be used for attempts at prediction, in this case, student achievement, on the basis of instructional activities and characteristics of the school setting.

3.4.2.4.2 Problems of Allocation of Amount of Variance

What is the order of importance of the instruction factors in determining student achievement? How do they compare in magnitude to the importance of learner factors? What is the interaction effect between instruction and learner factors in determining student achievement? Do the instruction factors retain the same significance in school settings having different sociocultural background?

3.4.2.4.3 Problems of Distributional Characteristics

Which practices are widespread, which are controversial? Does the size of the school make any difference, or the language being taught? Are there geographic differences? Or differences between teacher background: their age, where they were trained, whether they are native speakers, etc.?

3.4.2.4.4 Problems Related to Corrective Measures

Where and how fast can changes be introduced? Are there desirable priorities in certain areas? Can changes be made singly and independently or does a change in one area necessitate concomitant change in another?

We turn now to the next problem, the solution to which is indispensable to the success of the one just analyzed.

3.4.3 Problem: To Develop Adequate Evaluation Criteria for Assessing Success in the Study of a Second Language

3.4.3.1 Reference

See discussion of what it means "to know how to use a language" in Sections 3.1.1 and 3.1.2.

3.4.3.2 Tactics

3.4.3.2.1 Standardized Tests

As pointed out a number of times before, the only ones available here are the discrete-point variety and the goal is to develop standardized tests of communicative competence. The questionnaire and field observation techniques described below will be the principal methods for the development of such tests.

3.4.3.2.2 Interview Technique

The oral interview situation is a necessary component for the evaluation of communicative ability. The main problem consists of structuring the interview situation in such a way as to require the interviewee to make use of a sufficiently broad configuration of communicative activities to assess the range of his abilities. A number of these will now be suggested.

(a) *Opening a conversation and leave taking:* to be carried out in a simulated setting which specifies the relevant variables (who the addressee is, where the conversation takes place). The setting factors should vary in a number of ways to determine the individual's range of capacity in "striking up" conversations and appropriately ending them. Thus, addressees should vary in terms of their age, sex, status, familiarity to the speaker, occupation, etc.; place should vary in terms of location (street, restaurant, airplane, social gathering, etc.), time of day, etc.

(b) *Obtaining information to solve a particular problem:* a sufficient variety should be provided (travel instructions, buying an unusual item, filling out official forms, getting help in an accident, putting together a puzzle, making arrangements for a funeral, etc.).

(c) *Engaging in idle conversation and exchanging amities in a variety of settings.*

(d) *Carrying out a serious conversation on particular topics* (politics, religion, philosophy of life, etc.).

(e) *Executing socially defined formal activities:* some examples include making introductions, expressing condolences, asking for apology, congratulating the bride, telling a joke, etc.

(f) *Executing socially common but informal activities,* such as asking a girl out for a date, talking to a baby, getting rid of an unwanted salesman, reminiscing about childhood days, etc.

(g) *Reporting an event or describing an ongoing activity:* for example, reporting an accident to a policeman, or giving a description of a parade.

(h) *Effectiveness of information transmission:* the individual sits on one side of a screen and is required to transmit to and receive information from another individual who is a monolingual speaker in the second language and who sits, out of view, on the other side of the screen. Variations on this theme are, of course, possible: for instance, a telephone may be used. Complications may be arranged by introducing noise so that the participants have to shout, or "human chains" may be introduced so that the information passes through more than one individual. The task itself may be simple or as complicated as one wishes. For instance, one participant tells a story or reads a sentence or paragraph and the other participant must repeat it or paraphrase it. Or, a task may be arranged such that its solution depends on exchange of information between the participants.

These eight communicative situations, and their subparts, are obviously not exhaustive; one can easily suggest dozens of others. Where should one stop? This is essentially an empirical question and cannot be answered *ad hoc.* As more and more situations are added in such a testing procedure, one will no doubt find that less and less additional information is obtained, so that one must reach a balance between what is feasible within the demands of the testing situation and what is considered to be the minimum range of abilities the student must acquire for the purpose one has in mind (whether in the evaluation of a teaching program or the requirements of a job situation).

Serious attention must be given to the problem of scoring the individual's performance on these communicative tasks. Two approaches are possible, global and minute, and either or both can be used depending on the purpose for which the evaluations are made. Global ratings for each communicative act can be given in terms of some relative scale that uses as a reference point the expected or observed performance of a native who has background characteristics that resemble the interviewee (age, sex, education, occupation). Obviously, if the interviewee is a sixteen-year old girl from a small town in the Midwest, she should not be compared to a forty-year old Parisian housewife with a college education (if the test language is French). The interviewer would need some degree of sophistication and practice in evaluations of this sort (perhaps audiovisual materials with case histories can be made available for their training).

The minute approach would consist of evaluating specific features of the interviewee's utterances. Proposals for such analyses have been made in a number of places for paralinguistics and kinesics (see Hayes's review, 1964), stylistics (see the review in Jakobovits, 1969e), semantics and meaning (Jakobovits, 1968c) and many others. This is an open-ended task even if we limit ourselves to the analysis tools now available, which cannot be considered adequate or exhaustive. But this state of affairs is no cause for despair as far as concerns the present problem. After all, testing is a practical business and it is quite appropriate to stop being exhaustive at precisely the point where sufficient information has been obtained for a particular purpose and within the "cost" afforded by the situation. It is plain that the policy followed by the profession up till now, namely of stopping at discrete-point tests, is not going far enough (or going in the wrong direction); we can (must) go further. How much further, is both an empirical and a practical question.

There is another kind of possible objection to the approach being suggested here, and this must be dealt with. It is the obvious argument that tests of communicative acts are heavily contaminated by nonlinguistic factors. What if the interviewee is a shy person and functions badly under simulation conditions? What if he is socially inept? These other factors can have such a strong effect that we are not really measuring their *linguistic* knowledge. The objection is really inappropriate. It would have some force provided one were interested exclusively in linguistic competence and provided one could define linguistic competence independently of the use of language. But both provisions are inappropriate on theoretical as well as practical grounds. The latter is quite plain to any language teacher, the former is still a controversial issue in linguistics but only in terms of present limitations in that discipline. There is no doubt that linguistics would ultimately have to incorporate not only *how* one says things but also how one knows *what* to say, and the most recent formulations in generative semantics (see Steinberg and Jakobovits, in press) have come to grips with this problem (e.g., knowledge about the "appropriateness" of an utterance, which includes knowledge about the world and culture, is being incorporated in the theory of semantics).

One final point needs to be examined. Macnamara (1967b) has suggested that the contribution of nonlinguistic factors in what he calls "indirect" measures of language proficiency (i.e., other than discrete-point tests)—and tests of communicative acts would fall in this category according to Macnamara's definition—may be "controlled out" by subtracting an individual's performance score in a task requiring the use of the second language from the score obtained on the same task requiring the use of the native language. The difference in score would then be an indication of relative proficiency. Elsewhere (Jakobovits, 1967), I have pointed out several weaknesses to this argument, the major one being that there is no guarantee (or even high probability) that the interaction effect between the nonlinguistic and linguistic competence factors in the two languages is equivalent. This is especially true for coordinate bilinguals of dissimilar cultures where communicative acts cannot be considered equivalent since what is appropriate in one culture may be completely irrelevant in the other. In Section 3.1.2 we spoke of Fishman's concept of "bilingual dominance configuration." Note that there are two possible reference points for dominance: the bilingual himself, relative to his native language or, an idealized monolingual from the target culture. It is the latter that is being advocated here as most useful. Thus comparison of the interviewee's scores on the eight communicative tests described above with those of a relevant monolingual speaker of the target culture would yield his bilingual dominance configuration.

3.4.3.2.3 Written Questionnaires

This technique will be broadly interpreted as including written tests which are, however, nonstandardized.

(a) *Judgments of Appropriateness: Situations:* An event is described in which the participants engage in non-verbal behavior. The test consists of making judgments concerning the appropriateness of the behavior (perhaps on a six- or seven-point scale). The intent here is to assess the individual's awareness of which social behaviors are acceptable in the target culture.

(b) *Judgments of Appropriateness: Speech Acts:* The individual is required to make judgments of acceptability of utterances within specified contexts, or alternately, rating the stylistic appropriateness of certain expressions. An example of the former would be as follows:

> John Doe is telephoning his high school classmate, Bob Jones. An adult male voice answers the call saying "Jones residence, Hello!" John Doe might say one of the following. Choose the most appropriate utterance.
>
> (a) Hi! Is Bob there?
> (b) Good evening. This is Mr. John Doe. Can I speak to Mr. Robert Jones, please?
> (c) Hello. This is John Doe. Could I speak to Bob, please?

Some examples of the second alternative would be the following:

> Below are presented pairs of sentences that have similar meaning. In each case select the alternative that is more natural or more acceptable stylistically.
>
> A. 1. He was frightened momentarily.
>   2. He was fearful momentarily.
> B. 1. He took a long sip.
>   2. He took a long gulp.
> C. 1. He had been dozing for some time when the phone rang.
>   2. He had been dozing off for some time when the phone rang.
> D. 1. He criticized me only once.
>   2. He nagged me only once.

Probably both types of tests should be used since they measure somewhat different competencies. (The rationale behind these examples is given in detail elsewhere. See Chapter 4, Section 3.)

(c) *Judgments of the Affective Meaning of Words:* Individuals are asked to rate words or phrases on a seven-point bipolar scale whose ends are defined by appropriate qualifiers (adjectives in English). This approach is known as the "semantic differential technique" (see Osgood, Suci, and Tannenbaum, 1957) and an example is given below:

MONEY

sweet	:	:	:	:	:	:	sour
heavy	:	:	:	:	:	:	light
sharp	:	:	:	:	:	:	dull

The individual's ratings can then be compared to those given typically by monolingual speakers. Semantic differential scales have been developed for some thirty languages (Jakobovits, 1966; Osgood, 1964) and norms for monolingual, monocultural subjects are available for 600 words (Center for Comparative Psycholinguistics, in press; Jakobovits, 1969f). This test can be used to assess the individual's sensitivity to some important aspects of subjective culture.

(d) *Inferring the Implicative Meaning of Utterances:* The individual is given snatches of conversation and is required to infer their implications (emotion of the speaker, irony, undertones, etc.). Here is an example:

> Below are some snatches of conversation between two individuals. Following the last utterance (italicized) a few alternatives are given which guess at the state of mind of the speaker. Choose the best alternative on the basis of your interpretation of the situation.
>
> I. X. Hey, George! I just talked to the boss. I've got some news for you.
> Y. Great! I've been expecting something about that salary raise. Well, what did he say?
> X. He said you're fired.
> Y. *Thanks, clever man. I'll talk to him myself.*
> a. The speaker is thankful for the information received.
> b. The speaker is angry because he has been fired.
> c. The speaker thinks X is joking and does not believe him.

(e) *Assessment of Lexical Structures:* Psychologists have shown that the vocabulary of speakers is stored in structures and hierarchies, rather than in random or alphabetical sequence. Some aspects of such lexical relations are shared by members of a language/culture community, a commonality which is undoubtedly related to the conceptual framework proper to that culture. In learning a second language, the individual comes to acquire lexical structures that correspond to a greater or lesser degree to that of an idealized monolingual of the target culture. The assessment of the degree of this relationship may be important since there are indications that (i) such lexical structures reflect the individual's conceptual systems and (ii) they mediate the individual's interpretations of situations and events.

There are several techniques for estimating lexical structures, some of which are similar, others entirely different. It would not be useful to review them here (for some references see Chapter 4).

(f) *Performance under Conditions of Noise:* Spolsky (1968b) and his co-workers have shown that individuals who perform adequately on the traditional achievement tests or under typical classroom conditions show a marked decrease in listening comprehension (relative to native speakers) as soon as noise is introduced into the situation. They attribute this difference to a failure to learn adequately the redundancy relations in language (phonological, lexical, semantic) and culture (what is likely to happen or to be said under particular conditions). If Spolsky's hypothesis is correct, this kind of a test could prove to be most useful as a global estimate of several of the skills measured by the other tests described above. (Note that this test could be administered either orally in an interview or in a group situation with written answers to auditorily presented materials.)

Another test that seems also to measure knowledge of redundancy relations is the Cloze Procedure (Taylor, 1953) in which a paragraph is mutilated by deleting say, every fifth word in the text, and the individual is required to supply the missing words.

3.4.3.2.4 Descriptive Field Observations

The purpose of developing tests is to enable the teacher or investigator to estimate an individual's performance under natural conditions. While many tests have such obvious face validity that one can be fairly certain that they are relevant to performance in natural settings, not all have this characteristic, and furthermore, some tests that appear arbitrary and esoteric on the surface, turn out to have excellent predictive value for performance in natural settings. For this reason, it is highly desirable to develop observation techniques that allow for systematic description of individual performance in natural settings. Auditory and visual recordings of such performance supplemented by detailed notes on the communicative setting are indispensible techniques for such descriptions.

3.4.3.2.5 Field Evaluations

Evaluations can be made, indirectly, on the recorded observations or directly, by allowing the evaluator to be present in the natural setting. Training and the use of evaluation forms will help insure acceptable levels of interjudge agreement and reliability.

3.4.3.2.6 Manipulation by Selection

3.4.3.2.7 Manipulation by Induction

These techniques will be useful in assessing the effects of specialized training procedures on test performance. For instance, language games that involve "acting out" situations may help performance on tests of communicative acts of the type described above. Note that some of this training may be given in the learner's native language. Because of cultural differences, the individual may lack communicative skills that are common in the target culture but unusual in the native culture. For instance, degree of physical contact, eye contact, gestural expansiveness, mouth opening, and so on, which affect communicative skills, may be so foreign to the learner that practice in these nonverbal acts may be desirable in either simulated settings or artificial ones, through the medium of the native language. Finally, practice in listening to mutilated tapes may be a useful procedure to have subjects learn redundancy relations in language.

3.4.3.3 Procedure

3.4.3.3.1 Selection and Preparation of Observation Techniques

3.4.3.3.2 Selection of Setting

3.4.3.3.3 Analysis of Data

Each test must be carefully developed using standard principles of good test construction. Administration must be standardized, ambiguous items corrected, scoring bias or unreliability eliminated.

3.4.3.4 Overview

The problem reviewed in this section is extremely critical. Unless adequate evaluation criteria are developed, the effectiveness of instruction procedures cannot be properly evaluated. The task is admittedly complicated–and we are starting practically from the beginning–but it can no longer be avoided or postponed. Its result may have far reaching consequences for the profession. FL teachers may come to change completely their attitude with respect to what they are teaching: instead of teaching "French" or "Spanish" or "German," etc., they may view themselves as teaching "how to do things" in French, Spanish, German, etc. Course titles may take on a new image: instead of "French 101," say, we might have "How to Travel in France, 101" or "How to Win Friends in Russian, 304" and the like. With courses such as these, the "student motivation" problem is likely to be transformed into an overcrowded classroom problem.

3.4.3.5 Commentary

The most controversial aspect of this chapter, an argument that may be discouraging to many teachers, is the claim that the teacher's contribution to quality of instruction is often of a negative sort. It is important to keep in mind that "quality of instruction" has been defined here in a more restricted sense than is usually the case when such an expression is used. *It certainly does not mean that the teacher can make no contribution to the learning process.* In fact, the whole notion of "compensatory" education, as it has been discussed here, was introduced for the specific purpose of rendering the instruction process more effective and in explicit recognition of the belief that the teacher can have an extremely important role in the overall instructional activity. So it would perhaps be useful to briefly review the argument and in slightly different terms:

Whereas our ability to learn far outstretches our ability to explain in specific terms just *how* we learn and

Whereas we are unable to specify in specific terms just *what* it is to "know" a language, then

Therefore it follows that it is impossible to *teach* a language, in the strongest sense of that word.

This conclusion, while not a traditional one, is not as new and revolutionary as it might seem to many teachers. Socrates, in ancient times, and the contemporary psychologist Carl Rogers in modern times, to mention but those two, have held similar views about education. The notion that "teaching is an art, not a science" embodies this principle, although it appears to me that teachers have not always fully appreciated the implications of this dictum. In all matters relating to human interrelationships–art, medicine, politics, education, social work, psychotherapy–practice has always outstripped science, or to put it in reverse terms, scientific knowledge in these areas has always lagged behind practical knowledge. This is not to deny the proper role that scientific investigations have to play in improving our skills to perform certain tasks, although in matters of politics, education, and psychotherapy, the contribution of the scientific enterprise has been much less conspicuous than in medicine and engineering. Nevertheless, the strong tendency in recent times on the part of educators to believe in the supreme efficacy of "scientific principles" as the touchstone of their teaching practices has led to the erroneous and devastating belief that teaching is a matter of reinforcing certain known pieces of behavior and that when the teaching process fails and students don't learn, it is because they have a "motivation problem."

This has been no less true in FL teaching. And yet I believe that the arguments presented in this chapter show that the fault lies not in the "rebellious" student but in the FL teaching enterprise. To teach surface facts about a language by means of habit drills is not an efficient way of teaching communicative skills. To teach "speaking skills" when there is no opportunity to use the language for speaking is not efficient. To attempt to teach the same thing and by the same method a mass of students who demonstrably differ in FL aptitude is not a wise practice. To overlook the specific interests and needs of individual students, when these are determined by the wider social context in which they live, is foolhardy.

What, then, are the alternatives? I hope this chapter has pointed to some of the possibilities by discussing the notion of compensatory education. We must first be aware of how the larger sociopolitical context influences the interests and needs of students and take it from there. We must second have clearly in mind what the specific goals of a particular course are, not in terms of some abstract and irrelevant criterion as indexed by a discrete-point language test, but in terms of terminal behavioral tasks such as "the ability to engage in a conversation about the weather" or "the ability to ask directions" or "the ability to write business letters" or "understand a news broadcast," and so on. Then, finally, we must expose the student to practice situations which will enable him, in whatever mysterious ways learning takes place, to attain the specified goals within the limitations and restrictions imposed by the learning context: the student's aptitude, his willingness to spend the required amount of time in active study, the opportunities available to him for practice, the cumulative amount of time (in terms of months and years) that the curriculum affords, etc.

What about the carefully and painstakingly worked out language teaching materials, sentence patterns, vocabulary sequences, contrastive analyses, laboratory tapes, and other paraphernalia of applied linguistics, the stock and trade of the professional FL teacher? What role do they play in my visionary scheme? It would be foolhardy, in my opinion, to chuck them out the window, but their role must be honestly reevaluated in the light of individuated and compensatory FL instruction. There are those students who can, and will learn despite and without them (children do, and immigrants do). But the essence of compensatory instruction is to help the individual student where he needs help and at the time he is actively trying to solve a particular problem. The materials of applied linguistics are not to be used as a predetermined, rigidly applied set of procedures to be followed from A to Z as prescribed by a program or text, but rather as specific and explicit knowledge the teacher internalizes or has at his disposal and uses when and where it may be of help to a particular student who exhibits certain specific problems. The teacher should in effect adopt the model of the physician. The latter is a highly trained specialist who has incorporated the best scientific knowledge available at the time of his training; the paraphernalia at his disposal–the instruments and drugs–are not applied indiscriminately to all patients who knock at his door. Individuated and compensatory activity is based on similar principles whether in medicine or education.

How realistic is this proposal? One needs to look at this question from two points of view. On the one hand I think it is perfectly legitimate to consider utopian and idealized situations in order to set up a model of what we could be striving for, even if we cannot attain it within the foreseeable future. I have no doubt that many FL teachers and administrators would classify my proposal in that category. I happen to think that we are closer to such a model, that it will be a reality in the not too distant future. However, another aspect to the question is how can we render present-day instructional activities more compensatory in character than they are now? The first requirement is to reorganize the FL curriculum in such a way that it is made up of a set of specific courses with limited goals. This reorganization must be done within the limiting conditions that hold for any particular school: the number of teachers available and the number of students who opt for a particular goal in a particular language. These limiting conditions may vary from year to year in any school and the FL program must be responsive to such variations. The program should be defined in terms of the range of goals to be offered, not in terms of levels or years. Thus students of different grades may attend the same course, and the length of a course (in weeks or months) should be determined by the difficulty of its goal, not by the school year. For instance, a course on "understanding news broadcasts" or "reading newspapers" might take only 10 weeks, while "engaging in street conversation" or "writing business letters" might take 20 weeks, and "reading literature" or "social conversation" might take the full academic year. Criteria for admission to each course should be based on interest, aptitude, and the student's state of knowledge as assessed by a personal interview with the teacher or his aides, in terms of his actual capacity to perform certain specified tasks (e.g., being able to engage in "street conversation" before being admitted to a course on "social conversation"). Participation in a course should not be necessarily defined in terms of class attendance but rather in terms of performing certain activities that the student and the teacher agree would lead to the attainment of the goal of that course. For instance, in a reading course much of the requisite activity can be done by the student independently. In a conversation course the student can go out and spend so many hours with a speaker of the FL (which can be an available native in the community or an advanced student).

The FL curriculum must obviously be based on the available resources in the school and surrounding community. For example, if no Russian speakers are available, either natives, bilinguals, or advanced students, it makes no sense to offer a conversation course to 40 students when there is only one Russian teacher available to the school. I know this has been attempted, but the activity ends up to be a waste of time for most of the students. The goals must be determined within the restrictions of the case if we are seriously concerned with success rather than with going through the motions.

Will the students cooperate? Pessimistic expectations based on student attitudes to the current curriculum must not be taken too seriously. The reactions to the new curriculum proposed here cannot be predicted on the basis of present uncooperative reactions to the current curriculum. I think it will always be the case that a certain proportion of the student body simply will never be interested in FL learning. This is a sociocultural fact and we must accept it. On the other hand the student with an initial interest is likely to get involved when he clearly perceives the relevance of his study activities to the goals he has chosen himself and experiences progress within these limited goals.

But can they really learn more effectively in this rather free-floating manner than through the carefully worked out sequential steps of phonology, morphology, syntax, vocabulary, etc., of the usual text or materials? This is of course the ultimate question, and it is an empirical one. Arguments cannot resolve this issue. On the basis of my own experience and observation of experimental courses and of self-taught individuals, I believe this would be more effective. I intend to buttress my arguments with further observation and experimentation that are currently underway. The point is that we must try something else because what we are doing now is not working.

Chapter 4

PROBLEMS IN ASSESSING LANGUAGE PROFICIENCY

A criticism of current practices in FL education that recurs throughout the earlier chapters is that the traditional methods used for assessing language proficiency attained by students are inadequate. Grade-point averages obtained in FL courses and standardized discreet-point tests (both written and oral) are not sufficient indicators of the ability to use the FL for communicative purposes. One could even argue that these assessment procedures are not only insufficient, bur irrelevant. Furthermore, one important reason why research on the comparative effectiveness of different teaching methods has never yielded definitive results is that the methods and procedures employed for assessing what the student has acquired have been inadequate.

There is a critical need in the language testing field for tests of communicative competence. Some possible approaches to this problem were briefly outlined in the last section of Chapter 3 under the heading of "Criterion evaluation." (See p. 106). This chapter considers the problem of assessment in greater detail. The first section provides the rationale for a "functional" approach and gives a few illustrations on how one would go about developing tests of language skills. The last two sections have a more "molecular" orientation and are concerned chiefly with the assessment of transfer effects between the individual's two languages. This part of the book is more "experimentally" oriented than the rest, and here the FL teacher can gain a glimpse of the academic researcher in action. It is involved, esoteric, and sometimes abstruse, and may be of only peripheral interest to the practitioner. Nevertheless, I encourage the reader to plough through these sections, not only because he will gain a better understanding of the psycholinguist's mind (hopefully!), but also because they raise interesting and important issues on the nature of bilingualism: Are there different "types" of bilinguals? To what extent does the native language affect the acquisition of the second language? Under what conditions may we expect positive and negative transfer? And many others.

A FUNCTIONAL APPROACH TO THE ASSESSMENT OF LANGUAGE SKILLS

The problem of assessing language skills is a practical concern. Developments in this area have proceeded under the impetus of necessity rather than under the guidance of a coherent theoretical understanding of the nature of language and communication. There is nothing opprobrious in such a strategy, given the various social needs which the field of language testing has had to meet, and no doubt the activities associated with this endeavor will—and should—continue in the near future. On the other hand there is no wisdom or advantage in ignoring the potential contribution of theoretical developments in the fields concerned with the study of language and in this section I shall attempt to outline what I consider to be the implications of recent theoretical developments for the practical problems which are of concern to the language testing field.

4.1 COMMUNICATIVE COMPETENCE

Because of their practical orientation, the contributors to the language testing field are more aware than their theoretically oriented colleagues that language is primarily a communicative skill. Or so it would seem. And yet a cursory examination of the "state of the art" in language testing indicates that the progress of the work to date has been chiefly oriented towards the assessment of linguistic competence rather than communicative competence. Since much of the rationale of the proposal to be outlined relates to the distinction to be made between these two types of competencies, it is necessary to examine it in some detail.

The distinction is recognized intuitively at certain embarrassing moments in our social interactions when we don't know *what* to say or *how* to say something, when we fail to communicate "a point," when we "put our foot in our mouth," when we misunderstand "the words" of someone, or, at less awkward moments, when we infer intent and other psychological states on the basis of someone's utterances, when we identify a person's geographic origin and his social and educational background on the basis of his speech, and so on. The study of linguistic competence has traditionally excluded these wider considerations involved in the use of language as indicated by the emergence of "paralinguistic," "exolinguistic," "sociolinguistic," and "psycholinguistic" hybrid fields whose purpose was to cover various aspects of the communicative act. Linguists have acknowledged the fact that the study of language *use* must necessarily encompass these wider competencies, sometimes referring to the difference as linguistic competence versus linguistic performance, but they have generally maintained that the study of linguistic competence per se need not concern itself with social-psychological factors. The development of language tests as measures of linguistic skills derives its justification from this traditional position taken by linguists. However, the adequacy of such a position must now be challenged as a result of the evidence that has accumulated in these hybrid disciplines as well as from recent work in linguistics itself, especially, but not exclusively, that aspect of the field that has concerned itself with the semantic component of language.

Let us consider some specific issues involved in this argument. It has been established (see for example the review by Ervin-Tripp, 1967) that speakers of a language have a command of various "codes" that can be defined as a set of restriction rules that determine the choice of phonological, syntactic, and lexical items in sentences. These restriction rules form a code by virtue of the fact that they are related to the same set of variables such that, given the presence of a particular variable, it will then require a specifiable set of rules determining the choice of these items in speech. For example, the choice of address form in English (using the title "Mr." followed by last name), the choice of a particular phonological variant (the "-ing" ending of the progressive form of verbs), and the choice of certain lexical equivalents ("Good Morning" vs. "Hi") are all determined by the same social variable which relates to the status relation between the speaker and listener. (Contrast the utterance "Good morning Mr. Gibbs! How is your work coming along" with "Hi, John! How's your work comi*n*' along?"–both of which are possible for the same speaker, but he would not use both under the same situation: they belong to different codes.) The choice of "Tu" and "Vous" in French (and in German along analogous lines) is determined by specifiable social factors between two interlocutors. In Thai (and several other languages) it is impossible to carry out a conversation without explicitly encoding certain relations that hold between speaker and listener (status, age, degree of friendship, family ties, etc.).

These selection rules, and others of this type, are as necessary a part of the linguistic competence of a speaker as those with which we are more familiar in syntax such as accord in gender, number, and tense, and it would seem to be entirely arbitrary to exclude them from a description that deals with linguistic competence.

There have been a number of recent proposals (e.g., Katz and Fodor, 1963; Osgood, 1968) that attempt to describe the meaning relations among words in terms of a set of semantic features (e.g., "animate," "male," "human," etc.). Certain linguistic facts can be explained by assigning particular semantic features to words. For example, if one assumes that MAN is coded for an "animate" and a "human" feature (among others), DOG for "animate" and "nonhuman," TABLE for "nonanimate" and "nonhuman," SPEAK for "human" and RUN for "animate," then one can explain why the following sentences are permissible or nonpermissible, as the case may be:

The man did not wish to speak.
*The dog did not wish to speak.
*The table did not wish to speak.
The man ran away.
The dog ran away.
*The table ran away.

The nature and identity of the semantic features that must be postulated is still a matter of dispute. One practical criterion for the choice of a feature is whether it helps explain a linguistic fact. Thus to account for the fact that the expression "to beg proudly" is anomalous (as opposed to "to beg humbly" which is apposite), Osgood (1968) postulates a "supraordinate–subordinate" feature for interpersonal verbs ("to beg" is coded for "subordinate" and "proudly" for "supraordinate"–hence the anomaly of the combination). I have pointed out elsewhere (Jakobovits, 1968c) that OLD MAN is coded for "passivity" and "weakness" which accounts for the fact that the following two utterances are paraphrases of each other:

(a) Don't worry about him. He can't interfere. He's just an old man.

(b) Don't worry about him. He can't interfere. He's just a $\begin{Bmatrix}\text{passive}\\\text{weak}\end{Bmatrix}$ old man.

The addition of "passive" or "weak" in (b) is redundant, showing that OLD MAN is coded for a "passivity" and a "weakness" feature. Note further that (c) is anomalous:

(c) *Don't worry about him. He can't interfere. He's just $\begin{Bmatrix}\text{an active}\\\text{a strong}\end{Bmatrix}$ old man.

It is possible under certain circumstances to ask native speakers directly whether a particular word is coded one way or another for any particular feature. The *Cross-cultural Atlas of Affective Meanings* represents such an attempt in which a group of native speakers in some 20 language/culture communities were asked to code 600 words in terms of three generalized affective features: Evaluation, Potency, and Activity (see Osgood, 1964; Jakobovits, 1966; 1969). The relevance of this *Atlas* for the present discussion lies in the fact that the affective features of words that represent translation equivalents are sometimes universal (e.g., MOTHER is code as "+Evaluation," DEATH is coded as "–Evaluation," AIRPLANE is coded as "+Activity," ROCK is coded as "+Potency," etc.) and sometimes cross-culturally variable (e.g., PRAYER is coded "+Evaluation" in the United States but "–Evaluation" in Yugoslavia). The "+Evaluation" and "–Activity" coding of SUNDAY in American English accounts for the interpretability of the sentence "On this island, my friend, every day is Sunday." In Delhi Hindi, SUNDAY (meaning: the first day of the week, the Day of the Lord) is coded as "0 Evaluation" and "0 Activity" (i.e., "Zero") and the sentence in question would not be interpretable. Note, however, that in order to account for these linguistic facts it is necessary to take into account specific cultural differences between Delhi Hindi and American English cultures. Again it would be a matter of pure arbitrariness to declare that these cultural factors are to be excluded from an account of linguistic competence.

Finally I would like to mention one other specific issue which argues against a restricted view of linguistic competence. One would certainly insist that any serious account of linguistic competence would include the derivation of the meaning of a (well formed) sentence. Central to such an account is the fact that speakers of a language are capable of recognizing whether two sentences have the same meaning, that is, that they are paraphrases of each other. That the following two sentences are paraphrases of each other, namely

(a) Kiki chewed up the bathroom rug.

(b) The rug in the bathroom was chewed up by Kiki.

can be adequately demonstrated by showing the transformations which relate the two sentences to each other. But what would it take to demonstrate that the next two sentences are paraphrases of each other?

(c) You're on, Rex.

(d) You're next, Rex.

The relation between these two sentences is in terms of functional equivalence (of intent) within the context in which either of them may be uttered. It would do no good to argue that the relation involved is arbitrary, nonlinguistic as might be the case between two equivalent secret passwords, since it can be shown that functional equivalence in meaning can be rendered by novel paraphrases (e.g., the telephone is out of order, the telephone isn't functioning, the telephone doesn't work, the telephone is dead, etc.). In order to account for a speaker's ability to recognize the equivalence of these sentences, one will have to consider factors other than those usually included in a restricted sense of linguistic competence (for example, intention of the speaker, see below).

4.2 THREE LEVELS OF MEANING

In order to be able to account for the minimum range of linguistic phenomena involved in communicative competence, it will be necessary to incorporate in the analysis of an utterance three levels of meaning. I shall refer to these as linguistic, implicit, and implicative.

4.2.1 Linguistic Meaning

I shall retain this term to refer to the traditional concerns of linguists as outlined in such recent treatises as Chomsky (1965) and Katz (1966). Briefly, this includes a dictionary of lexical meanings and their projection rules, syntactic relations as defined by a derivative transformational theory, and phonological actualization rules.

4.2.2 Implicit Meaning

I shall use this term to refer to the elliptically derived conceptual event which an utterance represents. Let me use the following example to clarify what I mean. Consider the meaning of "agreed to" in each of the following sentences:

(a) The University agreed to pay his moving expenses.

(b) After the President invoked the Taft-Hartley Act, the strikers agreed to go back to work.

(c) Joan agreed to marry him.

(d) They agreed to settle the matter out of court.

Note that in each of the four instances "agreed to" has some different particular implications which one can infer on the basis of the situation to which the sentence as a whole refers. These particular implications are a function of the situational context that the sentence in which the verb is used refers to and therefore are potentially infinite. The dictionary meaning of the verb applies certain definite restrictions on the kind of particular implications it may have in a sentence and thus, although these implications are potentially infinite, they are not randomly variable. There are many other instances in which this type of nonrandom but infinite variability principle operates. The concept of "triangularity" can be particularized as a visual form (among others) with infinite, but nonrandom, variability: each particular triangle will have its own unique properties different from any other particular triangle. What I am arguing is that the effective information that is being transmitted in communication via sentences–that which the speaker intends the listener to understand–is the particular meaning, not the general, for this is what represents the conceptual event ("idea") that he attempts to communicate to the listener. In order to recover the particular meaning of a word intended by the speaker, the listener must engage in an inferential process which makes use of his knowledge of the general (dictionary) meaning of words as well as his knowledge of the overall situation to which the sentence as a whole refers. This inferential process yields what I have called "the elliptically derived conceptual event" which an utterance represents and which I have used as the definition for implicit meaning. Note that the effective carrier of the message is the *implicit* meaning of the sentence, not the linguistic one. Hence, we see once more that linguistic competence must include factors outside a narrow view of linguistic manipulations and that the assessment of such competence by means of language tests must therefore also include these larger issues.

4.2.3 Implicative Meaning

We have seen that words have a relation to a generalized abstract meaning (linguistic meaning) as well as to a particularized meaning that relates to a specific conceptual event (implicit meaning). Utterances as a whole have, in addition, a relation to several aspects of the speaker: his intention, his psychological state, his definition of the interaction and certain "claims" (both intentional and unintentional) he makes about the status of his utterance, etc. In some cases these implications are necessary to recover the intended meaning of the utterance (e.g., "Do you have a match?" is not a question to be answered verbally but a request for fire to light a cigarette). In other cases, the implications of an utterance are by-products not essentially related to conveying intended meaning (e.g., phonological clues that reveal geographic origin). I shall refer to both types of implications as the implicative meaning of an utterance.

4.3 A FUNCTIONAL APPROACH

Within the framework that I have outlined the problem of assessing language skills becomes the problem of describing the specific manner in which an individual functions at the three levels of meaning identified above. The relations that hold between the three levels, both for a speaker and a listener, is a matter to be determined empirically for each individual, although it is to be expected that such empirical studies will show that some of these relations will be universal for all language users. The development of specific tests for assessing these relations should be guided by an overall model of the functional elements in communicative competence. Because of the practical concerns involved in language testing, one need not postpone the task of developing language tests until such time as adequate theoretical models become available. In fact, it might even be the case that such empirical evidence that the language tester accumulates would constitute useful information for building such theoretical models. I would argue, however, that the development of language tests on a piecemeal basis and without considerations derived from a model that encompasses the full range of phenomena involved in communicative competence, can only yield artificial laboratory exercises that have little significant relationship to the use of language in real life situations. I believe it is presently possible to outline the major elements to be included in a model of language use even if it may be insufficient in details, and I have described elsewhere (Jakobovits, 1968c) a classification scheme based on an analysis of the three levels of meaning discussed above. I will not discuss the full classification scheme here but present below an overview of it:

1. *A functional analysis of meaning*
    - 1.1 linguistic meaning
    - 1.2 implicit meaning
        - 1.2.1 aspectual
            - 1.2.1.1 extended duration
            - 1.2.1.2 limited duration
            - 1.2.1.3 inception
            - 1.2.1.4 iteration
            - 1.2.1.5 gradualness
            - 1.2.1.6 chronicity
            - 1.2.1.7 termination
            - 1.2.1.8 collectiveness
            - 1.2.1.9 inaction
            - 1.2.1.10 directionality
            - 1.2.1.11 intensity
            - 1.2.1.12 nonchalance
        - 1.2.2 affective
        - 1.2.3 aesthetic
        - 1.2.4 contextual
        - 1.2.5 situational
    - 1.3 implicative meaning
        - 1.3.1 sociolinguistic
            - 1.3.1.1 geographic origin
            - 1.3.1.2 education and SES
            - 1.3.1.3 professional
        - 1.3.2 emotional
        - 1.3.3 intention
            - 1.3.3.1 mands
                - 1.3.3.1.1. request
                - 1.3.3.1.2. command
                - 1.3.3.1.3. prayer
                - 1.3.3.1.4. question

- 1.3.3.1.5. advice
- 1.3.3.1.6. warning
- 1.3.3.1.7. permission
- 1.3.3.1.8. call

1.3.3.2 pseudo mands
- 1.3.3.2.1. superstitious
- 1.3.3.2.2. magical

1.3.3.3 intraverbals
- 1.3.3.3.1. grammaticalness
- 1.3.3.3.2. word associations
- 1.3.3.3.3. conventions
- 1.3.3.3.4. expressions
- 1.3.3.3.5. recitations

1.3.3.4 private tacts
- 1.3.3.4.1. feelings
- 1.3.3.4.2. opinions
- 1.3.3.4.3. rationalizations

1.3.3.5 public tacts
- 1.3.3.5.1. instructing
- 1.3.3.5.2. describing
- 1.3.3.5.3. entertaining

1.3.3.6 autistic utterances
- 1.3.3.6.1. verbal fantasy
- 1.3.3.6.2. self-tacting
- 1.3.3.6.3. self-manding

1.3.3.7 autoclitics
- 1.3.3.7.1. importance
  - 1.3.3.7.1.1. stress pattern
  - 1.3.3.7.1.2. repetition
  - 1.3.3.7.1.3. adverbial intensification
  - 1.3.3.7.1.4 syntactic inversion
- 1.3.3.7.2. existential status
  - 1.3.3.7.2.1. assertion
  - 1.3.3.7.2.2. negation
  - 1.3.3.7.2.3. obligation
  - 1.3.3.7.2.4. possibility

1.3.3.7.2.5. probability
1.3.3.7.2.6. certainty
1.3.3.7.2.7. hear-say
1.3.3.7.2.8. permission
1.3.3.7.2.9. imperative
1.3.3.7.2.10. irony
1.3.3.7.3. relational status
1.3.3.7.3.1. explicit hinges
1.3.3.7.3.2. implicit hinges
1.3.3.7.3.3. zero hinges

2. *Elements of style*
   - 2.1 internal consistency
   - 2.2 appropriateness
   - 2.3 effectiveness
   - 2.4 aesthetic value
   - 2.5 affective value

3. *Selection factors in the act of composing*
   - 3.1 intention
   - 3.2 audience
   - 3.3 situation
   - 3.4 style
     - 3.4.1 intraverbal influences
     - 3.4.2 formal constraints
     - 3.4.3 blendings

4. *The structure of the message*
   - 4.1 syntactic
   - 4.2 conceptual

4.4 A PROGRAM OF TEST DEVELOPMENT

It is not possible within the context of this section to specify in detail a program of test development that will take into account the full range of linguistic phenomena covered by the classification scheme sketched out above. Furthermore, the development of such a testing program would require the collaboration of a team of workers with specialized skills which I do not possess. Nevertheless, I can perhaps offer some tentative suggestions with respect to some methodological approaches that may be used in connection with many of the linguistic phenomena involved in the classification scheme.

4.4.1 Judgments of Acceptability

This technique consists of asking a subject to make an evaluation of the acceptability or appropriateness of an expression, or alternately, presenting him with two similar expressions and asking him to choose the more appropriate of the two. The technique is well suited for assessing sensitivity to aspectual qualities of words. Aspectual quality (1.2.1) is part of the implicit meaning of a word and is based on inferences one can draw about characteristics of the specific conceptual event implied by a word. These characteristics are not specified directly by the dictionary meaning of the lexical items involved but are instead implied by them. Some examples of aspectual qualities in English are the following: extended duration (as exemplified by the following contrasts: "to stare" versus "to notice," "fearful" versus "frightened," "state of normalcy" versus "state of crisis"), limited duration ("to strike" versus "to beat," "to gulp" versus "to sip"), inception ("to doze off" versus "to doze," "obsolescent" versus "obsolete," "adolescence" versus "manhood"), and iteration ("to nag" versus "to criticize," "to sob" versus "to yelp," "wave" versus "line"). It is possible to construct phrases that contain modifying elements which are either consistent or inconsistent with the aspectual quality of the modified element. In each of the following examples the second phrase contains an inconsistent modifier; given a choice, the subject should choose the first alternative if he is sensitive to the implicit meaning of the expression:

He was frightened momentarily/He was fearful momentarily

He took a long sip/He took a long gulp

He had been dozing for some time when the phone rang/He had been dozing off for some time when the phone rang.

He criticized me only once/He nagged me only once

4.4.2 Semantic Differential Technique

The usual method requires a subject to rate a word on a set of seven-point bipolar adjectival scales (see Osgood, Suci, and Tannenbaum, 1957). The selection of scalar opposites varies with the purpose of the test. Scales for the assessment of three dominant and universal affective features have been identified empirically for English and some 20 other languages (see Osgood, 1964; Jakobovits, 1966). These consist of Evaluation (for American English: nice-awful, good-bad, sweet-sour), Potency (big-little, powerful-powerless, strong-weak), and Activity (fast-slow, alive-dead, noisy-quiet). For other affective features, different scales would be used. The technique is general enough to allow for changes in the stimuli that are rated (e.g., they may consist of phrases and sentences) as well as the nature of the scales used for the ratings (e.g., instead of the seven-step scale one may use an "either-or" two-step scale). Sensitivity to the aspectual quality of intensity (1.2.1.11.), for example, can be revealed by asking a subject to say which of two choices is *more* or *less* intense: "icy" versus "cold," "filthy" versus "dirty," "ravenous" versus "hungry," "to shatter" versus "to break," etc.

4.4.3 The Questionnaire Method

This approach is convenient for assessing a subject's sensitivity to implicative aspects of the meaning of utterances: sociolinguistic (1.3.1.), emotional (1.3.2.), and intentional (1.3.3.). Since nonverbal factors (e.g., gestural, visual, situational) provide particularly important clues to implicative meaning, the problem of assessing an individual's skill in this area is likely to be quite involved. Without implying that these nonverbal factors should be left out of the testing program let me suggest that utterances, even in the absence of such clues, do allow for the derivation of quite a bit of information about the speaker—and the skill involved in this can be assessed more readily within the confines of the usual testing situation. Phonological variables present in tape recordings offer clues to sociolinguistic characteristics of the speaker and his emotional state. Syntactic and contextual variables offer clues to intentions of the speaker. Here are some examples in connection with intentions (1.3.3.). "Pass the salt," "Hands up," "Take your coat off. It's hot in here," "Now listen to this," are utterances which reveal the speaker's interest in inducing some action in the listener. These utterances are classified as mands (1.3.3.1.) and the four given here are instances of a request, a command, an advice, and a call, respectively.

The speaker continually uses devices in utterances that have the function of commenting on certain aspects of the message. These are called autoclitics (1.3.3.7.). For example, stress pattern and repetition indicate that the speaker wants to lay emphasis on his utterance ("You should *not* infer from this that . . ."; "I like it very, very much"). Comments on the existential status (1.3.3.7.2.) of assertions include, among others, obligation ("I *had* to give in"), possibility ("Couldn't it happen?"), probability ("He is likely to forget"), hearsay ("The two accident victims are reported to have died"), irony ("Aren't we having *fun*!"), etc.

4.4.4 Acting out Situations

The questionnaire approach just described assesses decoding (passive skills). Reversing the task by asking a subject how he would say something under specific conditions becomes an encoding task that assesses corresponding active skills. He now assumes the role of the speaker by acting out the communicative act called for by the instructions. These may be simple or complex. An example of a simple situation would be to ask the person to transform an utterance in such a way as to express certain intentions. For instance, the sentence "He will be going to the meeting," which is an assertion, is to be transformed to indicate negation (He will not be going to the meeting), obligation (He has to go to the meeting), permission (He is allowed to go to the meeting), certainty (He most definitely will be going to the meeting), irony (Wouldn't he just *love* to go to the meeting!), and so on. More complex instructions might require the subject to construct public tacts (1.3.3.5.) appropriate to various situations (reporting a past event, describing an ongoing activity, telling a joke, etc.). Encoding and decoding skills are not necessarily related. Thus, one might successfully identify the geographic origin of a speaker without being able to imitate him; or, one may recognize that a speaker is angry without being able to talk like an angry man upon demand. (The latter case exemplifies a further distinction to be made between volitional control of encoding skills and the ability to carry out the same skills under natural conditions but without volitional control.)

4.4.5 Paraphrasing

"Rewording" is a traditional test for assessing understanding. But rewording often changes the tone or style of utterances, which means in fact that the alternative construction is not semantically equivalent: it may have different implicit and implicative meanings. I use the term semantic modulation to refer to the possibility of alternative phonological strings that are related in linguistic meaning but are different in their implicit and implicative aspects. Consider some examples in semantic modulation:

He spoke loudly/He spoke with a thunderous voice

The light was too bright/It was a blinding light

It was uncomfortably hot and humid/The weather was stifling

He worked extremely hard/He worked his fingers to the bone

The second sentences of each pair in these examples are recognized as paraphrases of their respective first sentences (they have equivalent linguistic meaning) but they are marked in their implicit meaning by the aspectual quality of intensification (1.2.1.11.). The ability to manipulate the implicit meaning of an utterance without changing its linguistic meaning is an important skill in "creative writing." Similarly, the ability to manipulate implicative meaning is a mark of the effective writer and speaker (contrast "That's not the way to do it" with "If I were you, I would do it differently").

4.4.6 Intraverbal Skills

Intraverbals (1.3.3.3.) refer to aspects of verbal behavior that are not marked for intent. The most obvious instance of intraverbal influences is grammaticalness. Another instance is the associative relation that holds between words as exhibited in the traditional word association test. Conventional phrases (greetings, acknowledgement of thanks, condolences, etc.), expressions (proverbs, idioms, platitudes), and recitations (lines of poetry, prayers, etc.) all involve intraverbal skills that should be included in any testing program that attempts to assess communicative competence.

4.5 SUMMARY

I have pointed out that the traditional approach to the assessment of language skills derives its rationale from a restricted definition of linguistic competence. I have argued that such a restricted view is totally inadequate to account for the most basic phenomena in language use and, hence, language tests based on this rationale are nothing but artificial laboratory exercises that have little in common with the skills involved in the everyday use of language. To study adequately the latter process, one must recognize the basic functions of communciation via language and the total information available in the communicative act. I have described in an outline form a classification scheme for identifying the functional elements to be taken into account in the study of communicative competence and have suggested some methodological approaches that one might adopt in the development of a testing program designed to assess skills involved in the use of language.

4.6 COMPOUND-COORDINATE BILINGUALISM

Since Ervin and Osgood's (1954) discussion of the problem, compound-coordinate bilingualism has received the attention of several investigators (see, for example, Lambert, Havelka, and Crosby, 1958; Jakobovits and Lambert, 1961; Preston, 1965; Kolers, 1963; and others: see the review by Macnamara, 1967). The distinction between the two types of bilinguals offered by Ervin and Osgood (1954) was a unidimensional one, in terms of the semantic relation between the bilingual's two languages. The compound bilingual was supposed to have a single meaning system hooked up to two different input (decoding) and output (encoding) channels corresponding to the bilingual's two languages. This type of bilingualism was assumed to come about as a result of learning the second language in the same environmental setting as the first, and using the first language as the indirect channel of acquisition. In this kind of a psycholinguistic system every word in the second language was a mere replica of a word in the first language with a one-to-one correspondence in meaning between the two translation equivalents. This is why the "compound" bilingual system is sometimes referred to as a "fused" system (Weinreich, 1953).

On the other side of this semantic continuum is located the "separate" system of the coordinate bilingual who is assumed to possess two independent meaning systems corresponding to his two languages. This situation is achieved, according to this view, as a result of direct language acquisition in a linguistic-cultural community different from one's own. There is no one-to-one relation between the two meaning systems and, in fact, translation equivalents are mere approximations, their closeness depending on the similarities in the two cultures involved. A direct test of the semantic distance between a few translation equivalent words for French-English bilinguals was carried out by Lambert, Havelka, and Crosby (1958). These authors divided their sample of bilinguals into three groups. One was composed of unicultural compounds who learned French in school by the indirect method through the medium of English. The second group was composed of unicultural coordinates who learned French by the direct method and often used it in a setting different from that where they habitually used English; the two settings, although different, were nevertheless both North American. The third group was composed of bicultural coordinates; these were often native speakers of French (in Quebec) who lived in the bicultural setting of Canada. Having selected a set of common words in English (HOUSE, DRINK, POOR, ME) and their French translation equivalents, the investigators then obtained semantic differential ratings for each word using the appropriate scales in English and French. The results showed that the semantic distances between translation equivalent terms were largest for the bicultural coordinates and smallest for the unicultural compounds (a statistically significant difference), with the unicultural coordinates falling near the unicultural compounds and not significantly different from them. These results, which represent partial confirmation of the predictions of Ervin and Osgood (1954), are further strengthened by a subsequent study (Jakobovits and Lambert, 1961) which demonstrated that reducing the meaning of a word (through semantic satiation brought about by verbal repetition, see Lambert and Jakobovits, 1960) in one language also brings about a corresponding reduction in meaning of its translated equivalent in the second language for compound bilinguals but not for coordinate bilinguals—as indeed the theory would predict.

The theory of compound-coordinate bilingualism as described above may be quite useful in understanding certain aspects of the semantic functioning of bilinguals. However, it may be advantageous to extend the compound-coordinate distinction to other areas of psycholinguistic functioning. The remainder of this section will explore some possible ways by which such an extension may be achieved.

It would be useful to recognize at the outset that bilingualism involves two different aspects of the question of interrelatedness of two distinct language/culture systems. One such aspect (R_A) deals with the relation between the bilingual's two language/culture systems, and may be represented as follows:

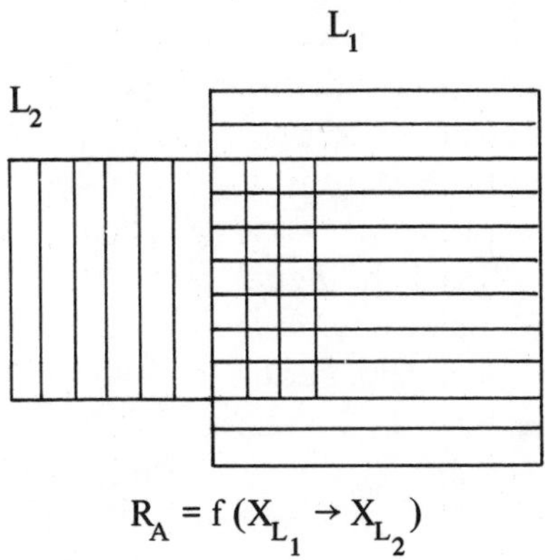

$$R_A = f(X_{L_1} \rightarrow X_{L_2})$$

where X stands for the speaker and L for the language spoken. In this diagram the first language is represented by a rectangle marked by horizontal lines (on the right), while the second language is represented by a rectangle marked by vertical lines (on the left). The overlapping area of intersection is marked by both horizontal and vertical lines and represents interference. In this example L_1 is larger than L_2 to indicate dominance. The second aspect of the question of interrelatedness deals with the comparison between each of the two languages of a bilingual to that of an idealized monolingual member of the two respective language/culture communities (R_B & R_C). This relationship may be represented as follows:

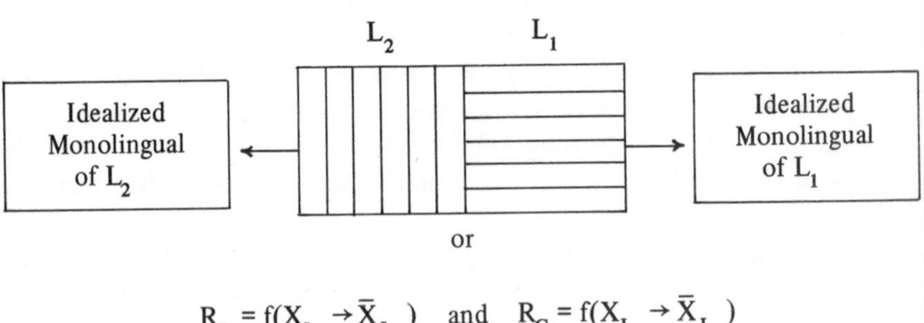

or

$$R_B = f(X_{L_2} \rightarrow \bar{X}_{L_2}) \quad \text{and} \quad R_C = f(X_{L_1} \rightarrow \bar{X}_{L_1})$$

where $\bar{X}$ stands for an idealized monolingual. It is possible to devise tests which would measure the extent of interrelatedness that exists for each of these two aspects within various areas of psycholinguistic functioning (e.g., semantics, grammar, decoding, etc.) and several of such tests will be described below. At this point, however, it would be useful to restate the definition of compound-coordinate bilingualism keeping in mind the extended perspective presented above.

The ideal coordinate bilingual represents a state of complete functional independence of two language/culture systems in all their aspects: semantic, lexical, syntactic, phonological, morphemic, cultural, attitudinal, etc. In his case, R_A (see diagram) has a minimum value while R_B and R_C have maximum values. In its extreme form, coordinate bilingualism represents linguistic schizophrenia: one individual with two separate and theoretically unrelated cultural-linguistic systems co-occur within the same body. In compound bilingualism, the two linguistic systems are so fused and interdependent that the second language represents a mere alternative channel for the overt manifestation of the same underlying system represented by the first language. In this state R_A and R_C have maximum values, while the other, R_B, has a minimum value. In its extreme form compound bilingualism represents a translation machine: for every coded bit in L_2 there must be a corresponding bit in L_1 with the relationship between the two exactly specified.

Let us now examine some implications which follow from these considerations.

4.6.1 Degree of Bilingualism

Under this topic we should include both the question of bilingual interference as well as bilingual proficiency. Bilingual interference can be defined, following Mackey (1965), as the use of elements in one language while speaking another. The consequence of such intrusions is an increase in the value of R_A and a decrease in the value of R_B: the bilingual's speech in L_2 (X_{L_2}) will differ from the idealized version ($\overline{X}_{L_2}$) in direct proportion to the extent of interference from L_1 (R_A); furthermore, the bilingual's first language may show uncharacteristic departures from the standard ($\overline{X}_{L_1}$)–a problem he did not encounter as a monolingual. One would expect that the most common form of bilingual interference would be in the direction of L_2: that is, high values in R_A would lead to low values in R_B leaving R_C relatively unimpaired. However, there is evidence (see Mackey, 1965) that in certain areas of psycholinguistic functioning, particularly in semantics, the value of R_C may decrease as a result of backlash interference (see below).

Bilingual proficiency has sometimes been defined (e.g., Macnamara, 1967) in terms of the relative competence of the bilingual in his two languages: where the two competencies are equal, bilingual proficiency is said to be maximal (sometimes referred to as a state of "balanceness," see Lambert, Havelka, and Gardner, 1959). Where competence in one language surpasses that in the other, a state of bilingual "dominance" is inferred. I have pointed out elsewhere (Jakobovits, 1967) the difficulty with such a definition. When bilingual proficiency is estimated, as has often been the case (see Macnamara, 1967), by means of indirect measures which may be contaminated by nonlinguistic factors, the relative or difference score would not be acceptable without prior determination of interaction effects. When bilingual proficiency is established by means of direct competence tests, then the difference score obscures the distinction between R_B and R_C, two elements which are theoretically independent. For these reasons it would be preferable in discussing the problem of degree of bilingualism, to keep separate these two relations expressed as $X_{L_2} \rightarrow \overline{X}_{L_2}$ (R_B) on the one hand and $X_{L_1} \rightarrow \overline{X}_{L_1}$ (R_C) on the other. The first of these must be measured by proficiency tests in the second language standardized on monolingual speakers. The second relation is of interest to the problem of what might be called "backlash interference"–the intrusions into and modifications of one's mother tongue due to the learning of a foreign language.

One may raise the question of the relation between the two aspects of bilingualism discussed above, namely *degree* and *compound-coordinatedness.* Let us recall the elements in our system:

Degree of Bilingualism (D)	*Compound-Coordinate Bilingualism (CP-CR)*
(i) Proficiency in L_2 (P_{L_2})	(i) $R_B = f(X_{L_2} \rightarrow \overline{X}_{L_2})$
(ii) Proficiency in L_1 (P_{L_1})	(ii) $R_C = f(X_{L_1} \rightarrow \overline{X}_{L_1})$
	(iii) $R_A = f(X_{L_1} \rightarrow X_{L_2})$

These relations have already been explicated above. Now let us consider the following two hypothetical cases:

Case Y: P_{L_2} is high; P_{L_1} is unimpaired
R_B is maximal; R_C is maximal; R_A is minimal

Case Z: P_{L_2} is low; P_{L_1} is unimpaired
R_B is minimal; R_C is maximal; R_A is high

As can be seen, case Y represents a bicultural balanced coordinate bilingual: proficiency in the second language is high while functioning in the mother tongue is unimpaired; furthermore, this bilingual functions as a native in both languages (R_B and R_C) without showing cross-linguistic interference (R_A). This case then is the linguistic schizophrenia referred to earlier. Case Z is weak in the second language (P_{L_2}) while he retains the characteristics of his language/culture group (P_{L_1} and R_C); he shows considerable interference in the second language (R_A) which renders his speech in that language uncharacteristic (R_B). In other words, case Z represents a unicultural dominant compound bilingual. The reader may explore for himself other possible combinations using this schema. By manipulating the various elements in a systematic fashion, one at a time, some interesting cases arise, but these will not be taken up here. Instead, let us consider the extension of the model by the addition of two other dimensions.

One dimension relates to the various areas of psycholinguistic functioning as might be indexed by such tests as semantic distance, word association structure, adequacy of translation, language switching, reading comprehension, pronunciation accuracy, and some additional ones which will be described below. The other dimension to be considered is that of development over time. Figure 1 is a schematic representation of a four dimensional model of bilingual description using the elements discussed above. The first dimension, that of degree of bilingualism (P_L), is given by the relative size of the two rectangles: the left hand rectangle with the vertical lines represents the second language (L_2) and the right hand rectangle with the horizontal lines represents the mother tongue (L_1). Proficiency in L_2 and L_1 is indicated by the size of their respective rectangles. The second dimension, that of compound coordinate bilingualism, is indicated as follows: R_A (i.e., $X_{L_1} \rightarrow X_{L_2}$ or interference) is given by the amount of overlap between the two rectangles; R_B (i.e., $X_{L_2} \rightarrow \overline{X}_{L_2}$) and R_C ($X_{L_1} \rightarrow \overline{X}_{L_1}$) is given by the density of the vertical and horizontal lines within the rectangles: high density represents a high degree of relationship. The third dimension, that of psycholinguistic area of functioning is represented on the vertical axis (a. vs. b. vs. c.), and development in time, the fourth dimension, lies along the horizontal axis (1 vs. 2 vs. 3). Let *a* stand for grammatical intrusions, let *b* stand for pronunciation accuracy, and *c* for a measure of word association structure (see below for details). Let *1* stand for the beginning stages of second language acquisition, let *2* be several months later spent in a bicultural setting, and let *3* be at the completion of the language acquisition process. Looking at part a.1 of the figure, we notice a dominant unicultural compound (L_1 on the right is dense and larger than L_2 on the left, which it envelops) whose

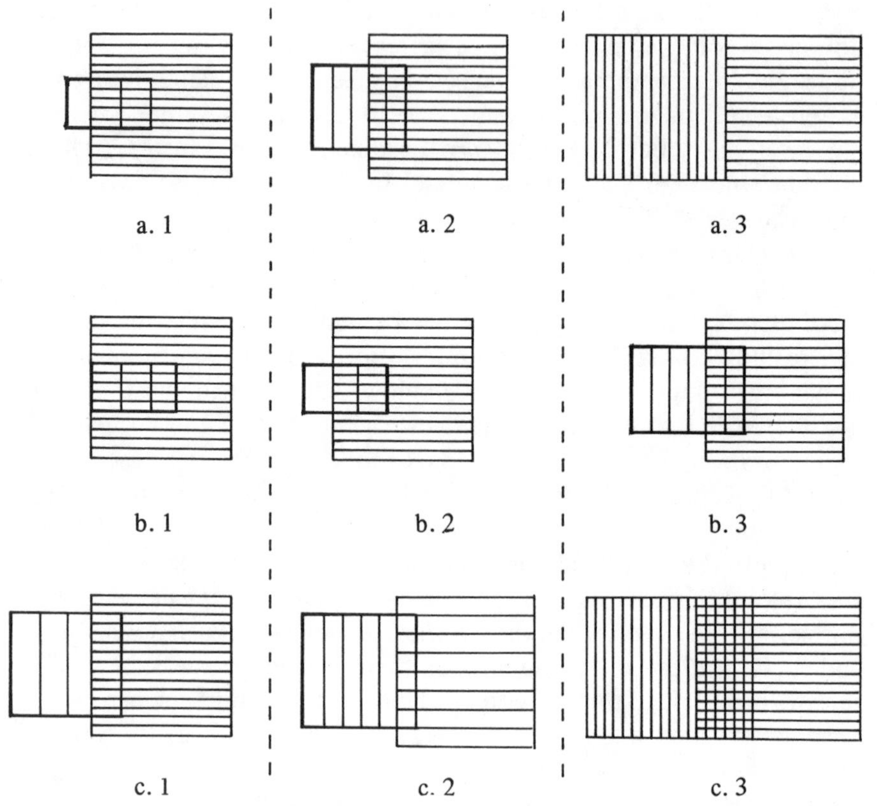

FIGURE 1. A FOUR-DIMENSIONAL MODEL OF BILINGUAL DESCRIPTION.

grammatical performance in L_2 is poor (note its small size). His pronunciation in L_2 (b.1) is practically unintelligible as the phonemic system of L_1 completely dominates it. A test of word association structure (c.1) shows relatively better performance (note larger size of L_2). A few months later, and with the opportunity of bicultural experience such as that offered by extensive travel in the foreign country, our language learner has considerably improved in grammatical performance (note larger size of L_2 at a.2), although his pronunciation still shows heavy contamination (b.2). His greatest progress is exhibited on the word association test where his performance increasingly resembles the cultural norm (note increase in size of L_2 at c.2 and greater density of vertical lines). At this point an interesting phenomenon occurs, "backlash interference." As a result of becoming more bilingual the individual experiences a typical departure from his mother tongue as compared to idealized monolingual speakers of that language. At the end of the successful acquisition process, the grammatical performance of this bilingual (a.3) shows the coordinate pattern (large, dense rectangles with no overlap). His pronunciation (b.3) is good but not native, and his word association structure (c.3) shows a curious pattern: his performance is excellent (large rectangles) and native-like (dense lines), but the two linguistic systems interact (note overlap): the bilingual has developed what might be called a "cross-cultural semantic system"—a kind of "coloring" or "flavoring" of semantic factors which comes about through cross-cultural contact (see Jakobovits, 1966).

Once again the reader may want to explore further the various combinations that are possible in this kind of a schema. The advantage of what may appear to be a gratuitously complex representation is that it facilitates systematic elaboration of possible stages of bilingualism and may thereby increase our understanding of the processes involved.

4.6.2 Translation and Language Switching

In their analysis of compound coordinate bilingualism, Ervin and Osgood (1954) are led to the hypothesis that extensive translation on the part of a coordinate bilingual will transform him into a compound system. They argue that continued interaction between the distinct meaning systems of the two languages washes out the differences between them. However, the opposite effect is also logically possible: continued interaction can act as discrimination training through contrast and forced differentiation and, in fact, experienced translators seem to be attuned to stylistic and connotative differences between translation equivalents to a degree not apparent in less experienced bilinguals. The Ervin and Osgood model furthermore neglects the problem of a language switching mechanism which must be postulated to account for the fact that bilinguals, and especially compounds, are able to function in one language without extensive interference from the other language. Figure 2 represents an elaboration of the Ervin and Osgood model by including hypothetical language switches on the decoding and encoding sides as well as filter mechanisms (separators) whose function it is to channel signs into their respective languages at the decoding and encoding stages. Consider first the compound bilingual. If the input switch is "on," incoming signs will be shunted into either L_A or L_B, depending on the "language set." In other words the switch has directional properties. The signs are then fed into the common meaning system where they are decoded. Now, if the output switch is also "on," the

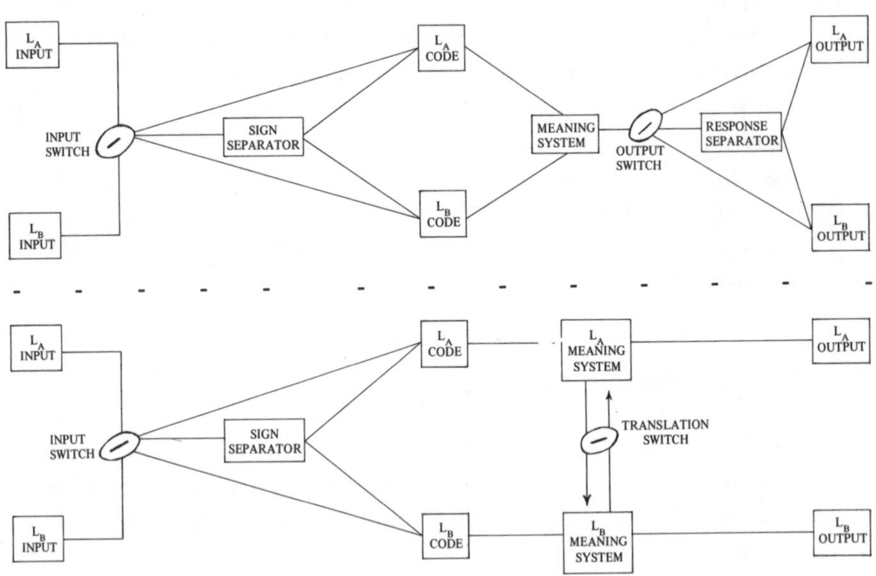

FIGURE 2. A MODEL OF COMPOUND (TOP) AND COORDINATE (BOTTOM) BILINGUISM.

encoding response will "exit" through L_A or L_B, again depending on the direction of the switch. One must also consider the case where the bilingual (compound or coordinate) is set to decode from either language (e.g., in a bilingual environment). In that case the switch is turned "off" and the incoming signals are filtered through the "sign separator" mechanism and fed into the meaning system through L_A or L_B. For the coordinate bilingual, there is no need for a "response separator" mechanism since the meaning systems in the two languages are distinct and feed into separate output systems. For the compound, however, such a filter on the encoding side must be postulated to allow for the possibility that the output switch be "off" (e.g., where the bilingual is set to encode in either language). On the other hand, it is necessary to postulate a "translation switch" for the coordinate to allow for his capacity to attend to L_A in the decoding stage and to render its equivalent in the encoding stage. Now let us see how the model depicted in Figure 2 can be used to make predictions about the behavior of bilinguals. The following are some outcomes of the assumptions that have been made:

1. For both compounds and coordinates decoding will be less efficient when the input switch is "off" (e.g., when he has to attend to signs in both languages at the same time–see Measures 17 and 18 below). The reason for this expectation is that the route through the sign separator is less direct and the filtering process should take measurable time.

2. The requirements to encode in either language (see Measures 16 and 19 below) should be more disruptive for the compound than the coordinate, again because of the time requirements of the filter separator.

3. Instructions to translate into a specified language should be a more efficient task for the compound than for the coordinate bilingual. The greater efficiency of this task for the compound can be seen in Figure 2: If the output switch is "on" and directed, say, toward L_B, the meaning system feeds directly into the output system. For the coordinate bilingual, there must first be an "equivalence search" between the two meaning systems through the translation switch, and this should take measurable time. It should be noted that if the translation time is very short, such as might be the case for word-to-word translation of common lexical items, the coordinate's

disadvantage relative to the compound would be difficult to measure. This might account for the failure of some investigators (see Macnamara's 1967 review) to find latency differences under these conditions. Where the translation task is less automatic (unfamiliar words, phrases, sentences) the present prediction should be verifiable.

The reader can explore further for himself several other predictions that Figure 2 suggests. Macnamara (1967) has discussed the kind of experimental data that would be required to verify the validity of the switch model—the number of switches it is necessary to postulate and whether switches take measurable time for operating. Some translation and switching tests are described below.

4.6.3 Degree of Interrelatedness

Under this topic we shall discuss some of the factors that lead to compound-coordinate bilingualism. We should consider three types of factors: language acquisition context and usage, attitudinal and motivational variables, and cross-cultural distinctiveness. Within each of these areas, it is necessary to distinguish among the various aspects of psycholinguistic functioning. In the semantic area the evidence on connotative distance between translation equivalent words resulting from separate acquisition contexts and usage has already been discussed above. The effects of some attitudinal variables on semantic change has been discussed by Lambert (1967) and his coworkers (see, for example, Lambert, Gardner, Barik, and Turnstall, 1963). In the latter report it was shown that semantic interdependence is positively related to higher achievement in an intensive language acquisition program. The measure involved was the semantic distance (as indexed by the semantic differential) between the meaning of some words in English (the mother tongue) at the beginning and at the completion of the course, as compared to the meaning of the translation equivalent words in French. Thus all three aspects of interrelatedness were presumably involved, although, unfortunately, they were not all directly measured. Let us examine how this type of change would affect the three aspects of interrelatedness discussed earlier in this paper. The value of R_C (i.e., $X_{L_1} \rightarrow \overline{X}_{L_1}$) may be presumed to have decreased from its previous maximal value: there is a decrease in coordinateness and the meaning of words in the mother tongue of this bilingual is no longer representative of monolinguals of his culture. R_A (i.e., $X_{L_1} \rightarrow X_{L_2}$) in the semantic area decidedly increased: as Lambert and his associates put it, the students "permit the two languages to interact, and this is to their advantage in the learning of the second language" (p. 368). This would lead to greater compoundness. However, change in the value of R_B (i.e., $X_{L_2} \rightarrow \overline{X}_{L_2}$) is in doubt: the students' semantic systems may have progressed towards the native pattern of L_2–in which case the value of R_B increased promoting coordinateness, or, also possible, their semantic system may have moved away towards a compromise position which is not characteristic of the culture and is colored by the mother tongue, as Lambert et al. put it: ". . . these students develop generalized superlinguistic concepts which incorporate the unique semantic features of the concepts in each of their two languages" (p. 368). Thus it would appear that contrary to what one might expect from an emphasis on "direct" teaching methods, an increase of compoundness in the semantic area of connotation during certain stages of the acquisition process may facilitate progress in a FL.

Figure 3 represents another hypothesized relation between attitudinal factors and compound-coordinateness. The two psychological variables considered here are ethnocentrism and language learning orientation. The former trait is measured by a questionnaire intended to ascertain the extent of the student's rigidity of belief in the superiority of his own culture, while the latter trait is ascertained by his answers to questions about his purposes for learning a foreign language: instrumental reasons (e.g., usefulness in work or travel, meeting the Ph.D. language requirements) versus integrative reasons (e.g., getting to know the people better; see Lambert et al., 1963, for greater detail). Figure 3 says that high ethnocentrism coupled with an instrumental orientation are psychological factors which promote compound bilingualism. The reason for this is presumably that a highly ethnocentric individual would not tolerate a decrease in the value of R_C (i.e., $X_{L_1} \rightarrow \overline{X}_{L_1}$) as this would estrange him from his own culture in whose superiority he so firmly believes. The over all implications of the relationship represented in Figure 3 are rather intriguing, since it indicates that the opposite number of the highly ethnocentric, instrumentally oriented student, namely the self-

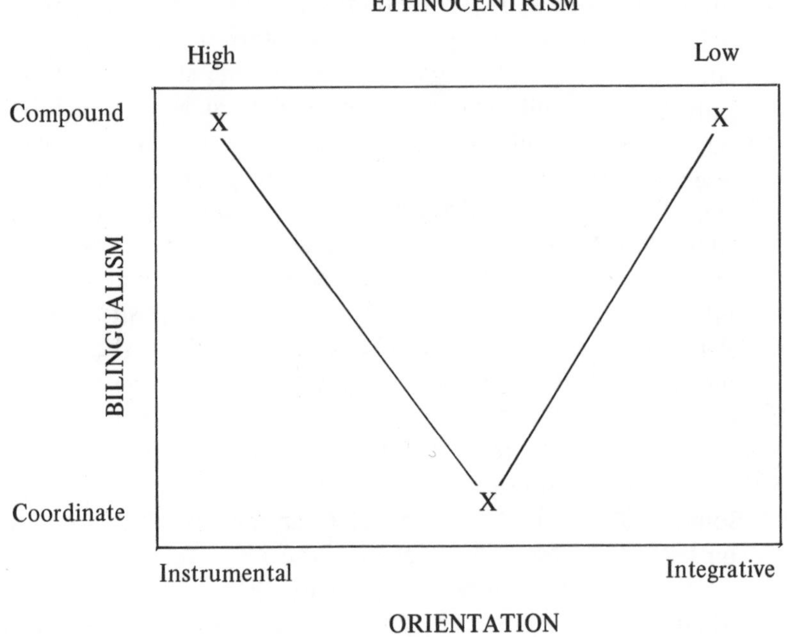

FIGURE 3. HYPOTHESIZED RELATION BETWEEN COMPOUND-COORDINATE BILINGUALISM AND ATTITUDINAL STRUCTURE.

deprecating, integratively oriented "culture grabber" characteristic of young, enthusiastic language learners eager for "foreign culture," would also promote compoundness: this comes about, presumably, because this kind of an individual freely allows a decrease in R_C (i.e., $X_{L_1} \rightarrow \overline{X}_{L_1}$) as he eagerly "leaves behind" the norms of his culture. Figure 3 also shows that coordinateness will be promoted by moderate levels of ethnocentrism and bi-directional tendencies in orientation: in other words the psychologically conflictual individual. Such a person would tend to maintain R_C (i.e., $X_{L_1} \rightarrow \overline{X}_{L_1}$) at a high level, while moving at the same time towards high values for R_B (i.e., $X_{L_2} \rightarrow \overline{X}_{L_2}$). This type of an individual would be expected to experience the "throes of anomie" as his linguistic schizophrenia develops into the full-fledged coordinate pattern.

The third type of factor to be discussed in this section, as mentioned above, is cross-cultural distinctiveness. A general hypothesis may be formulated as follows: cultural distinctiveness promotes coordinate bilingualism while cultural similarities inhibit it. It would be difficult for an Acadian in Halifax, Nova Scotia, or a Cajun from Louisiana, to be a coordinate bilingual. Similarly, one cannot expect a Japanese immigrant to San Francisco to be a compound bilingual, even after twenty years and half-a-dozen American monolingual grandchildren. Although it is true that certain semantic characteristics related to affective structure tend to be universal (see Osgood, 1962; Jakobovits, 1966), other characteristics tend to be uniquely peculiar to individual cultures, and these must be considered in evaluating the factors that determine compound-coordinate bilingualism.

4.6.4 Some Measures of Compound-Coordinate Bilingualism and Their Interrelatedness

In this final section we will consider a number of tests which may be used to index the various aspects of compound-coordinate bilingualism as discussed here. The following is a brief description of some 27 measures of compound-coordinate bilingualism. The first nine are in the semantic area; the tests numbered 10 to 14 are in the lexical area; those numbered 15 to 19 are translation and language switching tests; 20, 21, and 22 are grammatical tests that require transformation and paraphrasing; tests 23-25 deal with a judge's subjective ratings of various bilingual skills; and the last two (26 and 27) are proficiency tests in the two languages (discrete-point type).

4.6.4.1 Semantic Distance Test

The geometric distance formula *D* is used with the semantic differential to index connotative differences between words (described in Osgood, Suci, and Tannenbaum, 1957). When translation equivalent concepts are used for the same individual, as in Lambert, Havelka, and Crosby (1958), it becomes one index of R_A (i.e., $X_{L_1} \rightarrow X_{L_2}$) where a large *D* would indicate coordinateness. When a bilingual's ratings are compared with a monolingual (or with a norm profile for a monolingual group), it becomes an index of R_B or R_C, depending on whether one deals with L_2 or L_1 (large *D* values indicate compoundness).

4.6.4.2 Semantic Cross-satiation Test

This is an indirect test of semantic distance and is complicated by the unavoidable occurrence of language switching due to the nature of the test. The bilingual repeats a word in L_1 (or L_2) and a test is then made for the semantic satiation which is presumed to transfer to L_2 (or L_1). Jakobovits and Lambert (1961) have used this test with clearcut results: cross-linguistic satiation occurs with compound systems but not with coordinates.

4.6.4.3 Associative Interference Task

This test incorporates a transfer of learning design in which bilinguals first learn to memorize a list of commonly occurring words in one language, then receive further training on an interpolated list of words which is made up of the translation equivalent words in the other language of the previously learned list. The theoretical predictions based on transfer of learning theory are clear: because of the identity in meaning of the two lists for compounds, positive transfer is expected; for the coordinates, either less positive transfer or actual negative transfer should be exhibited. This test was successfully used by Lambert, Havelka, and Crosby (1958).

4.6.4.4 Semantic Congruity Test

The procedures for this test were developed by Osgood (1966) in connection with the investigation of semantic feature analysis. The subject is given a set of verb-adverb combinations and asked to make a judgment as to their acceptability. Take for example the following items involving the combination of the verb *to attack* and three adverbs.

	Apposite	*Permissible*	*Anomalous*
To attack violently	X		
To attack stupidly		X	
To attack meekly			X

The acceptability judgments appear on the right. Osgood assumes that the acceptability rating is determined by the interaction between the semantic features for which the verb and adverb are characteristically coded. This test, when used with bilinguals, would be a measure of both R_B and R_C. By careful selection of the items it should be possible to test quite subtle differences in meaning. Because of this, the test is likely to be more sensitive and efficient in detecting small differences than the previous ones described.

4.6.4.5 Metaphor Sensitivity Test

The principle involved here is similar to that in the previous test but it is considered separately here because the nature of the competence that underlies the judgment process is believed to develop differently in the two situations. More specifically, metaphor sensitivity is believed to originate "deeper" in the semantic structure of a language and represents a type of competence that cannot be learned adequately from dictionaries. This type of "Sprachgefühl" would be particularly sensitive to coordinate achievement in the second language (R_B).

4.6.4.6 Semantic Range Test

Mackey and Savard (1967) have described an index of "coverage" which assigns a numerical value to words on the basis of a combination of characteristics which include power of definition, inclusion, extension, and combination–all measures relating to some aspect of the semantic range of words. It is proposed that these or equivalent indices be adapted for the use of individual speakers in order to permit comparisons of individual scores to the population norm. These would then become indices of R_B.

4.6.4.7 Word Association Test

Words in both languages are given as stimuli and the subject is free to respond in either language by giving as many words as he can think of within a certain period of time, usually 60 seconds (see Noble, 1952). The following indices can be derived from this procedure: (i) number of responses to the stimuli in L_1; (ii) number of responses to the stimuli in L_2; (iii) the difference between (i) and (ii); (iv) number of responses in the language of L_1 for stimuli in L_1; (v) number of responses in the language of L_2 for stimuli in L_2; (vi) number of responses in L_2 for stimuli of L_1; (vii) number of responses in L_1 for stimuli of L_2; (viii) number of translation responses for stimuli in L_1; number of translation responses for stimuli in L_2; (ix) proportion of responses in L_2 for stimuli in L_1 [i.e., (vi)/(i)] ; (x) proportion of responses in L_1 for stimuli in L_2 [i.e., (vii)/(ii)] ; (xi) number of "bilingual" responses for L_1, where applicable (i.e., cognates or homographs for related languages); (xii) number of "bilingual" responses for L_2, again where applicable.

4.6.4.8 Paired Associate Task

This test is a measure of learning ability with meaningful materials. The bilingual's comparative performance in the two languages may be estimated, and the general level of his performance compared to the norm within the population. Various procedures for paired associate learning are possible. A convenient procedure which does not require a memory drum is that used in the Modern Language Aptitude Test (Carroll and Sapon, 1958).

4.6.4.9 Semantic Structure of Affective Meaning

This rather complex procedure consists of the following steps: (a) semantic differential ratings of concepts in both languages are obtained from the bilingual; (b) these ratings are then analyzed by means of Tucker's three mode factor analysis (see Levin, 1965) and compared to group factor analyses using various factorial similarity indices (see for example Kuusinen, 1967). These measures should reveal significant departures of semantic structure from the cultural norm (R_B and R_C).

4.6.4.10 Word Association Structure

There are several methods which have been used to arrive at indices of similarity in word association structure (see Deese, 1965). Kolers (1963), Rosenzweig (1959), Lambert and Moore (1966), Jenkins and Russell (1960), and Moran (1966) have made use of some of these indices in comparisons of word association structure across languages.

4.6.4.11 Semantic Cluster Analysis

This measure is an index of vocabulary structure based on factor analysis and cluster analysis techniques described in Osgood, Suci, and Tannenbaum (1957) under the heading "concept factor analysis." Visual representation of vocabulary structure is possible and facilitates comparisons (see for example, Osgood and Luria, 1954 and Jakobovits and Osgood, 1967).

4.6.4.12 Spew Hierarchy

Relying on certain complex arguments presented by Underwood and Schulz (1960) and summarized in their "Spew Hypothesis," Osgood, Archer, and Miron (1962) developed elicitation procedures which yield association data that when treated by means of the information statistic H, reveal a response hierarchy that is stable and characteristic of a language/culture group. Comparisons of such "spew hierarchies" (to which word frequency distributions are related in a crude way) should reveal the degree of the bilingual's coordinateness.

4.6.4.13 Word Categorization Task

There is considerable evidence (Mandler, 1966; Jenkins and Russell, 1952; Cofer, 1965) that the lexical items in the vocabulary of an individual are structured in his memory along patterns that are organized in clusters which can be revealed under conditions of free recall and spontaneous emissions. There would be considerable interest in determining the stages of development of such vocabulary clusters in learners of a second language and the extent to which compound-coordinateness affects the establishment of such clusters.

4.6.4.14 Word Stereotypy

This measure is related to the H index used in the determination of the spew hierarchy described above (4.6.4.12). It gives an indication of the "richness" of a concept and its stereotypy, that is the extent to which subjects under conditions of a restricted word association task will tend to give the same high frequency responses. Again, the interest here, as in the last few measures just described, lies in the determination of the degree of correspondence between the bilingual's vocabulary structure and that of the population norm.

4.6.4.15 Translation Test

Facility in translation as indexed by latency and accuracy measures may be related to compound-coordinate bilingualism in so far as it involves language switching and semantic correspondence, as discussed earlier in this section. It would appear that a translation test involving sentences or meaningful discourse should be more revealing than the translation of single words since the latter is likely to be either too simple and automatic—when the word in isolation has a single meaning, or too difficult and conflictual—when the word has multiple meanings. One should also keep in mind the possibility that translation may be a separate special skill only partially related to the usual skills of decoding and encoding required in everyday discourse. If this were the case, translation should not be used as a measure of language proficiency.

4.6.4.16 Language Alternation Test: Encoding

The purpose of this test is to force the bilingual to encode in both languages in rapid succession. The task has two levels of difficulty: one consists of naming objects shown to the bilingual in each language, alternating with each new stimulus; the other level consists of persuading him (a difficult task with some!) to tell a story while alternating languages for "chunks" of discourse as he goes along. The size of these chunks (i.e., words, phrases, sentences) at reasonable fluency is likely to be the significant variable.

4.6.4.17 Language Alternation Test: Decoding A

Here the bilingual's ability to understand written and oral material is being tested. The text is made up by alternating languages using phrase chunks. Here is an example of a sentence in such a text using English and French as the two languages: "The government of Henry the Seventh, de son fils, et de ses petits enfants was, on the whole, plus arbitraire, than that of the Plantagenets."

4.6.4.18 Language Alternation Test: Decoding B

This differs from the previous test in that the alternating chunks are smaller. Here is an English-French example: "A complex appareil used in deux ou plus parts de la world suggests un rapport between eux in very measure to leur complexity." Understanding of both kinds of texts can be evaluated by requiring the subject to answer questions based on the text. Latency measures may also prove to be useful.

4.6.4.19 Pronunciation Switch Task

This test is added for the special case where the two languages possess homographs either because of linguistic closeness (as in English and French) or because of linguistic contact (e.g., English origin words in the linguistically unrelated languages of India that use a common script). A list of homographs is prepared and the bilingual is instructed to read it as fast as he can by alternating languages with each word. Both speed and accuracy are recorded. Here is an example of such a list in English and French: FORMER, OR, CHAIR, SEIZE, LAME, POUR, TAPER, COMMENT, HABIT, MAIN, SON, COIN, FOUR, CASE, ON, CENT, RIDE, CHAT, DRESSER, BUT, PIN, SORT, DOT, LOIN, BOND.

4.6.4.20 Capsule Sentences

The peculiar (but nevertheless, regular) transformations that characterize newspaper headlines result in sentences whose meaning often eludes non-native speakers of a language whose proficiency otherwise is quite adequate. This test is designed to measure the bilingual's knowledge of these peculiar transformations by requiring him to recover the original sentence from the "capsule" sentence. For example: given the headline "Tells Parties for Army Aids by U.S. Firm," the subject may recover "He reveals that parties are given by a U.S. firm on behalf of army personnel." The recovered sentence should contain not only the factual information but also the *sub rosa* implications ("reveals" for "tells").

4.6.4.21 Sentence Transformation Test

The purpose of this test is to measure the bilingual's capacity to transform sentences from one mode to another (e.g., from active to passive; from negative question to active declarative, etc.; see Miller, 1962). Error and speed are the two relevant measures.

4.6.4.22 Cloze Procedure

In this test a text is mutilated by deleting every fifth word and the incomplete text is then given to the subject for completion. The choice of words in the bilingual's attempt to restore the text is compared to the original or to the performance of native monolinguals. Accuracy can be scored in terms of exact type or in terms of semantic correspondence to the original. The Cloze procedure was first described by Taylor (1953).

4.6.4.23 Subjective Evaluation of Competence

A competent bilingual judge, in a face-to-face interview with the subject, evaluates the bilingual's competence in five areas: phonology, syntax, vocabulary, oral comprehension, and fluency. The judge has available a rating sheet which he fills out while he is conversing with the subject. Here is an example of such a rating sheet:

Accent

foreign _____ : _____ : _____ : _____ : _____ : _____ native

Grammar

inaccurate _____ : _____ : _____ : _____ : _____ : _____ accurate

Vocabulary

inadequate _____ : _____ : _____ : _____ : _____ : _____ adequate

Fluency

uneven _____ : _____ : _____ : _____ : _____ : _____ even

Oral Comprehension

incomplete _____ : _____ : _____ : _____ : _____ : _____ complete

The six-point scale is defined, from left to right, as follows: extremely, quite, more left than right, more right than left, quite, extremely. A pretest of the reliability of this scale using two sophisticated judges rating French-English bilinguals yielded interjudge correlations in the high 80's and low 90's for the five scales.

4.6.4.24 Subjective Evaluation of Compound-Coordinateness.

During the interview the judge engages the bilingual in conversation about his language acquisition history and usage, asking sufficiently specific questions to enable him to rate the individual on four measures of compound-coordinate bilingualism: compound acquisition, coordinate acquisition, compound usage, and coordinate usage. In each case a rating is given which may vary from 0 to 100. In a pretest using French-English bilinguals, interjudge reliability was found to be in the high 60's and low 70's for the four measures. Compound acquisition and usage correlated positively with each other (in the 70's) and negatively (in the 60's) with coordinate acquisition and usage (the latter also correlating positively with each other, in the 70's).

4.6.4.25 Subjective Evaluation of Attitude

Two measures are included under this heading: an orientation rating (discussed earlier in this Chapter) and a rating of the attitude of the subject toward bilinguality: how advantageous or important it was to be bilingual, whether he'd require his children to achieve a high degree of bilingualism, and so on. Both of these ratings may vary from 0 to 100.

4.6.4.26 and 27 Proficiency Tests in Both Languages

In many languages special proficiency tests have been developed and are widely known and used. Where these are not available, achievement scores in language courses or some other substitute tests would have to be used. In all cases, the question of validity will have to be carefully considered. These problems cannot be dealt with here and the reader is referred to the discussions in Lado (1961) and Mackey (1965), and the discussion in Chapter 3 and at the beginning of this Chapter.

4.7 TRANSFER EFFECTS FROM ONE LANGUAGE TO THE OTHER

Transfer is perhaps the single most important concept in the theory and practice of education. In its most general form the principle of transfer refers to the hypothesis that the learning of task A will affect the subsequent learning of task B and it is this expectation that justifies educational training in schools as a form of preparation for the subsequent demands that society will impose upon the individual. In fact, some educators (e.g., Ferguson, 1956) consider transfer as the general case and learning as the specific case where task B is highly similar to task A and learning of task B thus constitutes further practice on task A.

The general paradigm that applies to all transfer studies can be summarized as follows:

Experimental Group:	Learn A	Learn B
Control Group 1:	——	Learn B
Control Group 2:	Learn X	Learn B

In the experimental group, the transfer effects that are presumed to operate are of two types: specific and nonspecific. The former are attributed to the habits acquired in learning task A which are utilized in the learning of task B. The latter are attributed to general factors involved in the learning of any task such as warm-up effects and the development of learning sets. By comparing the performance of the experimental group to that of Control Group 1, the combined effects of specific and nonspecific transfer can be assessed, whereas by comparing their performance to that of Control Group 2, the specific transfer effects can be assessed without the contamination of the nonspecific factors.

The interest in transfer in second language learning has been most explicit in attempts at specifying interference effects through contrastive analyses between the second language (L_2) and the first (L_1). The most extensive analysis of the potential mechanisms of interference between two languages is that of the classic work of Weinreich (1953). Today contrastive analysis is a widely accepted technique among second language teachers and is commonly used to guide classroom and laboratory activities in terms of the type of materials to be introduced at specific times and the nature of the practice exercises to which the learner is to be exposed. In addition the operation of transfer is implicitly assumed both within the language learning situation and in the applicability of the course instruction to skills the individual will be called upon in using the language outside the school. The expectation of transfer within the language instruction situation relates to the notion of cumulative gains to be obtained so that language acquisition is conceived of as a step-by-step building process of successively more complex stages and whatever is learned in the early stages is expected to be retained and transferred to later stages. There is the further expectation that knowledge of the common elements which constitute the structure of the language will transfer to the various skills; for instance, a grammatical relation learned orally is supposed to facilitate the acquisition of the same relation in reading or writing.

The external applicability of the classroom training similarly rests on assumptions of transfer effects so that a student drilled in pattern practice is expected to be able to transfer these skills to the real life situation of an ordinary conversation with a native speaker. Reading of literature in the second language and indirect exposure to the foreign culture through the content of sentences, pictures, and films are similarly justified in that such knowledge is expected to facilitate later understanding of "field-like" situations. Obviously then, a major portion of what constitutes second language teaching today rests its justification on the explicit or implicit recognition of the operation of transfer effects.

4.7.1 The Extrapolation of Knowledge

The literature on transfer (when the term is considered in its broadest sense) is possibly more extensive than that on any other topic in psychology and education. It can be subdivided into two categories: on the one hand, one finds a mass of experimental reports on highly specific aspects of transfer effects under laboratory learning conditions; on the other hand, one finds a substantial body of writings which deals with the operation of transfer in real life settings such as the school and industrial training programs. In a pattern now familiar in the social sciences whereby scientific exactitude is inversely proportional to realistic concerns, we find that whatever specific knowledge there is on transfer concerns tasks and settings that are largely irrelevant to crucially important educational concerns, and the amount of specific and reliable knowledge on the latter is practically nonexistent.

Careful reviews of the vast literature pertaining to transfer are invariably pessimistic. Concerning the work on paired-associate learning Betts (1966) concludes that "the data presented here and the equations derived from these data are much too tentative to be offered to educators as practical solutions to their problems" (p. 135). Concerning the work on interference theory in rote learning one of the most authoritative experts on the subject recently concluded that "thus far, there is little empirical evidence in support of [the] assumption [that] forgetting outside the laboratory is a function of the same variables and represents the same processes as are observed in formal studies of interserial interference" (Postman, 1961, p. 166). In an extensive, formal, and detailed report on restricted aspects of learning Russian under controlled laboratory conditions, Crothers and Suppes (1967) conclude that ". . . in these second language learning experiments the proportion of correct responses usually seemed to depend more on the detailed structure of the item than on the presentation-order variables that were examined" (p. 311). This pessimistic conclusion is particularly noteworthy because the work of Crothers and of Suppes is often cited as examples *par excellence* by proponents of the formalized experimental approach to problems in learning and teaching.

I am citing these conclusions, which are representative and describe accurately the "state of the art," because I want to draw attention to a tendency that has become quite widespread in the social sciences generally and in education, including second language teaching, specifically. This tendency consists of an attempt to justify teaching practices of a particular kind by appealing to experimental findings in the laboratory that deal with materials of an entirely different order of complexity than the learning task in question. An example of this, which by now ought to be notorious, is the description of language learning and language behavior that is based on conditioning principles developed through laboratory studies with rats and rote learning studies with human subjects. A more recent instance, one which is very much topical today, concerns the justification of pattern drill practice in second language teaching by appealing to laboratory experiments on motor skills and to principles of generalization and transfer derived from stimulus conditioning and verbal rote learning studies. While I think it is both justifiable and desirable to apply knowledge which one might gain from laboratory experimentation to educational and social concerns, I do not think that this extrapolation carries greater scientific merit than the extrapolation that comes from knowledge acquired outside the laboratory through observation, experience, and insight. The extrapolation process in both instances is not a rigorous matter and cannot be scientifically justified. Chomsky's evaluation of this tendency has been quite harsh: "... there has been a natural but unfortunate tendency to 'extrapolate,' from the thimbleful of knowledge that has been attained in careful experimental work and rigorous data processing, to issues of much wider significance and of great social concern. This is a serious matter. The experts have the responsibility of making clear the actual limits of their understanding and of the results they have so far achieved, and a careful analysis of these limits will demonstrate, I believe, that in virtually every domain of the social and behavioral sciences the results achieved to date will not support such 'extrapolation' " (1968, Preface).

I suspect that these remarks will be welcomed by those practitioners of the teaching arts who have always preferred to follow their flair and who have maintained a distaste for the analytic and molecular formulations of the experimentalists. However, I would like to dispel immediately any sense of security that a smug subjectivity may provide. It would be a mistake to assume that because extrapolation from the laboratory is not a scientific process, therefore we must give up all attempts at developing systematic evaluation criteria whereby teaching methods can be made more effective. It is possible to be systematic without at the same time being rigid about the manner in which we make additions to our knowledge. The analysis of transfer effects in second language learning which I sketch in this section is molecular and has, I believe, a systematic character which could potentially organize the knowledge that language teachers already have from their experience in the classroom in such a way that they could make more effective use of such knowledge by rendering it more explicit. Hopefully, it might have the additional quality of enabling them to increase the usefulness and signficance of the knowledge they may gain through additional and continuing experience in teaching.

4.7.2 Some General Principles of Transfer

In this attempt to summarize some principles of transfer I will rely on the experimental work that is extant without, however, the pretense that the statements are scientifically rigorous. One should more properly consider them as fairly specific descriptions of current knowledge about transfer effects, knowledge which was arrived at by various procedures, which include interpretation of experimental data, observational data gathered through the experience of educators, and selections from what is common knowledge in the culture (sometimes called "common sense").

A general formulation of the transfer problem must deal with five basic elements: task A, training or practice on task A, training or practice on task B, and the relation between task A and task B. Since our specific interest here lies in language learning, let us refer to the five elements as follows: P_{L_1} (proficiency on task A), P_{L_2} (proficiency on task B), t_{L_1} (training in L_2), t_{L_2} (training in L_2) and $R_{L_1-L_2}$ (the relation between L_1 and L_2). The transfer effects to be expected in second language learning can then be expressed by the following formula:

$$P_{L_2} = f(P_{L_1}, t_{L_1}, t_{L_2}, R_{L_1-L_2})$$

This formula says that attained proficiency in L_2 will be some joint function of attained proficiency in L_1, training in L_1, training in L_2, and the relationship between L_1 and L_2. Consider now some of the possible relations that may hold in this formulation (see Ferguson, 1956) and how they are reflected by this formula. In the case where $t_{L_2}$is constant and $R_{L_1-L_2}$ is fixed we have:

$$P_{L_2} = f(P_{L_1})$$

where $P_{L_1} = f(t_{L_1})$. This says that given fixed amounts of training, proficiency attained in L_2 is a function of native language proficiency, which no doubt reflects a general language ability. It is known that verbal ability and verbal intelligence are significant factors in second language learning although the shared common variance is fairly small. Furthermore, certain special abilities whose development may very well depend on t_{L_1} factors in early life, such as memory for coding phonetic materials and sensitivity to grammatical relations (see Carroll, 1966), seem to share substantial common variance with P_{L_2}.

In situations where t_{L_1} is very large and P_{L_1} has attained a stable value (e.g., an adult learning a second language), the general formula reduces to:

$$P_{L_2} = f(t_{L_2})$$

where $R_{L_1-L_2}$ is assumed fixed. This expresses the usually recognized function in second language learning where achievement is said to be a function of training in that language.

Where t_{L_1} is very large, P_{L_1} stable, and t_{L_2} fixed, the general formula reduces to:

$$P_{L_2} = f(R_{L_1-L_2})$$

which can be recognized as expressing the common knowledge that "exotic" languages are more difficult to learn than the more familiar ones.

An interesting feature which emerges by rearranging the elements in the general formula is expressed by the equation:

$$P_{L_1} = f(P_{L_2}, R_{L_1-L_2}).$$

This equation says that when $R_{L_1-L_2}$ has a particular value (e.g., with closely related languages) the learning of a second language may come to have interference effects on the mother tongue. This refers to what I have called elsewhere "backlash interference" as distinct from the more familiar linguistic interference which is expressed by the equation:

$$P_{L_2} = f(P_{L_1}, R_{L_1-L_2}).$$

One of the factors which is known to be important in the operation of transfer concerns the common elements between the two tasks; in the present discussion this refers to $R_{L_1-L_2}$. I have pointed out earlier that this relation has three different aspects, as follows:

1. $R_A = f(X_{L_1} - X_{L_2})$
2. $R_B = f(X_{L_2} - \overline{X}_{L_2})$
3. $R_C = f(X_{L_1} - \overline{X}_{L_1})$

where X refers to a particular speaker (either of L_1 or of L_2) and $\overline{X}$ refers to an idealized monolingual of L_1 or L_2. Equation 1 (R_A) refers to the relation between the bilingual's two languages; equation 2 (R_B) refers to the relation between the bilingual's second language and that of an idealized monolingual speaker of L_2, equation 3 (R_C) of an idealized monolingual speaker of L_1. These three relations are theoretically independent and their simultaneous value within the various linguistic domains defines the bilingual's position on the compound-coordinate continuum.

4.7.3 Transfer Effects in Second Language Learning

In attempting to assess the transfer effects in second language learning it will be necessary to consider the various relations separately since the same situation may have differential effects on each of them. Consider for instance the values to be expected for each of these relations on the basis of Osgood's three laws of interlist similarity (as reviewed by Jung, 1968). The three principles can be stated as follows:

1. Two tasks in which the stimuli are the same but the responses different (A-B, A-D) will yield negative transfer which increases the more the responses get dissimilar.[1]

[1] Following established practice in the literature on paired-associate learning, the first letter in expressions like A-B or A-D refers to antecedent stimulus factors while the second letter

2. If the responses are the same, but the stimuli are different (A-B, C-B), positive transfer is expected which increases the more the stimuli get similar.

3. When both stimuli and responses are different in the two tasks (A-B, C-D), negative transfer is expected which increases the more the stimuli get similar (see Figure 4).

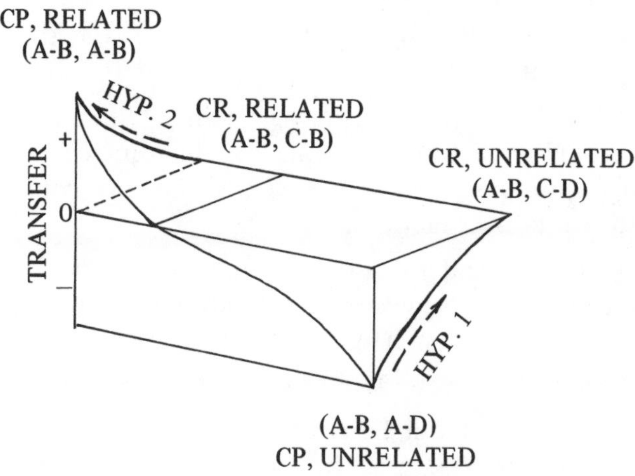

FIGURE 4. TRANSFER EXPECTATIONS IN SECOND LANGUAGE ACQUISITION BASED ON OSGOOD'S TRANSFER SURFACE. (OSGOOD, 1953, FIGURE 172, p. 532.)

---

refers to consequent response factors. The comma in expressions like "A-B, A-D" separates the first task from the second. Identity of letters is intended to indicate that the same factors are believed to hold in the two tasks. Thus, the expression "A-B, A-D" refers to two tasks in which the stimulus conditions are the same but the response conditions different. Please note that "stimulus" and "response" as used here do not carry the usual rigorous denotations and connotations which they have in the literature on "S-R theory."

In second language learning "stimulus similarity" may be taken to refer to the environmental conditions that are antecedents to linguistic utterances: these include the physical, external environment (to be referred to as E_{L_1} or E_{L_2}) as well as the mental, internal environment (to be referred to as e_{L_1} or e_{L_2}). "Reponse similarity" may be taken to refer to the structural relations between the linguistic systems of the two languages (to be referred simply as L_1 and L_2).

We are now ready to express the transfer expectations in second language learning which Osgood's three laws would suggest (see Figure 1):

1. In a compound setting with the indirect method of teaching (where E_{L_1} and E_{L_2} are highly similar, and so are e_{L_1} and e_{L_2}), we would expect negative transfer which increases the more L_1 and L_2 get dissimilar.

2. With closely related languages (where L_1 and L_2 are similar), we would expect positive transfer which increases the more E_{L_1} and E_{L_2} (and e_{L_1} and e_{L_2}) get similar, i.e., in a compound setting with the indirect method.

3. When E_{L_1} and E_{L_2} (and e_{L_1} and e_{L_2}) are relatively different (as with the direct method in a coordinate setting) and L_1 and L_2 are different (as with unrelated languages) negative transfer is expected which increases as E_{L_1} and E_{L_2} get similar.

These principles can be restated from the point of view of the interest in maximizing positive transfer and minimizing negative transfer.

Hypothesis 1. With unrelated languages a coordinate setting (symbolized as CR) will yield less negative transfer than a compound setting (symbolized as CP).

Hypothesis 2. With related languages a CP setting will yield more positive transfer than a CR setting.

Note that the second hypothesis here derived seems to be in conflict with the widespread inclination among most proponents of the audiolingual method to maintain as much as possible a direct learning method and to avoid as much as possible any use of L_1 in the learning situation. There is some evidence, however (Lambert,

Gardner, Barik, and Turnstall, 1963), which supports the expectation that individuals studying a second language that is closely related to their first language (in this case French being studied by Americans) do better in the course if they show evidence of allowing a CP interaction in their meaning systems. In our terms, e_{L_1} and e_{L_2} were not kept separate even though there was an effort on the part of the instructors to maintain overt environmental separation (E_{L_1} and E_{L_2}) by offering to the American students enrolled in the intensive summer course the distinctive French-Canadian atmosphere in bilingual Montreal and not permitting, under threat of expulsion, any use of English. Despite these efforts on the part of the instructors the students who acted internally as CP bilinguals achieved higher grades. To be sure, this evidence is only suggestive with respect to the transfer expectation expressed as Hypothesis 2 and, because it seems to conflict with our common sense expectations, we should be wary of it. Nevertheless, now that we are alerted to its possibility, we should watch out for possible confirming evidence whenever possible.

Jung (1968) describes an elaboration contributed by Martin of Osgood's three laws of similarity. Consider the three components of specific transfer in two successively learned paired-associate tasks. They are response learning, the establisment of forward associations, and the establishment of backward associations. The findings are apparently consistent with the following statements:

1. With the A-B, C-B paradigm (different stimuli, same response) there is positive transfer from the first task (A-B) to the second task (C-B) for response learning.

2. With the A-B, A-D paradigm (same stimuli, different responses), there is negative transfer for the establishment of forward associations (A-B connections in the first task conflict with the A-D associations in the second task).

3. With the A-B, C-B paradigm (different stimuli, same responses), there is negative transfer for the establishment of backward associations (B-A connections established during learning of A-B associations in the first task) and conflict with B-C connections that tend to be established during C-B learning in the second task.

4. Low degree of first learning and low degree of response meaningfulness facilitate response learning and minimize the establishment of backward associations. Hence these two factors in combination will result in greater positive transfer in the A-B, C-B paradigm (since they augment the positive transfer mentioned in statement 1 and decrease the negative transfer referred in statement 3). With the A-B, A-D paradigm, these two factors produce less negative transfer since they minimize the effect expressed in statement 2.

Now let us examine what kind of expectations these principles would lead us to in the second language learning situation to see if this exercise will help us organize our knowledge.

4.7.3.1 Coordinate Training with Related Languages

This corresponds to the A-B, C-B paradigm where E_{L_1} and E_{L_2} (and e_{L_1} and e_{L_2}) are made as different as possible and response learning (L_1 and L_2) are relatively similar. According to Hypothesis 2 derived earlier from Osgood's three laws of similarity (see also Figure 4), the overall effect to be expected is zero transfer (as opposed to the positive transfer effect with CP training). With Martin's elaboration of Osgood's three laws we can specify in greater detail the effects in several areas (see Table 1).

4.7.3.1.1 Encoding Skills.

Positive transfer is expected for response learning of the second language due to the similarities in structure to the first language; however, CR training may reduce this effect because of the emphasis on separate contexts and the discouragement of the use of the learner's first language. The net effect is therefore in doubt.

4.7.3.1.2 Decoding Skills.

Because the background context is made different through CR training while the structures of the languages remain similar, negative transfer is predicted due to the expected tendency of the learner to relate L_2 responses to L_1 environment. Symbolically, this inference pertains to the relation $L_2 - E_{L_2}$ or $L_2 - e_{L_2}$ which refers to back-

TABLE 1
TRANSFER EXPECTATIONS IN SECOND LANGUAGE ACQUISITION FOR SEVEN AREAS UNDER FOUR CONDITIONS

Area of Transfer	Conditions of Learning			
	CR, Related (A-B, C-B)		CR, Unrelated (A-B, C-D)	
	Transfer Effect	Explanation	Transfer Effect	Explanation
a. L_2 learning (P_{L_2})	?	Should be facilitative due to L_1 - L_2 similarity but CR training may minimize effect	?	Should be interfering due to L_1 - L_2 dissimilarity but CR training may minimize effect
b. L_2 - E_{L_2} relation (or e_{L_2}) (decoding)	–	Backward associations (B - A, B - C) are interfering	0	Backward associations are irrelevant
c. L_2 - E_{L_2} relation for early childhood bilingualism	+	Lower degree of first learning minimizes effect in (b)	0	See (b)
d. R_c [= $f(x_{L_1} - \bar{x}_{L_1})$ or backlash interference	?	Backward associations are interfering but similarity of cultures minimizes effect	+	CR training reduces effect on L_1
e. R_c for early childhood bilingualism	+	Less interference in (b) due to lower degree of first learning	0	See (b)

(continued)

TABLE 1 (Continued)

	Transfer Effect	Explanation	Transfer Effect	Explanation
f. R_A [= $f(x_{L_1} - x_{L_2})$	?	Facilitation due to high L_1 - L_2 similarity but CR training may minimize effect	?	Interference due to L_1 - L_2 dissimilarities but CR training may minimize effect
g. R_B [= $f(x_{L_2} - \bar{x}_{L_2})$ or nativeness in L_2]	?	Assuming cultures also similar, should be facilitative but CR training may minimize effect	+	CR training promotes nativeness
a.	+	L_1 - L_2 similar	—	Should be interfering due to L_1 - L_2 dissimilarity
b.	+	Backward associations (B-A, B-A) are facilitative	0	Backward associations (B-A, D-A) are not interfering
c.	0	Since (b), lower degree of first learning has no effect	0	Since (b), lower degree of learning has no effect
d.	0	Assuming that cultures are also similar	—	Assuming cultures are also dissimilar
e.	0	See (c)	0	See (c)
f.	+	Facilitation due to L_1 - L_2 similarity	—	Interference due to L_1 - L_2 dissimilarity
g.	+	Facilitation, assuming cultures are also similar	—	Assuming cultures also different, CR training inhibits nativeness in L_2

ward associations (where $E_{L_2} - L_2$ or $e_{L2} - L_2$ corresponds to the forward associations involved in 4.7.3.1.1 above). Since the $L_2 - e_{L_2}$ relation refers to the decoding process (understanding), we would therefore expect less efficient acquisition of the "passive" skills.

4.7.3.1.3 Decoding Skills (early childhood bilingualism).

Because a young child's experience with the mother culture is more limited, the negative transfer expected in 4.7.3.1.2 should be minimized. According to the transfer principles discussed earlier, lower degrees of first learning should facilitate backward associations ($L_2 - E_{L_2}$); hence, the expectation will favor early childhood bilingualism in decoding skills. (The same situation would hold for immigrants in a country where their L_1 usage becomes unstable.)

4.7.3.1.4 Backlash Interference.

Departures from nativeness involving one's mother tongue as a result of contact with L_2 are expected to be less serious if the two cultures, as well as the two languages, are similar, as is often the case. Since we are dealing with related languages, the negative transfer in backward associations (i.e., in the decoding skills represented by $L_2 - E_{L_2}$ and $L_1 - E_{L_1}$) will be a source of difficulty as stated in 4.7.3.1.3 above. Thus with a CR setting, $R_C = f(X_{L_1} - \bar{X}_{L_1})$ will be maximized. As will be recalled from the earlier discussion, this refers to the possibility of backlash interference (when it is minimized) which has the effect of reducing the nativeness of the developing bilingual in his mother tongue. It follows that a CP setting with the indirect method when the languages are related should minimize R_C.

4.7.3.1.5 Backlash Interference (early childhood bilingualism).

Less interference is expected with lower degrees of first learning (as discussed earlier), i.e., when experience with the mother culture is still limited as in early childhood bilingualism.

4.7.3.1.6 Interlingual Interference.

As in 4.7.3.1.1, positive transfer is expected due to the similarities between L_1 and L_2, leading to a reduction in response interference $[R_A = f(X_{L_1} - X_{L_2})]$.

4.7.3.1.7 Degree of Nativeness.

Degree of nativeness in L_2 [i.e., $R_B = f(X_{L_2} - \overline{X}_{L_2})$] would be expected to be high with CR training, although when the two cultures, as well as the two languages, are closely related, this factor of setting is not likely to be as important as in the case when the cultures are quite different. Note that similarities in culture and language are expected to facilitate nativeness in L_2, but CR training may not capitalize on this effect; hence, in relative terms, this is not the most efficient training condition.

A similar analysis can be undertaken for the three additional cases where CR training is given for unrelated languages and CP training for either related or unrelated languages. The results of the analysis for the four cases are summarized in Table 1. Seven areas of transfer are examined. As can be seen, the most efficient condition for second language acquisition is that of CP training with highly related languages; CR training with highly related languages is not as efficient, a conclusion which is in agreement with the statement in Hypothesis 2 considered earlier. The least efficient condition is that of CP training with unrelated languages; CR training with unrelated languages is more efficient. An interesting effect which the table points up is the fact that expected *facilitation* effects may *not* materialize due to training conditions (e.g., 4.7.3.1.1 and 4.7.3.1.7 for the CR, Related condition); similarly, expected interference effects may not materialize thanks to training conditions (e.g., 4.7.3.1.1 and 4.7.3.1.6 for the CR, Unrelated condition). In some instances, the training condition converts an expected interference effect into facilitation (e.g., 4.7.3.1.4 and 4.7.3.1.7 for the CR, Unrelated condition).

The effects summarized in Table 1 should be viewed in relative rather than absolute terms. For instance, a question mark indicates that relative to some other condition, the expectations of facilitation are not as good (e.g., 4.7.3.1.7 for the CR, Related condition relative to the CP, Related condition). Furthermore, the processes and conditions to which the table refers are abstract conceptualizations of aspects of language behavior and conditions of learning. In real life situations these neat abstractions become "fuzzy." Thus what has been talked about as "CR or CP training" becomes in fact degrees of compoundness and coordinateness, and what is referred to as "response learning" or "decoding skill" turns out to be in practice a conglomeration of a multitude of skills and innumerable facets of knowledge each of which can be focused upon for observation and analysis. These practical considerations do not invalidate the abstract analysis, but they indicate that one must always be clear about what particular condition or language behavior process is in question. In a subsequent section I shall discuss the kinds of techniques and instruments that are available for assessing particular language behavior functions.

4.7.4 Areas of Transfer in Language Learning

Up to now I have been considering transfer effects in language behavior without specifying the specific skills involved. A systematic analysis must concern itself with specific skills within specified domains (e.g., syntactic competence in speaking, or vocabulary knowledge in reading) and, in addition, with the degree of proficiency attained in each of these skills at the time the analysis is relevant. A model of CP-CR bilingualism which I have described earlier specified changes in second language acquisition along four different dimensions: attained proficiency in L_1 and L_2, a three-fold relation between L_1 and L_2 (R_A, R_B, and R_C), psycholinguistic area of functioning, and development in time. The general transfer equation described above [namely, $P_{L_2} = f(P_{L_1}, t_{L_1}, t_{L_2}, R_{L_1 - L_2})$] and its various derivatives did not specify the nature of the functional relation. Theoretically the nature of this function can be zero, positive, or negative, and can be linear or nonlinear. An example of a nonlinear transfer effect is provided by the case where degree of practice affects amount and type of transfer. Thus phonological interference effects due to dissimilarity between L_1 and L_2 (e.g., 4.7.3.1.6 in the table above) are known to be particularly strong during the early stages of second language learning and diminish with time and practice. On the other hand, backlash interference (e.g., 4.7.3.1.4 in the table above) is expected to be strongest at later stages of L_2 learning and to be minimal at the beginning.

Obviously, the transfer expectations expressed in the table above must be further qualified with respect to the nature of the transfer function that holds for each specified skill, within the specified domain, for specified time and amount of practice factors.

Let us turn to an analysis of the mechanism of transfer within the various language domains. Weinreich (1953) defines interference as "those instances of deviation from the norms of either language which occur in the speech of bilinguals as a result of their familiarity with more than one language" (p. 1). The terms "bilingualism" and "language," Weinreich suggests, ought to be defined in a technical sense so that they would refer to the presence of two linguistic systems whether these be recognized as separate languages or not. From a theoretical point of view the mechanism of transfer would seem to be the same whether the contrasting forms and patterns are taken from different languages, different varieties of the same dialect, or even different codes from the same dialect; the amount of interference will depend on the number of "mutually exclusive forms and patterns," according to Weinreich who, at the same time, expresses pessimism with respect to the possibility of specifying (at this stage of our knowledge) the "total impact of one language on another." I don't think this pessimism is justified since it is common knowledge that within standard learning situations existing in our High Schools and Colleges some languages are learned more easily than others and it would certainly be possible to make overall statements about transfer relations between L_1 and L_X, L_Y, L_Z, etc., on the basis of such learnability data. In fact, Cleveland, Mangone, and Adams (1960) present a table (p. 250-251) which specifies the time requirements for attaining specified levels of proficiency in various languages for individuals with certain predetermined levels of aptitude enrolled in a highly intensive language course. Their table shows that Americans with average aptitude, can attain proficiency in speaking Italian, French, Spanish, Rumanian, or German (among others) in two-thirds of the time it takes them to achieve the same proficiency in Russian, Greek, or Finnish (among others), and in only half the time it takes them to learn the same functional proficiency in Chinese, Japanese, or Vietnamese (among others). At any rate Weinreich's suggestion of estimating the overall impact of one language on another by describing the various forms of interference and tabulating their frequency would certainly be useful for teaching purposes as an aid in anticipating areas of difficulty. I would suggest that in addition we should be aware of the areas of overlap and similarity since, as pointed out in the discussion above, these similarities can be turned into facilitation effects through positive transfer by manipulating the teaching conditions in an appropriate fashion.

A transfer analysis between two languages is likely to be very involved. To indicate some appreciation of the complexity of such a task, here in summary form is the analysis which appears in Mackey (1965). He discusses the various relations between L_1 and L_2 along four levels: phonetics, grammar, lexicology, and stylistic usage.

1. Phonetics
    - 1.1. Articulation
        - 1.1.1. Vowel phonemes
            - 1.1.1.1. Presence or absence
            - 1.1.1.2. Present but different
        - 1.1.2. Consonant phonemes
            - 1.1.2.1. Presence or absence
            - 1.1.2.2. Present but different
    - 1.2. Catenation
        - 1.2.1. Permissible combinations
        - 1.2.2. Combinations causing sound changes
        - 1.2.3. Linking and separating words
    - 1.3. Rhythm
    - 1.4 Intonation

2. Grammar
    - 2.1 Differences in system
        - 2.1.1. Presence or absence of cases
        - 2.1.2. Type and function of inflections
            - 2.1.2.1. Verb systems
    - 2.2. Differences in structure
        - 2.2.1. Word-order
        - 2.2.2. Interdependence
    - 2.3 Differences in classes
    - 2.4. Differences in units

3. Lexicology
   3.1. Form
   3.2. Word meaning
4. Stylistic usage

Now let us consider a few specific examples of transfer effects to be expected between say English and French. The absence of a vowel phoneme (1.1.1.1. above) should be less interfering than its presence in a slightly different form (1.1.1.2.). The former corresponds to an A-B, A-D paradigm which, if B and D are sufficiently distinct should produce close to a zero transfer effect, while the latter corresponds to an A-B, A-Br paradigm which produces a distinct negative transfer effect. Thus an English speaker learning French should acquire without difficulty the vowels [o] *tôt,* [e] *thé,* and [oe] *boeuf,* which do not exist in English. If the vowels are very similar, as in the French [aj] *ail* and the English [ai] *eye,* we would expect facilitation through positive transfer. Similar transfer effects can be illustrated with an example from the grammatical domain. Presence or absence of cases (2.1.1) as between English and French on the one hand, and Latin and German on the other, would be less of an interference than instances where both languages have common types of inflectional categories which vary in function (2.1.2). For example, the English and French verb systems (2.1.2.1) overlap in tense system but differentiate as to their functions. Thus, English *I hear he's coming* (hear = present tense) is rendered in French *J'ai appris qu'il viendra* ('ai appris = perfect tense). Similarly, English *I hope he comes* (comes = present) is rendered in French *J'espère qu'il viendra* (viendra = future). At the lexical level the transfer effects of cognates are well known both in terms of their facilitative effect (as in the huge savings involved in learning French vocabulary for an English speaking person) as well as their negative effects (as with the notorious pitfalls involving the *faux amis*). The transfer problems involved in word meaning and stylistic usage seem even more complex than those involving the phonological and grammatical aspects, undoubtedly because our methods of analysis are so much less systematic at the moment in the former instance. However, I believe that systematization of our intuitive knowledge about meaning is possible at this ime (see my attempt in Jakobovits, 1968c).

4.7.5 Operation of Transfer Effects: A Surface Feature?

The implications for transfer effects in language learning of the current return of interest in the universal laws that underlie the structure of all natural languages and the related interest in nativistic theories of language deserve our attention. There are certain fundamental differences which must be noted between the acquisition of a second language beyond adolescence and first language acquisition during infancy. In the first place the notion of second or foreign language aptitude has no parallel in first language acquisition. The latter appears to be a maturational process whose development is universal and regular throughout the human species. Exposure to adult language and communication constitutes both the necessary and sufficient condition for the attainment of native proficiency. In the second place it is a highly probable fact that unless the first language is acquired by early adolescence, the capacity to acquire any human language is lost forever. No such effect is true of second language learning. Thirdly, the acquisition of speaking fluency in a second language under intensive training conditions by a well motivated adult with high aptitude is achieved in the order of between 400 to 600 hours and in slightly less than two months (see Carroll, 1963). The time factor involved in first language acquisition during infancy is of an order of magnitude that is nine times larger when one considers the time of onset of speech at 18 months and mastery of complex syntactic combinations at 36 months of age.

These three basic differences between first and second language acquisition strongly suggest that the processes involved in the two learning situations are distinct in some fundamental way. Conditions of teaching and transfer effects appear to be quite important in second language acquisition; they have little or no effect in first language acquisition (see Chapter 1). First language acquisition can aptly be described as a discovery procedure guided by innate universals, where the paradigms of concept formation and hypothesis testing appear much more relevant than the conditioning paradigms that have been applied to the second language learning process (e.g., in Rivers, 1964). I think these observations are significantly related to the fact that sophisticated linguistic descriptions of the competence of native speakers concern themselves to a considerable extent with the underlying structure of language, whereas contrastive analyses between two languages have dealt with relatively surface features of the two languages. The latter fact may of course be the result of the relative recency of transformational descriptions of grammar but I am suggesting that, in view of the distinctions just raised between the processes involved in first and second language acquisition, similarities and differences of surface features may be more relevant for the operation of transfer effects in second language learning than deep structure relations, especially when one believes that at some level of depth all natural languages are describable in terms of one universal system. Perhaps it would be more useful to talk about descriptions at different relative depths rather than surface versus deep structures, but until we know more about this problem I see no theoretical justification for giving a greater weight to transformational descriptions of grammar over phrase structure descriptions in guiding our teaching approach to second language learning.

4.7.6 Attitudinal Factors in Transfer Effects

In my analysis of the variables to be considered in the operation of transfer effects I have thus far limited myself to the structural factors that emerge from a contrastive analysis between the two languages and to the manipulation of environmental conditions of acquisition. But as Weinreich (1953) has pointed out it is necessary to consider nonstructural factors that relate to the individual's contribution to the realization of transfer effects in his speech. I shall refer to these as "attitudinal" factors. I would like to consider three of these, the first two being those discussed by Weinreich.

The first of these concerns the individual's tendency to resist transfer effects which would cause serious confusion in his attempt at communicating in L_2. Because the instances involved in these particular interferences are defined by the structural demands of L_2,

Weinreich considers them "structural resistance" factors. For example, in the case of phone substitution such as [r] for [R] where there is only one trill phoneme, the stimulus situation which is the occasion for interference relates to a structural difference between the two languages, namely different pronunciations of equivalent phonemes. The resistance factor to this interference is the danger of confusion with another phoneme in L_2. Another example, this time from the lexical field, is the outright transfer of words (such as the use of *Telephon* in German rather than *Fernsprecher*). The resistance factor for this type of transfer is the danger of potential homonymy as well as the uncongeniality of the word form in L_2.

The second type of attitudinal factor pertains to a nonstructural variable that may affect the occurrence of transfer such as resistance factors related to cultural and social-psychological considerations, especially loyalty to the recipient language and intolerance on the part of the community for linguistic importations. Thus French-English bilingualism in French Canada has for many years been marked by high tolerance for English importations both at the grammatical and lexical levels. Even Public road signs exhibit a strong English influence (mainly American English) (e.g., *CEDEZ* which is a direct translation of the English *YIELD*). In recent years the government of Quebec has embarked upon a vigorous program intended to counteract this drift (e.g., the CEDEZ signs are slowly being replaced by signs of *PRIORITE A GAUCHE* and *PRIORITE A DROITE,* literally "priority to the left" and "priority to the right") and there is increasing evidence of spreading social resistance to English importations in the speech of bilinguals in that province, a trend that is especially strong among the educated and the intellectuals.

The third attitudinal factor, also nonstructural, relates to the individual's learning strategy. One approach is characterized by the learner's attempt to make use of his knowledge of L_1 as a reference structure in terms of which the elements and relations in L_2 are being assimilated. The other approach is characterized by the learner's attempt to keep the two languages as separate as possible. Certain conditions of teaching may facilitate one or the other of these two approaches (e.g., direct vs. indirect methods). The structural relations between L_1 and L_2 may also influence the individual towards one or the other of the two strategies. Ultimately, however, the individual himself has the greatest contribution to make and the teaching method itself cannot totally control the manner in which the individual chooses to approach the learning problem. The expectation is that the assimilatory strategy will yield greater transfer effects than the "separative" strategy. The resultant facilitative or inhibiting effects will depend on the conditions of training and the relation between the two languages, as discussed previously. Where transfer effects lead to interference the individual with an assimilatory strategy will encounter greater difficulties than the individual with a separative strategy; on the other hand, where the conditions are such that transfer effects are facilitative the individual with the assimilatory strategy should have an advantage. I do not know to what extent learning strategies of this type are stable and relatively invariant, nor how they can be manipulated by the teaching situation. It is clear, however, that the training conditions and the choice of the second language to be taught (when such choice exists) ought to take into account such individual differences in learning strategy.

4.7.7 Transfer of Grammatical Rules

Earlier I indicated my belief that extrapolation of findings from laboratory experiments to real life learning situations is not a rigorous and scientific undertaking. The analysis of transfer effects presented in the previous discussion and the specific transfer expectations outlined in Table 1 must be viewed with the proper understanding of the limitations of extrapolation. Predictions and generalizations arrived at through this process that run contrary to the expectations of the experienced language teacher must be viewed with some suspicion; those that concur with his expectations are thereby reinforced and strengthened still further; those that are unexpected or not previously considered by the teacher deserve his careful consideration and it is these that ultimately justify systematic analyses of this type since they bring into focus generalizations and observations that otherwise would remain unnoticed. One problematic issue with which I have not dealt in any substantive fashion but which is no doubt in the mind of the reader concerns the question of what is it that we are really talking about when we refer to stimulus conditions, response conditions, associations, and the like in the context of language learning. It is quite clear that we do not mean by these terms what the strict S-R behaviorists mean since by no stretch of the imagination can one seriously claim that the antecedent conditions of an utterance are rigorously specifiable "stimuli" or that an utterance can be considered as made up of elementary "responses" that are identifiable in terms of separate and unitary motor or neurophysiological elements, and even much less that the two sets of factors can be functionally related to each other in a one-to-one fashion. Any such claims simply cannot be serious. It seems to me that the only senses which the terms "stimulus," "response" and "association" may properly have in the present context are the following: a *stimulus* is some event which is hypothesized to be an antecedent to another event and related to it in some cause-effect fashion; this second event is a *response; association* refers to the belief that the stimulus event is in fact a contributing cause to the occurrence of the response event. *Event* refers to an abstract elaboration of some perceived or imagined change in time and is always context dependent, i.e., it is like figure which stands out from ground. *Transfer* refers to the hypothesis that two response events are related in such a fashion that they share a stimulus event. Thus, the transfer expectation previously expressed in Table 1 that L_2 learning for related languages yields greater positive transfer under CP conditions of acquisition than CR conditions (also shown in Figure 1 as Hypothesis 2) asserts that L_2 as response events can be made to depend on stimulus events which are already related to L_1. Note that the possibility of such a dependence relation is presumed possible by the assertion of a similarity between L_1 and L_2 as response events. In the absence of such claimed similarity (as in the case of unrelated languages) the attempt to make L_1 response events depend on stimulus events already related to L_2 will be expected to hinder the acquisition of L_2 (as in CP training with unrelated languages). It is important to realize that the notion of transfer as defined here refers to the kinds of expectations that the language teacher has on the basis of *his* understanding of the similarity relations between the response events and the stimulus events to which they are presumed to relate. On the other hand the observable occurrence of facilitative and inhibitory effects exhibited by the learner depend on the similarity relations that *he* perceives (with or without his explicit awareness) and on the events that are in fact stimulus events for *him* (as determined by his past and ongoing experiences). Thus failure of observation to confirm expected transfer effects indicate that the teacher has misconstrued the effective learning situation as it in fact takes place.

This way of looking at the problem sheds new light on some old controversies. For instance, consider the long standing debate of whether or not one should teach grammatical rules explicitly. Arguments for the affirmative include the following: knowledge of a language is in fact knowledge of grammatical rules, hence rules ought to be taught directly; when general principles are understood, the learning is more thorough and can better be applied to new instances; it is simpler and more effective to teach a rule explicitly than to leave it up to the learner to discover it. Arguments for the negative include: language use is mostly the automatization of habits; rules can be confusing when stated explicitly; rules are just hypotheses about linguistic relations and when these hypotheses are in error they confuse rather than help the learner. As I have defined the transfer problem it is clear that this controversy comes about by the fact that there is some confusion between the teacher's understanding of the task on the one hand and the learner's approach to it on the other hand. The former point of view justifies expectations of transfer effects when rules are taught explicitly, the latter point of view fails to confirm these expectations by empirical observations. The question that is most relevant in this connection is not "Are rules useful or not?" but rather "Under what conditions does the learner find rules helpful?" Conditions under which rule learning is not expected to be helpful include: the learner does not understand the rules in the way intended by the teacher; the learner applies the rules to instances not covered by them; the learner spends an inordinate amount of time and effort in learning the rules; etc. Conditions under which rule learning is expected to be helpful include (in addition to the obverse of the preceding conditions): the learner supplies his own rules and generalizations and these are erroneous or inefficient hypotheses; the learner fails to supply his own generalizations and proceeds by rote learning of patterns; the learner already knows the rules by virtue of his L_1 knowledge and the explicit statement of the rules shows him how to use them in the applicable instances in L_2; etc.

Stephens (1960) suggests some principles by which transfer effects can be maximized in any given situation:

(1) *"Bring out the feature to be transferred."* Whatever the "thing" that is to be transferred (a fact, a method, a general principle, an attitude, a way of life) it "should be highlighted and brought into focus" (p. 1542). Thus, the course should not "hope" that the student will see a relation, a similarity, or a difference: such things should be explicitly pointed out (e.g., $L_1 - L_2$ differences or similarities in cognates, syntactic analogies between L_1 and L_2, phonological similarities in phonemic contrasts, etc.). When the two languages are related we can expect the learner to have a strong tendency to approach the task with an assimilatory strategy (as discussed previously). This can be quite advantageous for all those instances where the response events and stimulus-response associations are sufficiently similar in the two languages. Likewise, it is necessary to isolate and point out explicitly those instances in which the expectation of similarity does not hold. Failure to do so could not only lead to negative transfer but may also vitiate the positive effects of the assimilatory strategy by confusing the learner with respect to where he may and where he may not use his previous knowledge. Under such punishing conditions he may, as Wolfe (1967) points out, adopt an escapist strategy of choosing new forms which do not parallel either language. When the two languages are unrelated the student quickly learns the futility of the assimilatory strategy although a CP setting may unduly retard its discard.

(2) *"Develop meaningful generalizations."* . . . Transfer is more likely to take place when the thing to be transferred is a generalization, a conscious insight, a constant error to be dealt with, or a rule that can be understood" (Stephens, 1960, p. 1542). In the context of grammatical rules or generalizations it is not clear how one is to characterize what is "meaningful" or "understood." In his review of the literature on the "transfer value of grammar" to writing skills, Meckel (1963) concludes that there is no good research evidence either to support or to negate the value of grammar as traditionally taught in developing writing skill. He argues that "commonly

accepted principles of transfer of training would not lead an experimenter to expect much transfer value from knowledge of grammar which has not included the knowledge and ability to apply grammatical principles to the construction of the pupil's own sentences" (1963, p. 981). Meckel does not preclude the possibility of transfer in this situation; his point is that adequate research on the question has not been carried out. He calls for research on (a) "what specific items of grammatical knowledge hold the greatest promise for improving composition skill" and (b) "what degree of mastery of this knowledge is required before we may reasonably expect transfer to writing skill" (p. 982).

Recent advances in linguistic theory are important in this context since they provide the teacher with more powerful generalizations than have been hitherto available in traditional grammar books. However, their formalized nature may not render them suitable for teaching many categories of students. The degree of adaptation necessary for transformational grammar to be a meaningful experience to the language learner and the kind of practice required to bring out their usefulness represent problems for which we do not at present have systematic knowledge for their solution. A student of linguistics who is also learning a second language would be more likely to profit from a transformational description of the language than a High School student who would have to spend an inordinate amount of time mastering the formalized metalanguage involved. There are also individual differences in grammatical aptitude to be taken into account. Two of the major abilities which Carroll and his associates have identified as important in foreign language aptitude consist of "grammatical sensitivity" and "inductive language learning ability" (see for example Carroll, 1966). One deals with the individual's ability to recognize the function of words in various contexts in the mother tongue; the other is the ability to "infer linguistic forms, rules, and patterns from new linguistic context with a minimum of supervision and guidance." These special abilities are likely to be a function of some early experience in the mother tongue and, when we come to isolate just what this experience is, we would no doubt be able to improve the success of second language teaching later in life.

(3) *"Provide a variety of experiences."* . . Whenever it is a principle or generalization that is to be transferred, it is most important to use a variety of experiences to develop the generalization" (Stephens, 1960, p. 1542). Many current applications of pattern drill seem to be based on the opposite notion of uniformity. The justification given for invariant patterns (with substitutions of 'equivalent parts of speech') is presumably that 'only one thing at a time' is to be taught and that, when considered over sets of lessons or even the course as a whole, all the patterns considered together do exhaust the important variatons. However, one can argue that piecemeal presentation of patterns inhibits the attainment of broad generalizations and encourages the formation of restricted hypotheses which later have to be unlearned after many false starts. Wolfe (1967) gives the following example: practice on:

Where does he live?
Where did he go?

may interfere with later occurrences of:

Can you tell me where he lives?
Do you know where he went?

and points out the mistakes the earlier practice leads to:

*Can you tell me where does he live?
*Do you know where did he go?

Nevertheless, everything cannot be taught at once, so we need to develop more systematic knowledge with respect to the degree of "variability of experience" that maximizes generality of rules within the limits of demand for practice and drill required to develop fluency and automatization. Even if it may be true that such variability of experience may retard automatization of fluency, this consequence may in the long run be the better outcome. Ferguson (1956) cites evidence that "cognitive abilities play a more important role in the earlier stages of the learning of a motor task than in the later stages, when performance becomes organized in the form of a habituated psychomotor response pattern" (p. 127). Although we should heed his warning that generalization on this point may be precarious, since the distinction between cognitive and motor abilities is arbitrary, I would like nevertheless to suggest that in language learning we can maximize transfer effects by concentrating in the early stages on the acquisition of general principles and only later should we worry about automatization of phonological habits, fluency, and correct pronunciation. (Note that this is the reverse of audiolingual practice.)

4.7.8 Transfer to Nonlinguistic Areas

In this section I want to consider briefly the kinds of transfer effects that we expect from learning a second language to areas of behavioral functioning that lie outside a direct interest in linguistic performance. A major justification for the teaching of foreign languages in school is the belief that such study has desirable consequences on the individual's intellectual capacities. It is argued that language is the carrier of culture and, therefore, language study provides an opportunity for contact with a culture other than one's own. Such contact, even if indirect, is supposed to broaden one's horizons, lead to a better understanding of one's own culture thus viewed in perspective, reduce ethnocentrism, and generally affect in a desirable way one's perception of the world.

I would like to point out that these various claims can be viewed as statements about the operation of transfer effects from one task (learning a foreign language) to another (understanding one's own culture, interpreting the behavior of other peoples, interacting with foreigners, etc.). As such, everything we have considered thus far about the nature of transfer is also relevant in this context. For example, CP training with unrelated cultures is expected to lead to strong interference effects which means that the second culture will not be understood as intended by the teaching goals. Or, CR training with related cultures that are highly similar will fail to capitalize on positive transfer effects that may occur in CP training. Furthermore, areas of transfer are to be considered separately, as they were in the case of linguistic processes, since they may vary in the specific transfer function that characterizes them. To give an example, consider the expectations we may have about transfer effects relating to perception of social distance in a particular foreign culture. With the study of a related culture in a CP setting, such as the study of French in most American High Schools, the student is expected to learn quite easily the French system of address forms by transferring the English system which it closely resembles (see Brown, 1965), particularly when the relations involved are explicated by a sociolinguistic analysis. When the student is in a CR setting, such as learning French during a year of study abroad, the superficial differences between the forms of address that he may observe (such as the fact that in English there is no pronominal marker for formal versus intimate style) may interfere with the realization that both systems mark the same differentiations even though they use different methods (e.g., French *Vous* sometimes parallels English Title + Last Name). With unrelated cultures the transfer expectations under the two conditions are exactly reversed. Thus, the study of Korean in a CP setting makes it difficult to learn certain features of its system of address forms which differentiates among at least four levels of intimacy that attach special significance to such factors as the relative age of the addressee, his sex and marital status, and whether or not he is a classmate of the speaker (see Howell, 1968). CR training on the other hand minimizes the tendency to apply the English system in an environment that constantly belies similarities in culture.

The transfer effects of second language learning to nonlinguistic areas of functioning are likely to be greatly magnified under conditions of early childhood bilingual experience. This transfer problem is often discussed in the literature as the "balance effect," which refers to the expectation that the more time is spent on practice in L_2 the greater its detrimental effect on L_1 and on cognitive functioning in general. Thus the "balance effect" is essentially a negative transfer hypothesis. Macnamara (1966) has recently presented an extensive review of the literature on this question and has carried out a careful investigation of his own on the balance effect as it applies to the current bilingual instruction program in the public elementary schools in Ireland. His findings and conclusions lend strong confirmation to the negative transfer hypothesis: native speakers of English in Ireland who have spent roughly half of their school time learning Irish achieve a substantially lower standard in both written English and written Irish when compared with their native English or Irish counterparts whose education is monolingual. Furthermore, the bilingual children show a substantial handicap in problem arithmetic tests, a fact which Macnamara (1966) relates to their linguistic difficulties (because numerical or mechanical arithmetic tests yield no differences between bilingual and monolingual children). In sharp contrast to these findings and conclusions, the study reported by Peal and Lambert (1962) shows that bilingual children in the French-Canadian setting of Montreal are distinctly superior in both verbal and non-verbal intelligence to their French speaking monolingual peers. These authors hypothesize that early bilingualism "might affect the very structure of intellect": ". . . a large proportion of an individual's intellectual ability is acquired through experience and its transfer from one situation to another" (p. 6). They argue that bilingual children are exposed to "wider experiences in two cultures" and these will give them "advantages which a monolingual does not enjoy": "Intellectually [the bilingual child's] experience with two language systems seems to have left him with a mental flexibility, a superiority in concept formation, and a more diversified set of mental abilities. . . "

There are many differences in the Irish and Montreal settings and somewhere in these differences is to be found the resolution to the contradictory positions which Macnamara and Peal and Lambert were led to espouse on the basis of their respective findings. Knowledge is lacking to resolve the issue at the present time.

4.7.9 Some Measures of Language Functioning

In this section I would like to review some techniques that are available for the assessment of language functioning in relation to the various areas of transfer that were discussed in this chapter. Four general areas will be explored:

Functional relation between the two languages
Language functioning in the second language
Changes in nativeness in the first language
Attitudinal factors

4.7.9.1 Functional relation between the two languages.

This has been represented symbolically in the earlier discussion by the equation $R_A = f(X_{L_1} - X_{L_2})$ and refers to the interaction effects between the learner's two language systems. Two types of tests appear appropriate: (a) translation and language switching tasks and (b) semantic distance tests. Included in the first type are latency measures for word translation, sentence translation, and language alternation for decoding and encoding tasks. Included in the second type are measures of affective distance by means of the semantic differential technique, cross-satiation index, and an associative interference task.

4.7.9.2 Language Functioning in the Second Language.

This has been symbolized earlier as $R_B = f(X_{L_2} - \overline{X}_{L_2})$ and refers to the learner's knowledge of and behavior in the second language relative to native speakers. Five types of measures are appropriate here: (a) *Mechanical Skills:* these consist of standard proficiency and achievement tests within the four levels of skills: reading, writing, listening, and speaking; (b) *Semantic Sensitivity:* these include judgments of acceptability of participial and adverbial phrases which measure the speaker's sensitivity to implicit, aspectual, and metaphorical facets of meaning, as well as semantic differential measures which compare the learner's evaluations with those given by native speakers; (c) *Utterance Meaning:* these are intended to assess the learner's understanding of the functional communicative value of utterances both in terms of the intended message they carry and the implications they allow about the speaker (his intentions, psychological state, social background, etc.); (d) *Communicative Competence:* the purpose of these measures is to assess the learner's capacity to function in a communicative context through the medium of the second language. Various techniques are available with perhaps the "acting out" method being the most versatile and simple and one which reveals the extent to which the learner has command over various "codes" that are differentially appropriate to particular sociolinguistic contexts; (e) *Cognitive Structure:* the measures included under this heading are intended to reveal the extent to which the learner has incorporated the cognitive structure of the native speakers of the foreign language insofar as knowledge about one's culture is represented by lexical and semantic relations in language. Specifically, they are word-association structure, measures of semantic range, and word categorization behavior.

4.7.9.3 Changes in Nativeness in the First Language.

This has been symbolized earlier as $R_C = f(X_{L_1} - \overline{X}_{L_1})$ and refers to backlash interference: upon learning a second language the individual may come to adopt new cognitive, attitudinal, as well as linguistic modes of functioning. He is no longer a "typical" and representative speaker of his native language. Such changes may be quite subtle, even though significant in the long run, and can be assessed by comparing the learner's word-association structure and semantic differential evaluations to monolingual speakers of his own culture. A test which can be quite sensitive to such changes is the "Cloze procedure."

4.7.9.4 Attitudinal Factors.

The subtle changes in nativeness just referred to can manifest themselves through feelings of "anomie" (which can be assessed) and changes in perceptual and cognitive orientations that are part of an individual's personality pattern. Depth interviews, measures of ethonocentrism, and the "personality differential" (which is an index of interpersonal perception) are techniques that might prove useful here. A different but yet highly relevant attitudinal factor relates to the sociolinguistic context of second language learning: What is the social status of the particular language being studied? How do the learner's reference groups (friends, parents, neighbors) view the second language and the culture with which it is identified? These and related questions can be incorporated in depth interviews and should be supplemented by ethnographic information that can be provided by knowledgeable resource persons within the community. Finally, the learner's strategy and orientation with respect to the learning task must be examined: where and how much does he use the assimilatory strategy? the separative strategy? What is his stated motivation for studying the second language? The latter question can be assessed by Lambert's Orientation Index; the former can be investigated by making observations of interferences and direct questioning during learning sessions.

4.8 SUMMARY

Extrapolation from laboratory experiments to real life learning situations is not a scientifically rigorous process. Nevertheless, it is possible to be systematic without at the same time being rigid about the manner in which additions to knowledge are made. The analysis of transfer effects in second language learning should be molecular and have a systematic character that could potentially organize the knowledge language teachers have developed through their experience in the classroom. The analysis presented in this chapter outlines some specific transfer expectations under four different conditions of second language acquisition: coordinate and compound training for related and unrelated languages. Some unexpected predictions are generated; for example, with related languages a compound setting will yield more positive transfer (hence be more facilitative) than a coordinate setting. Similarities between two languages in terms of their surface features are more relevant to the operation of transfer effects than deep structure relations. A distinction must be made between structural factors based on contrastive analyses and nonstructural factors pertaining to the learner's attitudes and the sociolinguistic context of the learning situation. Transfer effects operate at various levels of language functioning (e.g., mechanical skills, semantic sensitivity, communicative competence) and measures to assess these effects are suggested.

Chapter 5

FOREIGN LANGUAGE APTITUDE AND ATTITUDE

The purpose of this section is to outline some major issues in foreign language teaching today, issues that bear upon the current, profession-wide examination of FL requirements. This report does not attempt to give a general review of the literature on FL learning and teaching; instead, it relies on previous extensive reviews (see References), taking them as the starting point, and it attempts to outline those principal conclusions which seemed to have the most empirical justification. The report is organized into six segments:

1. Teaching Methods in FL Instruction.
2. The Case for FL Aptitude.
3. The Attainment of FL Proficiency.
4. The Effects of Motivation and Interest in FL Learning.
5. The Goals and Benefits of FL Study.
6. Recommended Changes in FL Requirements.

5.1 TEACHING METHODS IN FL INSTRUCTION

Two theoretical approaches take up most of the attention of language teachers today. One, the habit-skill approach, views language behavior as a chain of habit units, the main problem in teaching being defined as making these habit chains automatic. The other, the rule-governed grammar approach, views language competence as the ability to generate novel utterances on the basis of a finite set of rules, the main problem in teaching being the impartation of an adequate knowledge of these rules. The habit-skill approach emphasizes oral practice techniques with a minimum of explanation of grammatical rules (such as repetitive sentence pattern drills). The generative approach discounts the usefulness of traditional concepts in learning theory such as practice, conditioning, reinforcement, and concentrates instead on arranging the linguistic input to the learner in a way that would maximally facilitate his acquisition of structural patterns and rules. It should be made clear that emphasis on rules and structure of the generative approach is not to be confused with the traditional (now archaic, except perhaps for the teaching of Latin) approach of the so-called grammar-translation method, which attempted to impart to the student a knowledge of the formal grammatical distinctions between his native language and the target language. In the generative approach the structure and rules of the target language are imparted inductively without the use of a formal meta-language and without translation exercises. Both the generative approach and the habit-skill approach may make use of modern linguistic theory on the nature and structure of language relying on generative transformational theory and contrastive analysis. Both tend to give greater emphasis to speaking and understanding, but the extent to which reading and writing skills are also taught varies greatly within either approach.

The debate on the relative merits of the two approaches, which occupies a significant share of the attention of FL teachers and applied linguists in their deliberations at conferences and in literature, is not merely of academic interest. The polemic character of the debate is kept alive by two disturbing aspects of FL teaching today: one is the widespread dissatisfaction expressed by both students and teachers with the repetitive pattern drills required by the habit-skill approach, which makes the former feel like idiots and the latter more like drill masters than teachers. The other reason has to do with the distinct malaise that came to permeate the ranks of FL teachers upon the realization that the level of proficiency attained by a large, if not major, proportion of public school and college FL students is disappointingly poor. Given this situation, it is necessary to examine in some detail the nature of the arguments in this debate.

Some standard arguments were recently outlined in a critique by Bernard Spolsky (1966). He summarizes the major assumptions upon which the habit-skill method is based:

1. FL learning is a mechanical process of habit formation.
2. Habits are strengthened by reinforcement.
3. Language is behavior made up of habit sequences at the phonemic, morphological, lexical, and syntactic levels.
4. Repetition, practice, and reinforcement of units and their concatenation are effective ways of developing language performance.

These principles are said to be derived from Skinner's behavior theory. Skinner's (1957) major attempt to apply the principles of behavior originally derived from work with rats and pigeons to the language behavior of humans has been persuasively demolished by Chomsky (1959) in his review of Skinner's book, *Verbal Behavior.* In this review Chomsky shows that the operational concepts in Skinner's theory of verbal behavior are gratuitous extensions from his work on animal behavior and lose their explanatory power completely when applied in the context of human verbal behavior. For example, the concept of "response strength"–his basic measure of learning–is defined in the work on rats as number of bar presses in a box rigged to deliver pellets of food upon depression of a lever by the animal. In the pigeon, response strength is equated with number of pecks. But what is it in language behavior? Frequency of emission of words, rate of speech units, intensity of vocal response, and the like, have been proposed, but all these are clearly inadequate (think of the absurdity of the conclusion that a language is known less well when it is whispered–low response strength–than when it is shouted!). Another example concerns the concept of "control," which is said to be the end result of the learning process, viz., when a particular "response" is "brought under the control" of a particular "stimulus" through the consequences of the response (i.e., reinforcement). These processes, which have operational meaning in the animal laboratory (e.g., stimulus = a light, response = bar press, control = presence of bar press when light is on, reinforcement = pellet of rat food), lose their specificity and become completely obscure in language behavior and can be said to apply to this new area only by analogy and metaphor, hence devoid of scientific explanatory value (think of what might be the "stimulus" of an utterance, in what sense an utterance is a "response," and by what means can one say that one "controls" the other through what reward). Yet it is precisely these specific tenuous extensions upon which the habit-skill method of language teaching is said to be based by its proponents.

With respect to the role of repetition and practice, recent investigations of natural language acquisition in children clearly show that overt practice on specific grammatical examples carries little or no weight in "implanting responses" and that "imitation" of novel grammatical forms occurs infrequently (for a detailed discussion of this argument see Chapter 1). Thus these concepts (repetitive practice, implanting of responses, imitation), cherished and carried to the ultimate in repetitive pattern drills, have only the most tenuous scientific justification. The habit-skill approach to FL teaching curiously rests its justification on a sequentially controlled model of language, despite the fact that such an approach has been clearly refuted in both psychological (see Lashley, 1951) and linguistic (see Chomsky, 1957) literature.

It is important to consider the implications of the above critique for a new development in FL teaching, namely programed instruction. Several instructional programs are now commercially available in the form of language texts for French, Spanish, and German. The invention of programed instruction is attributed to Skinner (the "father of teaching machines"), and the basic scientific justification upon which this new technique rests is similarly related to the principles of behavior he developed in his work with animals. All the difficulties discussed above apply here with equal force, but there is even an added complication: progamed instruction requires the isolation of "units" which compose the competence to be taught or the knowledge to be acquired. It has been clearly shown (Chomsky, 1965; Lenneberg 1967, and many others) that the significant knowledge a user of a language has to acquire does not constitute "units" but patterns and relations. This holds true for all levels of linguistic analysis: phonological, semantic, syntactic, and morphological. For example, recent research has shown that a phoneme is not a physically distinct acoustic unit: it cannot be taught as a "unit," only as a class of variable phones which have certain relations to each other as well as to other classes of phones. Similarly, one cannot acquire "true" language competence by learning specific grammatical patterns as "units" since the number of sentence patterns understood by a native speaker is infinitely variable—one cannot seriously hope to teach true language competence by mechanical mastery over a limited number of sentence patterns.

However weak the theoretical position of the habit-skill approach may be, one can nevertheless inquire as to its comparative effectiveness to that of the generative rule or grammar approach. Numerous studies in the last twenty-five years or so have attempted to resolve the issue of effectiveness of various methods of FL teaching, none of which have been adequate enough to permit any definitive conclusions. The reason for this disappointing state of affairs is that it is practically unfeasible to vary one element of instruction experimentally without at the same time modifying the effects of other elements in an unknown manner. Hence, as in all complex educational problems, it is perhaps unwise to expect a scientific assessment of language teaching methods. In a recently completed extensive project carried out at the University of Colorado by Scherer and Wertheimer (1964), an ambitious attempt was made to compare the effectiveness of two different instructional programs for teaching German in college: one approach emphasized audiolingual skills while the other method emphasized reading and writing. At the end of one year of instruction the audiolingual group was found to be "far superior" in speaking and listening skills, while the more traditionally trained group was "significantly better" in reading and writing. During the second year the two groups were merged and given common course instruction. At the end of the year the first group was better at speaking while the second group was better at writing, neither of them differing in listening and reading. The authors concluded that "the two methods, while yielding occasionally strong and persisting differences in various aspects of proficiency in German, result in comparable overall efficiency." The results of this and several other studies of the same scope reviewed by Carroll (1966, 1965) lead him to "the rather commonplace conclusion that by and large, students learn (if anything) precisely what they are taught" (1965, p. 22).

Many other experiments of lesser scope have been carried out in attempts to evaluate relative effectiveness of various methods of teaching phonology, grammar, and vocabulary, but it is not within the purview of this section to give an evaluation of these attempts. The interested person is referred to the review by Carroll (1966). Attention is brought to recent efforts to develop self-instructional programs, especially to the work of Valdman (1964), who has proposed the idea of giving college students FL credit proportionate to their level of achievement rather than to the amount of time they spend taking courses. Carroll is very optimistic about the possibilities of such a program: "It is evident that self-instructional programs in foreign languages are not only perfectly feasible but also highly effective–more effective, in general, than conventional teacher-taught courses. When used by sufficiently well-motivated students, they can produce high levels of attainment in all four skills of language learning–speaking and writing as well as listening and reading" (Carroll, 1966, pp. 27-28). It should be made clear that the effectiveness of programed self-instruction has not been adequately assessed for the general college population. It is known that individuals with different aptitudes and rates of learning require adjustment in learning programs and the technical problems involved in adjusting FL self-instruction programs to the individual learner have not been worked out.

5.2 THE CASE FOR FL APTITUDE

In order to be able to evaluate the manner in which learner characteristics, such as aptitude and motivation, interact with methods of instruction, it is necessary to consider the definitions for certain terms that will be used in this discussion. These definitions are based on Carroll (1963a), and are also discussed in Chapter 3.

5.2.1 Learning

A task to be acquired; performing an act which previously could not be accomplished; understanding a concept previously not understood.

5.2.2 Transfer

When something learned in situation A also manifests itself in situation B because of the inferred commonality between the two situations. (The elements in common are often not specified or even understood.)

5.2.3 Learning Time

Amount of time spent on the act of learning. (Not to be confused with elapsed time which includes such activities as sitting at the desk dreaming, "wasting time" looking for a book or pencil, etc.)

5.2.4 Aptitude

Learning time under best teaching conditions; the shorter the learning time the higher the inferred aptitude. (Note that for a difficult task combined with a low aptitude, learning time may be indefinitely long.) Aptitude is specific to tasks and depends on possession of certain characteristics by the learner. These characteristics may be either genetic (innate) or they may be dependent upon prior learning or exposure to certain situations.

5.2.5 Ability to Understand Instructions

This is conceived of as dependent upon two factors: general intelligence and verbal ability. The first enters into the ability of the learner to infer the concepts and relationships needed for the task–especially when these are not carefully spelled out (which, one might add, is the usual situation in any complex learning task). The second comes into play in the understanding of the language used in the instructions.

5.2.6 Quality of Instruction

The extent to which it is made clear to the learner what it is he is supposed to be learning. Note that this refers to highly specific elements within the overall learning task. Thus telling the learner that he is supposed to acquire "a reading knowledge of this FL" says absolutely nothing about what he is supposed to be learning: does he begin by learning the "writing system," "vocabulary items" (which ones?), sentence patterns, phonology (how?), etc. Even in sub-tasks such as listening comprehension, the learner is confronted with the problem of just what he is supposed to be paying attention to: phonemic contrasts, segmentation, contour, grammatical relations, etc. It is evident that "quality of instruction" deals with such highly complex (and unsolved) problems as the identification of relevant contrasts, their sequencing, the amount of exposure needed at each level, and so on. It should also be noted that, as defined here, quality of instruction does not have an absolute criterion but relates to the learner's point of view, viz., whether or not the task has been made clear *to him.* His aptitude, previous knowledge, and ability to understand instructions will influence the specific requirements for making it clear what he is supposed to be learning. It follows that "a standard" method of instruction which does not vary with the learner's characteristics could not be of high quality.

5.2.7 Perseverance

The time the learner is willing to spend in learning to a specified criterion. (This definition may not be quite adequate since a learner may "be willing" but "is unable" due to distraction, frustration, etc. However, to resolve this issue one would have to go into a discussion of the type, Is he *really* "willing" when he "allows himself" to be distracted? etc.—a type of discussion which would take us too far afield from the central purpose of this section.)

5.2.8 Opportunity to Learn

The learning time allowed by the method of instruction and the environmental conditions. (Applies to sub-steps as well as to the overall task.)

We have now considered the definitions of all the concepts, stated or implied, required in the following formula given by Carroll:

$$\text{Degree of Learning} = f\ \frac{\text{time actually spent}}{\text{time needed}}$$

The numerator in this equation will be equal to whichever of the following three terms is *smallest:* opportunity to learn, perseverance, instruction and ability to understand instructions.

The problem to which this section is addressed concerns, of course, a review of the factors that enter into an evaluation of the degree of learning of FLs in the school situation, in particular the college or university. The discussion in the previous section on methods of instruction is particularly relevant to two concepts implied in the equation: quality of instruction and opportunity to learn. The next section on the measurement of proficiency deals with a specification of the criterion to be achieved, which has not been dealt with so far. The fourth section on motivation will deal with perseverance as defined here. The rest of the present section will deal with the remaining two concepts implied in the equation: the ability to understand instructions and aptitude.

It is known that the acquisition of any learning task is influenced by what has come to be called a "general intelligence factor." As defined here, ability to understand instructions is a joint consequence of this general intelligence factor and verbal ability. The challenge involved in developing programed instruction can be viewed as an attempt to reduce the limiting effect of the general intelligence factor by sequencing the learning task in sufficiently small and clear steps so that the learner doesn't have to depend on his ability to guess just what he is supposed to be learning. It is this feature rather than its purported relation to Skinner's behavior theory that makes this new development such an exciting prospect. But the "state of the art" in programed instruction, particularly in FL teaching, is at such a crude level that the learner's general intelligence remains an important limiting factor in degree of learning. It is not surprising, therefore, that grades obtained in FL courses correlate with grades obtained in other school subjects. In a survey conducted in 1965 at the University of Illinois (Flaugher, 1967) involving the grades in nine fields for all entering freshmen, the intercorrelations at the end of the first semester of work ranged from .18 to .66 with a mean of .38. Intercorrelations involving FL grades ranged from .34 (with Speech) to .51 (with Natural Sciences) with a mean of .42. This last figure is of the same order as that found by other surveys (see Pimsleur, Sundland, and McIntyre, 1964). These figures indicate that, while general intelligence is a contributing factor to success in courses, it accounts for only a modest proportion of the variance in success (a correlation of .42 accounts for 18% of the variance, leaving 82% of the variance to be accounted for by other factors). Indeed, as is well known, many students who obtain high grades generally do very badly in their FL course, and vice versa. This has led many to postulate "a special talent" for FL study. During World War II the U.S. government became involved in FL training programs designed to impart a "practical speaking knowledge" of many FLs to personnel assigned to overseas duties of a diplomatic, military, and paramilitary nature. These programs, known as "intensive FL training programs," apart from their costliness, were associated with a sense of wartime urgency which led to efforts of selection of trainees to "weed out" from the beginning those persons who had insufficient talent to complete the intensive program successfully. These initial attempts at prediction of success in FL study found that the best predictor of success in an intensive program was the student's performance in an intensive trial course that usually lasted three to four weeks (Carroll, 1965). On the basis of this experience, tables of expectations of success were developed, one of which is presented here as Table 1.

TABLE 1
TIME REQUIREMENTS FOR FOREIGN LANGUAGE ACHIEVEMENT (IN MONTHS)

Languages	Class Hours	Levels of Proficiency I		II		III	
		Hi Apt.	Aver. Apt.	Hi Apt.	Aver. Apt.	Hi Apt.	Aver. Apt.
Italian, French Spanish, German	1	4	6	No	No	No	No
Danish, Portuguese, Dutch, Swedish,	2	2	3	4	6	9	12
Rumanian, Norwegian	2	1½	2	3	5	6	9
Russian, Polish, Persian, Greek,	1	6	8	No	No	No	No
Finnish, Hungarian	2	3	4	9	12	15*	18*
	3	2	3	6	9	12*	15*
Chinese	1	6	9	No	No	No	No
Korean	2	4	6	15	16	24*	30*
Japanese	3	3	4	12	15	18	24
Arabic	1	6	9	No	No	No	No
Vietnamese	2	4	6	12	15	18*	24*
Thai	3	3	4	9	12	15*	18*

Notes: (a) "No" entries indicate that it is not practical to achieve that level of proficiency on a one-hour-a-day basis.
(b) Entries with an asterisk indicate that one must add three months in part-time training and using the language, preferably in the field.

The table appears in Cleveland, Mangone, and Adams (1960, pp. 250-251) and estimates the time requirements (in months) for FL achievement in intensive programs for individuals with "high" and "average" aptitude. Three levels of proficiency are defined as follows:

Level I: "Sufficient proficiency in speaking a foreign language to satisfy routine travel requirements."

Level II: "Basic familiarity with the structure of a language with sufficient proficiency in speaking to conduct routine business within a particular field. Sufficient familiarity with the writing systems to read simple material with the aid of a dictionary."

Level III: "Fluency and accuracy in speaking with sufficient vocabulary to meet any ordinary requirements which do not involve the speaker in a technical subject outside his own specialty. Ability to read newspapers and documents with limited reference to a dictionary." The time estimates are further divided into three degrees of intensiveness of the program: "1 Class Hour" refers to one hour of instruction per day supplemented by "2-3 hours of drill and study." This "low" level of intensiveness is not considered practical as an intensive program to go beyond Level I. (Note, however, that it is far more than the usual college FL course.) The target languages to be learned are divided into four groups. The "easiest" in terms of time requirement (for native Americans) include the most frequently taught FLs in American schools (Spanish, French, German) but also include languages that few college students normally think of taking (Dutch, Danish, Swedish). The next group of languages in terms of difficulty includes Russian, which is becoming increasingly more popular, and Modern Greek, as well as more "exotic" languages such as Persian and Hungarian. The most difficult languages for Americans are the "Asian" varieties including Chinese, Japanese, Vietnamese, and Thai, but also Arabic. The difficulties involved in mastering the writing system of these languages (at Level III) add a very appreciable amount to the time requirements.

The superiority of the "high aptitude" individual over persons with "average aptitude" can be seen to be considerable (people with "low aptitude" are not considered capable of attaining any significant level of achievement under the time requirements of an intensive program). For the easiest languages, the "high aptitude" person can attain Level III proficiency in one-half to two-thirds the time needed for the "average" aptitude individual. For the difficult languages, the time is between 20% and 33% faster. Carroll (1960) estimates that only one-third of the general population in the U.S. has a sufficiently high degree of FL aptitude to complete successfully intensive language training programs designed on the order of 400 hours of study (a four-year high school FL program represents on the order of 600 hours of study).

As aptitude was defined earlier in this section, it is clear that a low level of aptitude can be compensated for (up to a point) in two ways: increasing time for opportunity to learn and lowering the level of proficiency to be attained. It can be seen that, assuming adequate motivation to learn (perseverance), and fixing an upper limit for time of study–say four years of school work–one can set the maximum level of proficiency that individuals with a given aptitude could attain. If we now set the minimum acceptable level of achievement–say in terms of a score of X on a proficiency test–as the requirement for "success," there will then be a certain proportion of the population that will not achieve success in FL courses. Pimsleur, et al. (1964), estimate that up to twenty percent of the student population in high schools and colleges are "beset by a frustrating lack of ability" in FL study. They refer to these students as "underachievers" in view of the fact that their grades in FL courses are "*at least* one grade point lower than their average grade in other major subjects." These investigators set about on an ambitious project to identify the characteristics and specific abilities that constitute FL aptitude. They administered a battery of tests to high school students in a state school system that they considered typical of the Midwest and the Eastern Seaboard and correlated the scores on these tests with obtained school grades in FL courses. An evaluation of their effort is given by the comparison of variables that correlate with FL course grades (Table 2).

As can be seen, their Language Aptitude Battery (which takes less than two hours to complete) is as good a predictor as Grade-point average (which represents a whole semester of work in several subjects). When these two variables are combined, the multiple correla-

TABLE 2

Variable	Correlation with FL grade	Percent of Variance explained
I.Q.	.46	21
English grades	.57	32
Grade-point average	.62	38
Aptitude Battery	.62	38
(Last two combined)	.72	52

tion affords more than double the predictive value of an intelligence test, and one-half of the total variance to be accounted for.

It would be instructive to examine the tests of the Language Aptitude Battery as it may give an indication of what constitutes a "talent for FL's." Here is a brief description:

Interest Test 1: A series of questions designed to index how eager the student is in studying the language he is taking.

Interest Test 2: A series of questions evaluating the student's belief in the general value of FL study.

Linguistic Analysis Test: "A fifteen-item test of verbal reasoning in which the students are given a number of forms in a FL and asked to deduce from them how other things are said in that language."

Vocabulary Test: A vocabulary richness test as a rough measure of verbal ability.

Pitch Test: "A test of auditory discrimination in which the student must distinguish Chinese tones."

Rhymes Test: A test to measure fluency with words.

Sound-Symbol Test: A "rapid-fire test in which the student hears a nonsense syllable and must match it with the correct spelling in his booklet."

Not all these tests are equally related to FL aptitude. In fact, the results of a matched-group experiment, in which "underachievers" were compared to "normal" students, showed no difference between the groups on the "Linguistic Analysis Test," the "Vocabulary" tests, and the "Rhymes" test. On the other hand, on three of the tests the underachievers scored significantly lower: these were the *Interest Test 1,* the *Pitch Test,* and the *Sound-Symbol Test.* The conclusion Pimsleur, et al., reach is unambiguous:

> "According to this investigation, there does exist a "talent" for learning foreign languages–that is, a special factor beyond intelligence and industriousness which accounts for how well an individual succeeds in a language course. Our evidence indicates this special factor is *auditory ability,* which may be defined as the ability to receive and process information through the ear" (1964, p. 135).

A similar conclusion is reached by Carroll (1963), whose extensive work on the *Modern Language Aptitude Test* (MLAT) was carried out independently of and prior to the Pimsleur, et al., investigation:

> "These propositions [which this chapter will attempt to demonstrate] are (a) that facility in learning to speak and understand a foreign language is a fairly specialized talent (or group of talents), relatively independent of those traits ordinarily included under 'intelligence' and (b) that a relatively small fraction of the general population seems to have enough of this talent to be worth subjecting to the rigorous, intensive, expensive training programs in foreign languages . . . [However,] . . . the question of whether a student of lower than average aptitude should study foreign languages for purposes of general and liberal education depends upon a number of considerations which do not bear upon the selection of students for intensive foreign language courses of the type described here" (p. 89).

According to Carroll, FL aptitude consists of at least the following four identifiable abilities as measured by the MLAT: (1) *phonetic coding,* which is "the ability to 'code' auditory phonetic material in such a way that this material can be recognized, identified, and remembered over something longer than a few seconds." This ability is then very similar to that identified by Pimsleur, et al. (1964), as discussed above. The word "coding" in the description takes on added significance when it is realized that "phonetic discrimination" *per se* is not an important predictor of FL success. A test of the ability to perceive phonetic distinctions by requiring the listener to distinguish between similar sounds presented as "foreign syllables" was included in earlier versions of the MLAT Battery but was later abandoned: its "validity coefficients were consistently low in comparison to those of other tests, and the conclusion was reached that phonetic discrimination ability is not crucial in FL learning. Most normal people have enough discrimination ability to serve them in learning a FL, and in any case, it is more a matter of *learning* the discrimination over a period of time than any fundamental lack of auditory discrimination which can readily be tested in an aptitude battery" (Carroll, 1965, p. 96). Thus it appears that the popular notion of "having a good ear for languages" is an ability that doesn't depend so much on one's "ear" but on the brain's capacity to code and store for later recall auditory information of a phonetic type.

(2) The second major ability measured by the MLAT is *grammatical sensitivity,* which is "the ability to handle 'grammar'," i.e., the forms of language and their arrangements in natural utterances. The subtest which measures this ability ("Words in Sentences Test") requires the individual to recognize the function of words in various contexts using English sentences. For example, a word or phrase in a longer sentence is underlined and the subject is required to underline that word or phrase in a second sentence which has the same grammatical function as the underlined element in the first sentence. Thus the test does not require formal training in the metalanguage of grammar, although such training may improve this trait.

(3) The third variable measured by the "Paired-Associates Test" of the MLAT is "*rote memorization ability* for foreign language materials," and "has to do with the capacity to learn a large number of . . . associations in a short time." It is well known in the psychological literature on verbal learning that rote learning ability is not related to intelligence to any substantial degree.

(4) The fourth variable in FL aptitude is "*inductive language learning ability,*" which is the "ability to infer linguistic forms, rules, and patterns from new linguistic context with a minimum of supervision and guidance." Unfortunately, this ability is not measured by the present commercial version of the MLAT.

The validity coefficients of the MLAT vary greatly, depending on the subject sample and the population they are drawn from. For example, its correlation with two groups of students enrolled in the Five-University Semester Program in Middle Eastern Languages was .40 in one group and .58 in another. The course was an eight-week intensive program in various languages including Arabic, Turkish, Persian, and Modern Hebrew. In further extensive tests of the MLAT, Carroll (1960) obtained twenty-eight validity coefficients for high school courses; these ranged from a low of .25 to a high of .78 with a median of .55. In twenty-five coefficients obtained with college courses the range went from a low of .13 to a high of .69 with a median of .44. These coefficients were superior to those obtained with intelligence tests and there apparently "was no systematic fluctuation of validity dependent on teaching methodology."

An interesting aspect of the MLAT is the claim Carroll makes that it is equally valid for predicting success no matter what the target language is. The status of this claim, however, is uncertain in view of the ambiguous data available on this question (see, for example, Table 4.11 in Carroll, 1965). Nevertheless, the evidence for the positive, significant validity of the MLAT in all languages is strong and there is little evidence so far that particular languages require special abilities.

Another interesting aspect of the MLAT is its potential use as a diagnostic tool. At the present time, it is not known to what extent one can improve the various separate abilities in FL aptitude by remedial training. On the other hand, a type of instruction that takes into account an individual's specific weaknesses as revealed by his scores on the subtests of the MLAT would seem to be a helpful strategy. Even if individual attention is not possible, separate classes based on the MLAT as a placement test would be indicated.

5.3 THE ATTAINMENT OF FL PROFICIENCY

It is not the purpose of this section to review existing tests of proficiency for FLs or the principles involved in the development of such tests. Rather, the intent is to examine the nature of the goal of FL achievement, what Edgerton and his associates (1968) have called "liberated expression" in their report to the Northeast Conference on the Teaching of Foreign Languages. An extended quote from their report will introduce the problem to which this section addresses itself:

> "Most existing materials for classroom instruction in foreign languages–especially audiolingual materials–concentrate on teaching the overt "machinery" of the language. . . . When the question of meaning arises in the context of foreign-language instruction, "culture" must necessarily be considered since the semantic component, the "meaningful content," of a language cannot be separated from the culture of which it is a vehicle. . . . Blunder after blunder (of the very sort the student's experience with a native or near-native "monitor" would sort out for him) is due not to lack of adequate conditioning in the manipulation of the mechanical aspects of the language he is trying to speak, but to a failure properly to associate the "pieces" of that language with what they denote and connote in the foreign culture itself. . . . Very often it is assumed that the primary aim of study of a foreign language

> in the context of a general education is to train the student so that he can make practical use of his acquired skill and knowledge. However, on close inspection this aim seems quite unrealistic. The great majority of students who study a particular foreign language in the course of their schooling never make very much actual use of it for either professional or casual purposes" (pp. 100-101).

FL requirements in colleges and universities, both entrance and graduation, are usually stated either in terms of number of credit hours taken or in terms of some vague statement such as "a speaking knowledge" or "a reading knowledge" of the language. In evaluating the success of the FL training program in the American educational system, it is necessary, as the above quote suggests, to consider the attained proficiency on two levels. The first level concerns the mechanical manipulation of the FL, while the second, "higher" level, relates to the student's attainment of "liberated expression"—the ability to use the FL as a vehicle of communication, what might be called communicative competence.

With respect to the first level, it is well known that successful completion of "so many" course credit units is a very poor indicator of the degree of proficiency attained. Even standardized tests of FL achievement are ambiguous in this respect for, as Carroll (1960) points out, they allow an assessment of competence only in terms relative to a comparison group which is considered "typical." Percentile scores do not indicate the absolute level of achievement of a student. Carroll gives an example of what he considers "a meaningful scale on which it would be desirable to report proficiency" (1960, p. 72). This scale was established by the Foreign Service Institute of the U.S. Department of State. The standards in *speaking proficiency* are:

S-0– no practical knowledge of the language

S-1– able to use limited social expressions, numbers, and language for travel requirements

S-2– able to satisfy routine social and limited office requirements

S-3– sufficient control of structure and adequate vocabulary to handle representation requirements and professional discussions in one or more fields

S-4– fluency in the foreign language

S-5– competence equivalent to English

A similar series of standards has apparently been established for reading and writing. An example of such a scheme has already been provided in Table 1, previously discussed, which also gives, as will be recalled, the time requirements for attaining the various defined levels of proficiency. As long as school requirements of FL proficiency fail to specify the levels of achievement in terms similar to these, no meaningful assessment of the success of their programs is possible. Furthermore, until such an assessment procedure is adopted, the requirements for FL study are likely to continue to appear to the student as arbitrary and irrelevant, a condition that is not likely to foster the kind of interest and motivation that promotes FL study (see next section).

It is often stated that full native language achievement is an impossible goal for FL training in the school. While such an expectation is undoubtedly unrealistic under present conditions of instruction, considering the limited time available for FL study for most students in high schools and colleges, it need not imply that because full communicative competence is impossible instruction should be geared to merely a knowledge of the mechanical manipulation of the language. The various levels of *speaking proficiency* as defined by the Foreign Service Institute scale (see above) assume the mastery of various levels of communicative competence before complete mastery of mechanical manipulation is attained. For example, level S-4 (fluency in the FL) is preceded by S-2 (able to satisfy routine social requirements), which is short of the proficiency in mechanical manipulation achieved by many FL students in school courses yet is far ahead of the latter in terms of ability to use the language in a practical situation. It would appear that the low level of communicative competence achieved by students in FL courses in school is due more to a failure in the method of instruction than to lack of sufficient time devoted to FL study.

Hayes (1965), in a most perceptive discussion, has outlined the "new directions" that FL teaching ought to take to remedy the "gap" between a knowledge of "structural manipulation" and communicative competence. It is instructive to review briefly the nature of the knowledge that must be subsumed under communicative competence.

A. *Paralinguistic factors.* These refer to features of speaking such as pitch, range, tempo, clipping, etc., which may make one react to a speaker with the comment "It's not *what* he said, but *how* he said it . . ."

B. *Kinesic factors.* Formal, visual (facial, gestural, etc.) features that carry meaning such as the slightly protruded tongue whose significance varies not only cross-culturally and cross-linguistically but, also, contextually within a culture. (Consider the difference in meaning of this act in our culture when done by a child concentrating on a task, by a young woman to her intimate friend, or by an effeminate male.)

C. *Sociolinguistic factors.* Linguistic features (phonetic, lexical, grammatical) correlated with geographical origin (dialect), socioeconomic background, context of interaction (speech style), speech mode (writing vs. speaking), etc.

D. *Psycholinguistic factors.* Features of the communication situation (including all of the above) as they affect the listener. For example, the person who uses the "High" version of a language in a speech community characterized by diglossia (see Ferguson, 1964) where the "Low" version is required (as in Arabic, Greek, or Swiss German) is an object of ridicule, while the reverse blunder in a school situation may land the teacher in jail (in some Arabic-speaking countries). Or, to give a more familiar example, the use of informal phonological style by a non-native speaker evokes an unfavorable reaction (e.g., "I'm gonna go home," with a less than native accent on "gonna").

When these aspects of communicative competence are considered, it is clear that they may profitably be included in a FL teaching program whose goal is admittedly less than full native competence. It is well to consider that if communicative competence (at some realistic level) is the desirable goal of FL study, then a so-called "speaking knowledge" is not closer to it than a "reading knowledge." It would appear that communicative competence in reading and writing (with no comparable competence in aural skills) would in many circumstances be more desirable than a "speaking knowledge" of the audiolingual course variety that includes adequate structural manipulation but excludes practical use. Hence an automatic preference for developing so-called "speaking skills" in many modern FL courses would seem to be arbitrary and unjustified.

5.4 THE EFFECTS OF MOTIVATION AND INTEREST IN FL LEARNING

It will be recalled that one of the elements in the learning model outlined earlier was "perseverance," which was defined as the time the student is willing to spend in active learning. This section will examine some of the relevant factors that enter into the term "willing" in this definition.

There is a distinction to be drawn between "being interested" and "being motivated." Interest usually refers to the condition where the source of the drive to study lies in the student; the latter sees the intrinsic value of the effort to be expended and the goal to be achieved. "To motivate a student," on the other hand, refers to a condition where it is felt that there is an absence of interest and hence the drive to study lies in some area extrinsic to the goal to be achieved. It is often assumed that intrinsic interest is a more favorable condition for learning than supplied motivation, although the evidence on this matter is ambiguous. Thus, Lorge (in Carroll, 1960) reported that, when in the depression adults were paid to follow experimental courses in Russian, they learned equally well regardless of their stated interest in the task (p. 66). Dunkel (also in Carroll, 1960) found in a 1948 report that monetary rewards did not significantly improve performance in an artificial language learning task (p. 66). Carroll himself reports that a person's likes or dislikes for FL study were unrelated to aptitude or achievement (1960, p. 66). He concludes: "From these results one may infer that as long as learners remain cooperative and actively engage in learning *whether they want to or not,* motivational differences will not make much difference in achievement. Motivation will be related to achievement only when it affects how well students will persevere in active learning efforts in a situation in which they are relatively free to lag in attention, as in public schools" (1960, p. 66). However, it will be recalled that Pimsleur, et al. (1964), reported that their "Interest Test 1" was one of the tests on which underachievers were significantly lower than the controls, and they found it helpful to include it in their Aptitude Battery as a useful predictor of success. Similarly, after a series of investigations on the study of French in the Montreal, Maine, and Louisiana settings, Lambert (1963) reaches the following conclusion: "The results indicate that, similar to the Montreal studies, two independent factors underlie the development of skill in learning a second language: an intellectual capacity and an appropriate attitudinal orientation toward the other language group coupled with a determined motivation to learn the language" (p. 117).

The investigations of Lambert and his associates at McGill University raise some important questions for a "social psychology of bilingualism" which are not normally considered within the scope of FL training, yet indicate that the study of an FL may have some psychological consequences not unlike those experienced by immigrants in their efforts of acculturation. The individual's reactions to these psychologically significant processes are believed to affect the learner's motivation for study and, hence, his success in achievement. Lambert puts it this way:

> "This theory, in brief, holds that an individual successfully acquiring a second language gradually adopts various aspects of behavior which characterize members of another linguistic-cultural group. The learner's ethnocentric tendencies and his attitudes toward the other group are believed to determine his success in learning the new language. His motivation to learn is thought to be determined by his attitudes and by his orientation toward learning a second language. The orientation is 'instrumental' in form if the purposes of language study reflect the more utilitarian value of linguistic achievement, such as getting ahead in one's occupation, and is 'integrative' if the student is oriented to learn more about the other cultural community as if he desired to become a potential member of the other group. It is also argued that some may be anxious to learn another language as a means of being accepted in another cultural group because of dissatisfactions experienced in their own culture while other individuals may be equally as interested in another culture as they are in their own. However, the more proficient one becomes in a second language, the more he may find that his place in his original membership group is modified at the same time as the other linguistic-cultural group becomes something more than a reference group for him. It may in fact become a second membership group for him. Depending upon the compatibility of the two cultures, he may

experience feelings of chagrin or regret as he loses ties in one group, mixed with the fearful anticipation of entering a relatively new group. The concept of 'anomie' . . . refers to the feelings of social uncertainty which sometimes characterize not only the bilingual but also the serious student of a second language" (1963, p. 114).

It can be seen that the question of motivation in FL study may be a very complicated factor indeed. Lambert has found that "integratively oriented" students are more successful than "instrumentally oriented" learners, and he apparently believes that the latter are not normally aware that they are "trying less hard," if indeed they are. Carroll (1960) is of the opinion that the instrumentally oriented student in fact perseveres less at FL study, which he thinks accounts for Lambert's findings. Evidence consonant with this interpretation is provided by Politzer (1953-54), who reports that there is a direct correlation between performance in course examinations for college students and number of hours spent in *voluntary* language laboratory periods (the latter presumably being an indication of intrinsic interest), while the correlation with time spent in *doing homework* (presumably an indication of extrinsic interest) is curvilinear (the students getting A's and D's did the least amount of homework).

In view of the apparent importance of the learner's interest in the subject being studied, it is necessary to examine the evidence on this matter. Only two studies were found which report college student's interest in FL study. One was carried out at Harvard in the early 1950's by Politzer (1953-54), the other at the University of Illinois in 1968 by the Liberal Arts and Sciences Students Council (unpublished). The situation at both institutions was similar in that the students were enrolled in the FL courses for the purpose of fulfilling the FL requirement. (See Chapter 2.)

Two questions in the Politzer survey have direct relevance to student interest in FL study. The first deals with the student's selection of a particular language for study; the following options were given in the question:

(a) no particular reason

(b) language happened to be more easily available in the secondary school or college schedule

(c) it is easier than any other

(d) it is more likely to be of specific use

(e) reason for choice was a particular interest in French (or Hispanic) civilization or literature or people

The results are tabulated by type of course in which the students were enrolled: courses lettered A and C are those with admitted emphasis on reading; courses lettered B and D lay greater emphasis on speaking. A and B are first year courses, C and D are second year courses. The total sample consisted of 455 students. Of these, the majority were in the A and C courses (184 and 189, respectively, versus 49 and 33 for the B and D courses, respectively). The figures in the table refer to percentages.

	French		Spanish	
	a+b+c	d+e	a+b+c	d+e
A	36	64	48	52
C	40	60	57	43
B	18	82	12	88
D	28	72	37	63

The answers in this table are lumped by category of response indicating clearly extrinsic interest (a, b, and c) versus probable intrinsic interest (d and e). The following points are evident upon inspection: (1) the students who enroll in a course with a greater emphasis on speaking (B, D) have a more intrinsic interest in the language they are studying; (2) the extent of intrinsic interest held in the first year course decreases in the second year course; (3) anywhere from 1/3 to 1/2 of the students in the A and C courses have no intrinsic interest in the language they are studying. In addition, a breakdown of answers by grades indicates that more of the good students (in all courses) have an intrinsic interest (75%) than the bad students (53%), as indicated by their course grades.

The second question asked the students to indicate their opinion on what they felt ought to be the primary purpose of instruction. The choices given were:

(a) acquisition of reading knowledge

(b) ability to speak with some fluency on everyday topics

(c) acquaintance with some major literary works in the original

(d) better understanding of French (or Hispanic) culture

The results were:

	French			Spanish		
	a	b	c+d	a	b	c+d
A	64	31	5	62	34	4
C	48	43	9	52	44	4
B	39	61	0	17	79	4
D	25	71	4	0	100	0

Inspection of the table permits the following conclusion: more students in the A and C courses believe that reading should be the primary purpose of FL study, while the B and D students believe in the primacy of a speaking knowledge. Separate tabulation combining the opinion of the total sample of 455 students reveals that more students believe in the primary importance of reading over speaking (46% vs. 41%). Furthermore, the distribution of answers for "good" students and "bad" students for this question is about equal.

Two significant pieces of information emerge from the Politzer survey. One is that one-third to one-half of the students taking a FL to fulfill a college requirement have no intrinsic interest in the particular language they are taking. The other is that a reading knowledge of the language is held to be of equal or greater importance than a speaking knowledge. Both of these conclusions are further confirmed by the pattern of results at the University of Illinois survey, which was answered by about 838 students. (Participation was voluntary; about 5,000 questionnaires were distributed to the student body.) The results showed that 50% preferred "a language course oriented toward understanding of grammar and reading comprehension," versus 47% who preferred "a course oriented toward oral-aural comprehension." The fact that they have little intrinsic interest in FL study is shown by the following pattern of answers: only 28% read any material voluntarily in the language they are taking, 80% feel that they have to work harder in FL courses, a situation which they consider unfair, and for 61% of the students this extra work prevents them from taking other courses that they are interested in. Furthermore, 53% don't even feel that they would be able to use the FL they studied to meet graduate school requirements, and 80% doubt that FL study is helpful in developing "discipline" or "better study habits." Finally, 76% disapprove of the FL requirement and 40% feel that FL study in college has actually been detrimental to them.

In considering the dissatisfaction which FL teachers experience with respect to the low degree of success of the FL training program, it is necessary to pay attention to at least the following three factors: (1) the method of instruction, (2) the distribution of FL aptitude in the general school population, and (3) the apparent lack of intrinsic interest on the part of students in studying FLs. The general considerations relating to the first two factors have already been discussed in previous sections. The remainder of this section will consider the specific ways in which student interest is affected by his FL aptitude and the decisions the FL teacher can make about the method of instruction he practices.

In the definition of aptitude given earlier, it was stated that aptitude may be either innate or dependent upon transfer or prior learning or exposure to certain situations. One of the exposure conditions that may affect FL aptitude for college students might be prior FL study in high school. There are indeed some indications that the study of a FL in high school facilitates success in study of another FL in college (Carroll, 1966, p. 31), and students entering college who have had no lapse between high school and college in FL study do better than either students who have had no previous language study or students who have had a lapse of at least two years (Carroll, 1960, p. 68). However, the quality of FL study in high school appears to be generally low, as suggested by the fact that, at the University of Illinois, more students are enrolled in 101 and 102 type courses (considered remedial) than 103 and 104 type courses despite the fact that practically all incoming freshmen have had two years of study in high school (and 40% of them have had more than two years). It is well known that lack of achievement in a subject lowers student motivation and thus the lack of intrinsic interest in FL study at the college level may, to a certain extent, be the result of previous and concurrent failure in FL study. At any rate, tests with the MLAT have shown that FL aptitude remains fairly stable throughout one's life history past puberty, and the distribution of scores in the general population indicates that the FL teacher must be resigned to the fact that a certain (undetermined) proportion of students have aptitude scores too low to achieve at what he might consider an adequate level under the time requirements and instruction conditions of the school environment.

If this conclusion is accepted, the FL teacher may have to adjust his expectation of the proficiency to be attained by the student with a given aptitude, and he may profitably ask himself what steps he can take in his instruction to make FL study more worthwhile and more relevant to the student within the latter's capacities. Carroll (1966) reports certain cases in which "well-developed programs of instruction, particularly of the 'programed' variety, yielded low correlations between [FL] aptitude and performance suggesting that the obstacle of low aptitude may sometimes be surmounted by the use of small-step increment materials that do not challenge language aptitudes" (p. 29). Language study is unlike the study of most other school subjects in that the student has in it very adequate feedback of his failure to reach the goal. Unless sub-goals are clearly defined for him, he may get discouraged and lose interest or stop trying. The FL teacher ought to be aware of the psychological importance to the student of the latter's self-evaluation of his progress and take steps to help him to define his progress in realistic and relevant terms. Some students (and, indeed, FL teachers) tend to measure progress by inappropriate criteria. They may judge their progress in terms of how closely they come to a native speaker model instead of in terms of the attainment of sub-goals. They may insist on the early command of a large vocabulary disregarding the fact that the biggest problem in language acquisition lies in the mastery of phonological and syntactic skills, not the extension of vocabulary. They may insist on native-like pronunciation and frustrating phonetic exercises despite the fact that there is no evidence that such accuracy is essential for communicative competence, which, actually, is unlikely, quite apart from the fact that many learners have too low an aptitude for this degree of achievement. The aesthetic value placed on a "good accent" may be too high a price to pay when such insistence hinders the attainment of communicative competence. The student should also be given more help in the choice of an FL. An individual with low aptitude will experience more problems with languages that have a complex grammatical structure or a difficult writing system. Ferguson (1964) has outlined certain criteria that may be used for evaluating the intrinsic complexity of the grammar of a language (morphophonemic simplicity, number of obligatory categories marked by inflections or concord, extent of symmetry of paradigms, degree of strictness of concord). One might consider preparing rankings of modern languages in terms of difficulty for Americans based on norms of time requirements (such as in Table 1) and counsel the student for a choice on the basis of his aptitude and interest. The level of proficiency to be required may be set in advance on the basis of aptitude test results and either require substitute work to fill in the rest of the time or award less credit. Another possibility is to set different proficiency requirements for different skills. While existing aptitude tests, such as the MLAT, are not quite suitable for this purpose, a try-out course might be: thus, if it is found that a student's audiolingual attainment will be low, he can switch to a reading course where his chances of success might be better. Finally, FL study can be rendered more relevant by making it useful; for example, its requirement for readings in the student's major area of study and its use for communication purposes at an early stage without insisting on prior mastery of mechanical manipulation.

5.5 THE GOALS AND BENEFITS OF FL STUDY

To the question of what are the goals or benefits of FL study one usually obtains answers that fall into four categories (not necessarily independent): a reading knowledge, a speaking knowledge, communicative competence, and cultural awareness. The traditional goal of FL training and the one still dominant in the minds of undergraduate and graduate university students is the attainment of a reading capacity sufficient to serve library research requirements and to provide the possibility of enjoying major literary works in a language other than one's own. The major goal of the Intensive Foreign Language Program which sparked the "new" audiolingual approach during World War II was to produce a "practical speaking knowledge" in the shortest possible time. This result satisfied the immediate requirements of a need at hand: to train military, paramilitary, and diplomatic personnel assigned to overseas duty. As a result of these efforts, coupled by the increasing number of private American citizens who travel abroad, there has developed a strong feeling among many individuals connected with education, that the primary goal of FL study in the school ought to be the development of oral skills. With respect to this change of emphasis, Moulton raises certain important questions:

> "As part of a liberal education, however, we may also want the student to retain an understanding of the structure of the foreign language, just as we want him to gain and retain an understanding of the structure of his native language. . . . Likewise, as part of a liberal education we must be interested not only in teaching our students to speak, but also in teaching them to say something worth listening to; and this means that part of their work must consist in reading some of the great things which have been said in the particular language, some of its best works of literature" (1962, p. 90).

While most teachers today would not dispute the fact that reading literature in an FL is beneficial, and indeed such is required in advanced language courses, yet the emphasis on oral skills in the popularized audiolingual courses shows that when study time is short and a choice has to be made, the preference is for a development of oral skills and literature reading is left largely to the student who wants to specialize in FLs. The rationale for this preference is not obvious and the decision needs justification, for in fact it may not have any. The fact is that the practical considerations for FL study such as travel and a job abroad are still not sufficiently important for most Americans, and given the dominance of English in the world, which is still increasing, these considerations may never by themselves fully justify the emphasis of oral skills in FL study. The present wide insistence on a goal that is justifiably felt unwarranted by many students in our educational system may be responsible in large measure for the lack of high motivation in FL study. The choice of which skill to emphasize in FL instruction ought to be made in response to the goal or need felt by the student, not by some arbitrary decision. The emphasis on oral skills in the Intensive Foreign Language Program of World War II, in many current efforts such as the Peace Corps Training program, and in private FL training programs designed for business men, is a rational choice justified by the trainee's particular needs. Such a single purpose goal for FL training in our schools is not similarly responsive to the potentially variable needs of the general student population.

Irrespective of whether the goal of FL study is specified as a reading knowledge or a speaking knowledge, or both, there is one ultimate benefit that receives universal consensus. This is that FL study increases cultural awareness, reduces ethnocentrism, and is an effective "antidote to cultural myopia." Despite the undisputed status of this benefit, FL teachers often are incapable of making an efficient case for it to the student who often remains skeptical. It may be instructive to examine, in some detail, the arguments that some writers have used relative to this question.

The relationship between language and culture is often discussed in the literature in relation to the so-called linguistic or cultural relativity hypothesis, whose best known modern proponents have been Sapir and Whorf (sometimes also called the "Whorfian hypothesis" or the "Sapir-Whorf hypothesis"). Writers have disagreed concerning the strength of the influence of the language system upon thought, perception, and motivation. The strong formulation of the hypothesis posits that with each different language system there is correlated a unique thought pattern which determines the speaker's world view. The consequence of this position is the denial of the possibility of an exact correspondence between two linguistic expressions that belong to different language systems. The weak formulation only admits that coding systems in general, of which language represents one example, facilitates or inhibits memory functions. This position denies a direct influence of the language system on perception, and admits the possibility of "equivalent expressions" across different language systems.

Carroll has edited a book on some selected writings of Benjamin Lee Whorf (1956), but he seems to reject the strong version of the relativity hypothesis. He inclines toward the weaker proposition that language "predisposes" an individual toward a particular view insofar as the grammatical and semantic classes peculiar to a language emphasize certain aspects of experience and the environment in a way that is different from another language. He writes: "Insofar as languages differ in the ways they encode objective experience, language users tend to sort out and distinguish experiences differently according to the categories provided by their respective languages. These cognitions will tend to have certain effects on behavior" (Carroll, 1963b, p. 12). Some examples will illustrate the process Carroll has in mind. It is well known that the Eskimos have some dozen different words for varieties of snow, and so a person who is to communicate in their language must change his usual perceptions of snowflakes by learning certain differentiations he failed to make before. The realization that classification of objects as expressed by the names we give them is arbitrary may come when an English speaker learns Chinese and discovers that two categories of things that he has hitherto considered very different ("fruits" and "nuts") are in this language lumped into one class having but one name. To give an example that might be more familiar, when an American learns German his attention is drawn to the fact that German speaking people must specify the manner of transportation when they talk about displacing themselves: A German cannot just "go" to his country house; he must either walk (*gehen*), use a vehicle (*fahren*), ride on horseback (*reiten*), or whatever. Where English uses the verb "to pick up" something, Navaho uses several variants depending on the shape of the object that is handled–a difference which may account for the fact that Navaho speaking children pay attention to the form of objects at an earlier age than American children (Carroll, 1963b, p. 16). An American learning Spanish must consciously make a type of distinction about the concept of "to be" (*ser* versus *estar*) which he normally doesn't think of when speaking English. The student of a second language becomes sensitized to the fact that many of his values are not shared by members of another culture when he learns the different connotations of so-called "translation equivalent" words: The word "fat" in American English has a negative connotation, while in the Hindi language, among others, it carries a positive affect. It is sometimes argued that this kind of "cultural awareness" could be taught in an anthropology type course and one need not go to the trouble of acquiring a particular FL. Actually this is highly unlikely for it assumes that all or most cultural differences can be explicitly identified and stated verbally—a claim that no serious student of anthropology would dare make. In fact, recent developments in anthropology use a type of linguistic contrastive analysis to isolate cultural differences ("componential analysis"), and in psychology methods of "comparative psycholinguistics" are employed to isolate cross-cultural differences of a psychological nature (Jakobovits, 1966). There is recent evidence that linguistic differences in the connotation of translating equivalent words provides a clue to deep psychological factors related to the need system (personality) of individuals that distinguish economically "advanced" from economically "disadvantaged" societies (Jakobovits, 1969f). One recalls in this context Lambert's observation that becoming bilingual is more than just acquiring a "third signalling system": it may have weighty consequences not unlike the acculturation process of the immigrant. Ervin-Tripp (1955) has shown that the personality profile of a bilingual as revealed by his responses to the Thematic Apperception Tests picture cards varies depending on which of the two languages he uses. In extreme instances one may even speak of 'bilingual schizophrenia.'

Of course, one would not expect such strong effects to take place as a result of FL study in the school situation. But it is a question of degree only, and Carroll's following remark is expected to apply, to some extent, to all students engaged in FL study: "An individual learning a second language must be taught to observe and codify experience as nearly as possible in the same way as native speakers of that language" (1963b, p. 17). It is in this, much more than in his pronunciation, that the native speaker becomes a worthwhile object to be modelled.

5.6 SUMMARY AND CONCLUSIONS

The main conclusions that emerge from a review of the research on language learning and teaching as it is relevant to an evaluation of the FL requirement will now be summarized.

a. Two major approaches in method of instructing FLs can be identified: the habit-skill approach that emphasizes oral skills through a method of repetitive pattern drills and the rule-governed grammar approach that emphasizes the knowledge of structure. Both approaches draw upon modern linguistic theory, but the extent to which reading and writing skills are also emphasized varies greatly within either approach.

b. The habit-skill approach is based on a theoretically untenable position and the justification given for repetitive pattern drills appears invalid.

c. A scientific assessment of effectiveness of different methods of instruction is not now possible. Comparative studies that have been carried out support the following generalization: the student learns, if anything, precisely what he is being taught and there are no mysterious transfer effects across different language skills.

d. A proposal to give FL credit on the basis of attained proficiency in self-instructional programs for some students with high FL aptitude appears to be feasible.

e. The quality of instruction depends on the extent to which it is made clear *to the learner* just what he is supposed to be learning at each level. Hence a "standard" method of instruction which does not vary with the learner's characteristics (aptitude and ability to understand instructions) cannot be of high quality.

f. Evidence is now available that an important factor determining success in FL study is a special talent for languages and that this FL aptitude can be estimated by a short test.

g. Given a certain known level of FL aptitude, one can specify how long it will take to attain a particular level of proficiency.

h. Given a certain limited amount of time available for study, one can predict what proportion of students will fail to attain a certain level of proficiency on the basis of their estimated FL aptitude score.

i. Phonetic discrimination per se (i.e., hearing ability) is not an important factor in FL aptitude. What is crucial is the ability to code phonetic material so that it can be stored in memory. In all, four separate abilities have been identified as components of FL aptitude.

j. Existing FL aptitude tests can be used for placement and diagnostic purposes. When they are combined with a trial course, it should be possible to predict the level of attainment for each of the separate language skills. These expectations could then be used to establish variable FL requirements for each student.

k. Standard proficiency tests are inadequate on two accounts: (i) they do not indicate the student's absolute competence–only his relative standing to a "typical group"; (ii) they are intended to test mastery of mechanical manipulation or structural knowledge and say nothing about communicative competence. What is needed is a specification of levels of standards in terms of practical requirements in communication.

l. Attainment in FL study can be evaluated on two levels: degree of mastery of mechanical manipulation and extent of communicative competence. There appears to be no good reason for withholding training in the latter until advanced mastery of the former. Teaching at both levels conjointly would be preferable on several grounds.

m. As it is usually defined in FL courses or requirements, a "speaking knowledge" is not closer to communicative competence than a "reading knowledge." The emphasis of the former over the latter does not appear to be justified.

n. A consideration of motivational and attitudinal factors in FL study is relevant from two points of view: (i) a way in which these affect learners' perseverance (an intrinsic-integrative orientation has been found to be superior to an extrinsic-instrumental orientation); (ii) the way in which these affect the individual's reactions to contact with a foreign culture (there is evidence that becoming bilingual carries with it the tendency of becoming bicultural).

o. Two available surveys of college students' interest in FL study indicate that (i) one-third to one-half have no intrinsic interest in the language they are taking; (ii) one-half consider the primary goal to be the development of a reading knowledge of the language; and (iii) most of them disapprove of the college graduation FL requirement and almost one-half actually feel that FL study has been detrimental to them.

p. Given the wide distribution of FL aptitude scores in the general student population, it is unrealistic to expect a uniform level of achievement. The FL teacher must adjust his expectation of achievement to be attained to the student's particular aptitude.

q. The low level of intrinsic interest in FL study on the part of many students may be a result of a number of undesirable features of present practices in FL instruction. Some of these can be mentioned: (i) a failure to clarify appropriate criteria for student self-evaluation of his progress; (ii) insistence on a degree of phonetic mastery that is not justified by the requirements of communication; (iii) inadequate counseling on the choice of an FL in terms of considerations appropriate to the student's perceived needs; and (iv) failure to make FL study seem relevant to the student in terms of its practical use.

r. A single-purpose goal for FL study, such as the development of oral skills in the "progressive" audiolingual courses, is not responsive to the potentially variable needs of the general student population.

s. Although proponents of FL study agree that one of its main benefits is increased cultural awareness, they have apparently failed to communicate this idea to many students. It is possible to justify this claim on a number of grounds and it behooves the FL teacher to try to make a better case for it.

5.7 RECOMMENDED CHANGES IN FL REQUIREMENTS

In this section are some observations on present FL requirements and some alternatives which I offer as recommendations for consideration by the profession.

At the outset, I would like to affirm my belief in the unique value of the knowledge of a FL, both to the individual person as a liberation of linguistic and cultural chauvinism and to the larger community of men, nations, and the world. In a previous section, I have outlined some specific arguments on the nature of this benefit to the individual. Despite this feeling, I would be in favor of eliminating the present FL graduation requirement in colleges; I would offer the following arguments in support of this recommendation:

a. It is my opinion that most college students who successfully meet present requirements fail to achieve a level of proficiency that allows them to reap the benefits of FL study, whether it be at the humanistic level or the practical level of communicative competence.

b. I believe that this failure of the intended goal has several causes, the most important ones being the following: (a) FL study is not perceived by the students as relevant to their educational needs and aspirations. This feeling is strengthened by blanket college requirements which they view as archaic, arbitrary, and insensitive to their wishes; (b) serious study of an FL, of the type from which intrinsic benefits can be derived, entangles the student in a psychological involvement that may lead him to invidious comparisons between the foreign culture and his own. To some individuals, this involvement may be threatening, especially when he feels that it is being "forced down his throat." Failure to achieve any meaningful proficiency is an effective protection against such perceived threat; (c) present methods of instruction are geared toward a standard goal, while the students' needs are variable. This helps reinforce the feeling of the irrelevance of FL study. Apart from neglecting individual needs, such instruction disregards the variation that exists in FL aptitude.

c. The acquisition of a meaningful level of language competence cannot be achieved without intrinsic motivation on the part of the learner. No amount of duress in the form of a barrier against graduation can change this. In this sense, the FL requirement is self-defeating.

Given these considerations, I would like to suggest some alternatives, which, in my opinion, will be more effective in promoting the goal that the present requirement attempts, but fails, to promote.

a. The student ought to be given as much latitude as he feels he needs in the following areas: (i) the choice of a language (he ought not to be pressured to "stick to" a language he took in high school at a time when his needs may have been different and when the choices available to him were restricted); (ii) the type of instruction and the skills to be emphasized (he ought not to be made to suffer in self-respect by choosing a "starred"[1] course when his interests lie in developing reading and writing skills; typically, starred courses are for "D" students). The high aptitude student ought to be given the opportunity of pursuing self-instructional programs where he can achieve a desired level of proficiency at a rate much faster than the typical course affords; and (iii) the amount of credit he wishes to

[1]A term used at the Univ. of Illinois to denote sections for individuals with special problems.

receive in FL study. This last point is elaborated in the following recommendation.

b. A variable credit allotment ought to be made available based on the student's attainment of certain defined levels of standards stated in terms relevant to competence in language use. The following plan is intended as an illustration rather than a firm proposal (See Table 3):

The scheme of variable credit illustrated here is flexible enough to meet the variable needs and interests of the student body. Credit

TABLE 3
WRITTEN SKILLS

Levels	*Definition*	*Units of credit*
W_1	Be able to understand simple written material of a non-technical nature with the use of a dictionary	1
W_2	Same as the above without the use of a dictionary	2
W_3	Be able to understand written material of a technical nature (student's choice of area) with the use of a dictionary	2½
W_4	Same as the above without the use of a dictionary	3½
W_5	Be able to write a non-technical composition without the use of a dictionary	4
W_6	Be able to write a technical paper with the use of a dictionary	4½
	Oral Skills	
O_1	Be able to carry on a conversation (in formal style) with a native speaker on simple everyday subjects (weather, travel, shopping, etc.)	3
O_2	Be able to carry on an active discussion on various subjects (political, social, cultural) with native speakers, and in a group	6
O_3	Be able to speak effectively with command of different stylistic varieties required in social situations	9
	Humanistic Skills	
H_L	Demonstrated knowledge of FL literature (test to be taken in English)	2½
H_C	Demonstrated knowledge of the history and culture of the target language (test to be taken in English)	2½

can be obtained at any level with three types of skills. An ambitious student with high aptitude can pile up as many as 18½ credit units with the combination $[W_6 + O_3 + H_L + H_C]$. Or, a student may simply choose to write a technical paper on his major subject and receive 4½ credit units for W_6, etc. The exact credit allotments and levels of standards should be worked out more carefully and with some justifiable rationale.

c. I would also recommend that each department in a college spell out for its majors the desired levels of standards, types of skills that it recommends, and in which language(s). These recommendations ought to be flexible and be based on demonstrable usefulness to the program in question.

It is my belief that if these recommendations are put into effect, FL study will quickly lose its notorious status as "the bad child" of the college curriculum and will provide the type of benefits that we all want the liberally educated person to experience.

5.8 FOREIGN LANGUAGE ATTITUDE QUESTIONNAIRE: INTRODUCTION

The notion that student attitude toward FL study and culture is one of the major determinants of achievement has been stressed and discussed in several places throughout this book (see for instance Chapter 2, Section 2.4 and Chapter 3, Section 3.2). Some additional evidence and discussion is given in the first half of this chapter, and this is followed by the presentation of several questionnaire forms which were designed to measure attitudes towards a number of factors related to FL learning. These are presented here with the hope and expectation that the FL teacher and administrator will see the value of making use of them. Systematic evaluation procedures are not the sole prerogative of the academic researcher. They can be powerful tools in the hands of the educator for assessing where the students are, psychologically and attitudinally, so that they might take these factors into consideration in the over-all instructional effort. In my opinion these psychological tools should be used routinely by the teacher and administrator. It should be stressed that these are not additional "psychological tests" to be imposed on the hapless student: these are special communication devices whereby the students and their parents tell the school officials what they are interested in and where their satisfactions and dissatisfactions lie.

Sections 5.8.1 through 5.8.19 present 19 questionnaire forms, most of which were designed to index attitudes (called "Scales"). The first 11 scales are intended for students, while the last 8 are for their parents. These scales, many of which were originally developed by Professor W. E. Lambert and his collaborators at McGill University, reflect a specific interest in the study of French as a second language in Canada. However, these can easily be adapted by the teacher for his specific purposes; in most cases nothing more is needed than replacing references to "French," "French culture," "Canada," etc., by the appropriate equivalent terms.

The teacher who is planning to administer to his students a "test battery" for assessing FL aptitude, study habits, FL attitudes, and communicative skills should consider not only the choice of the specific tests but also the climate of test taking in the classroom. In my opinion tests should never be "forced upon" students who resent taking them, for, besides the ethical issue involved, the quality and reliability of information obtained under conditions of duress is questionable, and furthermore, the resentment that is generated outweighs whatever advantages there are to be gained by the test administration. Nevertheless, I believe that in the vast majority of instances students will gladly cooperate in test taking if their participation is voluntary and if the true purpose of the testing program is made clear to them, namely, that it is a two-way communication device rather than a punitive or manipulative attempt. Such a favorable attitude on the part of the students is practically assured if the teacher has respect for their feelings and shows understanding of them. Frank discussions of test results, where disagreements are accepted as legitimate, will not only draw students and teachers together in a community of fellowship and mutual respect, but can be an occasion for dynamic "attitudinal movement" and change.

Section 5.9 of this chapter presents an attitude questionnaire form that contains parts of several of the scales just discussed and a few additional others. It was prepared for the purposes of providing the teacher with a convenient test form that would measure several aspects of FL attitudes and which could be administered in approximately half-an-hour. The instructions of the original form (here reproduced) invite the teacher to send the results to me through the Northeast Conference organization. I hereby extend the same invitation to the readers of this book to send the data directly to me so that we may all share in the advantages to be accrued by comparing information obtained in diverse school and community settings. (My address: Dr. Leon A. Jakobovits, Department of Psychology, University of Illinois, Urbana, Illinois 61801).

5.8.1 French Attitude Scale

This is made up of 20 positively worded statements about French-speaking people. The higher the score obtained by a student on this form, the more favorable his attitudes are towards French-speaking people and their culture. The total score for this form (as well as for measures 2-5 which have the same instructions) is obtained by summing algebraically the plus and minus values. (Care must be taken to invert the sign of the score for items that are inversely worded.) Students with favorable attitudes toward the culture and people whose language they are studying are expected to be more successful in achievement (other factors being equivalent), especially in oral communicative skills. If the teacher finds that some of the students have negative attitudes toward the specific foreign culture they are studying, he should discuss this matter with the students concerned. In many cases frank discussions and explorations may turn up misconceptions about the foreign culture and threats to cultural identity which can be corrected and alleviated. In some cases, however, the negative attitudes may be too deep (for whatever personal or family reasons), and in these instances the student should seriously consider switching to another language.

FRENCH ATTITUDE SCALE

The following statements are ones with which many people agree, and many people disagree. There are no right or wrong answers since many people have different opinions. Please indicate your agreement or disagreement by writing on the line preceding each statement the number from the following scale which best describes your feelings:

+1 slight support, agreement
+2 moderate support, agreement
+3 strong support, agreement

–1 slight opposition, disagreement
–2 moderate opposition, disagreement
–3 strong opposition, disagreement

_____ 1. The French who have moved to this country have made a great contribution to the richness of our society.
_____ 2. The more I get to know French-speaking people, the more I want to be able to speak their language.
_____ 3. French-speaking people are very democratic in their politics and philosophy.
_____ 4. French-speaking people have produced outstanding artists and writers.
_____ 5. By bringing the old French folkways to our society, they have contributed greatly to our way of life.
_____ 6. French-speaking people's undying faith in their religious beliefs is a positive force in this modern world.
_____ 7. The French-speaking person has every reason to be proud of his race and his traditions.
_____ 8. If Canada should lose the influence of French-speaking people, it would indeed be a deep loss.
_____ 9. French-speaking peoples are much more polite than many Canadians.
_____ 10. We can learn better ways of cooking, serving food, and entertaining from the French-speaking people.
_____ 11. French-speaking people are very dependable.
_____ 12. Canadian children can learn much of value by associating with French-speaking playmates.
_____ 13. French-speaking people set a good example for us by their family life.
_____ 14. French-speaking people are generous and hospitable to strangers.
_____ 15. Canadians should make a greater effort to meet more French-speaking people.

______ 16. It is wrong to try to force the French-speaking person to become completely Canadian in his habits.

______ 17. If I had my way, I would rather live in France than in this country.

______ 18. London would be a much better city if more French-speaking people would move here.

______ 19. The French-speaking people show great understanding in the way they adjust to the Canadian way of life.

______ 20. In general, Canadian industry tends to benefit from the employment of French-speaking people.

5.8.2 Anomie Scale

This consists of 12 statements designed to index an individual's dissatisfaction with his role in society. The successful development of communicative skills in a second language often involves a prior tendency to "identify" with people who are native representatives of the foreign culture. Such an identification process appears to facilitate the acquisition of communicative skills, but at the same time it can create feelings of dissatisfaction with one's own culture and "ways of doing things." These feelings of dissatisfaction are referred to as "anomie." Frank discussions of anomic reactions by students with themselves and with the teacher can reduce their potentially negative effects (e.g., withdrawing or reducing involvement).

ANOMIE SCALE

The following statements are ones with which many people agree, and many people disagree. There are no right or wrong answers since many people have different opinions. Please indicate your agreement or disagreement by writing on the line preceding each statement the number from the following scale which best describes your feelings:

+1 slight support, agreement
+2 moderate support, agreement
+3 strong support, agreement

−1 slight opposition, disagreement
−2 moderate opposition, disagreement
−3 strong opposition, disagreement

______ 1. In Canada today, public officials aren't really very interested in the problems of the average man.
______ 2. Our country is by far the best country in which to live.
______ 3. The state of the world being what it is, it is very difficult for the student to plan his career.
______ 4. In spite of what some people say, the lot of the average man is getting worse, not better.
______ 5. These days, a person doesn't really know whom he can count on.
______ 6. It is hardly fair to bring children into the world with the way things look for the future.
______ 7. No matter how hard I try, I seem to get a "raw deal" in school.
______ 8. The opportunities offered young people today are far greater than they have ever been.
______ 9. Having lived this long in this culture, I'd be happier living in some other country now.
______ 10. In this country, it's whom you know, not what you know, that makes for success.
______ 11. The big trouble with our country is that it relies, for the most part, on the law of the jungle: "get him before he gets you."

5.8.3 Ethnocentrism Scale

The present version is designed for children and is made up of 7 statements. High scores on this scale indicate an ethnocentric orientation. One of the traditional goals of FL study has been the reduction of ethnocentric attitudes (or "cultural myopia"), but there are indications that this desired effect is not an automatic consequence for all students engaged in FL study. In some instances high ethnocentric values may stand in the way of FL achievement. Ethnocentrism, cultural allegiance (Measure 5.8.4), and authoritarianism (Measure

5.8.5) tend to go together and usually reflect parental and wider sociocultural influences. The specific ways in which these attitudes interact with anomie and interest and success in FL study are not well understood but correlational evidence usually indicate a negative relationship. The FL teacher ought to be aware of the presence of these attitudes, although at the moment we do not quite know how to induce changes in them and what might be the full psychological ramifications of such changes.

ETHNOCENTRISM SCALE

The following statements are ones with which many people agree, and many people disagree. There are no right or wrong answers since many people have different opinions. Please indicate your agreement or disagreement by writing on the line preceding each statement the number from the following scale which best describes your feelings:

+1 slight support, agreement
+2 moderate support, agreement
+3 strong support, agreement

–1 slight opposition, disagreement
–2 moderate opposition, disagreement
–3 strong opposition, disagreement

_______ 1. The worst danger to real Canadians during the last 50 years has come from foreign ideas and agitators.

_______ 2. Now that a new world organization is set up, Canada must be sure that she loses none of her independence and complete power as a sovereign nation.

_______ 3. Certain people who refuse to salute the flag should be forced to conform to such a patriotic action, or else be imprisoned.

_______ 4. Foreigners are all right in their place, but they carry it too far when they get too familiar with us.

_______ 5. Canada may not be perfect, but the Canadian way has brought us about as close as human beings can get to a perfect society.

_______ 6. It is only natural and right for each person to think that his family is better than any other.

_______ 7. The best guarantee of our national security is for Canada to get the secret of the nuclear bomb.

5.8.4 Cultural Allegiance Scale

The following statements are ones with which many people agree, and many people disagree. There are no right or wrong answers since many people have different opinions. Please indicate your agreement or disagreement by writing on the line preceding each statement the number from the following scale which best describes your feelings:

+1 slight support, agreement
+2 moderate support, agreement
+3 strong support, agreement

–1 slight opposition, disagreement
–2 moderate opposition, disagreement
–3 strong opposition, disagreement

_______ 1. Compared to French-speaking people, Canadians are more sincere and honest.

_______ 2. Family life is more important to Canadians than it is to the French-speaking.

_______ 3. Canadian children are better mannered than French-speaking children are.

_______ 4. Canadians appreciate and understand the arts better than do most people in France.

_______ 5. Compared to Canadians, the French are a very unimaginative people.

_______ 6. The French way of life seems crude when compared to ours.

_______ 7. The French would benefit greatly if they adopted many aspects of the Canadian culture.

_______ 8. People are much happier in France than they are here.

_______ 9. The opportunities offered young people in Canada are far greater than in France.

5.8.5 California F-Scale

(As mentioned above, these forms are designed as additional indicants of attitudes towards a specific foreign culture (Measure 5.8.4) and attitudes towards authority in general.)

The following statements are ones with which many people agree, and many people disagree. There are no right or wrong answers since many people have different opinions. Please indicate your agreement or disagreement by writing on the line preceding each statement the number from the following scale which best describes your feelings:

+1 slight support, agreement
+2 moderate support, agreement
+3 strong support, agreement

–1 slight opposition, disagreement
–2 moderate opposition, disagreement
–3 strong opposition, disagreement

_______ 1. Obedience and respect for authority are the most important virtues children should learn.

_______ 2. What youth needs is strict discipline, rugged determination, and the will to work and fight for family and country.

_______ 3. Nowadays when so many different kinds of people move around and mix together so much, a person has to protect himself especially carefully against catching an infection or disease from them.

_______ 4. What this country needs most, more than laws and political programs, is a few courageous, tireless, devoted leaders in whom the people can put their faith.

_______ 5. No weakness or difficulty can hold us back if we have enough will power.

_______ 6. Human nature being what it is, there will always be war and conflict.

_______ 7. A person who has bad manners, habits, and breeding can hardly expect to get along with different people.

_______ 8. People can be divided into two distinct classes: the weak and the strong.

______ 9. There is hardly anything lower than a person who does not feel a great love, gratitude, and respect for his parents.

______ 10. The true Canadian way of life is disappearing so fast that force may be necessary to preserve it.

______ 11. Nowadays more and more people are prying into matters that should remain personal and private.

______ 12. If people would talk less and work more, everybody would be better off.

______ 13. Sometimes I can't see much sense in putting so much time into education and learning.

______ 14. Most people don't realize how much our lives are controlled by plots hatched in secret places.

5.8.6 Orientation Index

This form lists eight reasons for studying a FL. Four of these reflect an "instrumental" orientation (odd numbered questions) and four are indicative of an "integrative" orientation (even numbered questions). Degree of instrumental and integrative orientation can be assessed by summing over the two sets of questions after assigning a numerical value to each alternative (e.g., definitely my feeling = +2, pretty much my feeling = +1, slightly my feeling = 0, not very much my feeling = −1, definitely not my feeling = −2). An individual thus receives an overall instrumental score as well as an overall integrative score. For certain purposes it might be useful to classify an individual as either an "instrumentalist" or an "integrationist" depending on which of the two over-all scores is higher. There is evidence that under certain conditions an integrative orientation leads to greater success in oral communicative skills, although under the conditions that hold in most American schools an instrumental orientation is not necessarily an indication of lower expected achievement. Nevertheless, an integrative orientation is more likely to be predictive of willingness to engage in activities that supplement the regular classroom work (independent study, travel abroad, language camps). This would be particularly important under conditions of compensatory instruction.

Orientation Index

Below are eight reasons which might be given for studying French. Please read each reason carefully and rate it, indicating the extent to which it is descriptive of your own case. Circle the letter in front of the answer that best represents your feeling.

THE STUDY OF FRENCH CAN BE IMPORTANT TO ME BECAUSE:

1. I need it in order to finish high school.
   a) definitely my feeling
   b) pretty much my feeling
   c) slightly my feeling
   d) not very much my feeling
   e) definitely not my feeling

2. It will enable me to gain *good* friends more easily among French-speaking people.
   a) pretty much my feeling
   b) slightly my feeling
   c) not very much my feeling
   d) definitely my feeling
   e) definitely not my feeling

3. One needs a good knowledge of at least one foreign language to merit social recognition.
   a) definitely not my feeling
   b) not very much my feeling
   c) slightly my feeling
   d) definitely my feeling
   e) pretty much my feeling

4. It will help me to understand better the French-speaking people and their way of life.

a) definitely not my feeling
b) not very much my feeling
c) slightly my feeling
d) pretty much my feeling
e) definitely my feeling

5. I think it will some day be useful in getting a good job.

a) slightly my feeling
b) definitely not my feeling
c) pretty much my feeling
d) not very much my feeling
e) definitely my feeling

6. It will allow me to meet and converse with more and varied people.

a) definitely my feeling
b) pretty much my feeling
c) slightly my feeling
d) not very much my feeling
e) definitely not my feeling

7. I feel that no one is really educated unless he is fluent in French.

a) definitely not my feeling
b) not very much my feeling
c) slightly my feeling
d) pretty much my feeling
e) definitely my feeling

8. It should enable me to think and behave as do the French-speaking people.

a) pretty much my feeling
b) slightly my feeling
c) not very much my feeling
d) definitely my feeling
e) definitely not my feeling

5.8.7 Desire to Learn French Scale

1. Place a check mark anywhere along the line below to indicate how much you like French compared to all your other courses.

French is my *least* preferred course. ___: ___: ___: ___: ___: ___: ___: French is my *most* preferred course.

2. When you have an assignment to do in French, do you:

______ a) do it immediately when you start your homework

______ b) become completely bored

______ c) put it off until all your other homework is finished

______ d) none of these (Explain)________________

3. During French classes, I:

______ a) have a tendency to daydream about other things

______ b) become completely bored

______ c) have to force myself to keep listening to the teacher

______ d) become wholly absorbed in the subject matter

4. If I had the opportunity and knew enough French, I would read French newspapers and magazines:

______ a) as often as I could

______ b) fairly regularly

______ c) probably not very often

______ d) never

5. After I have been studying French for a short time, I find that I:

______ a) have a tendency to think about other things

______ b) am interested enough to get the assignment done

______ c) become very interested in what I am studying

6. If I had the opportunity to change the way French is taught in our school, I would:

   ______ a) keep the amount of training as it is

   ______ b) increase the amount of training required for each student

   ______ c) decrease the amount of training required for each student

7. I believe French should be:

   ______ a) omitted from the school curriculum

   ______ b) taught only to those students who wish to study it

   ______ c) taught to all high school students

8. I find studying French:

   ______ a) very interesting

   ______ b) no more interesting than most subjects

   ______ c) not interesting at all

9. In my French class, I:

   ______ a) am generally not prepared unless I know the teacher will ask for the assignments

   ______ b) am always prepared for each lecture having done my assignments or read the material we are to cover

   ______ c) am sometimes prepared for the lecture, but mostly not

   ______ d) none of these (explain) ______________________

   ____

   ____

   ____

   ____

   ____

5.8.8 Motivational Intensity Scale

The answers to the next two forms may be summed to give an overall score of "motivation intensity" (by assigning a numerical value to each alternative on the basis of their meaning and direction). The expectation is that the higher the score is, the greater the effort the student might be willing to spend in active study ("perseverance").

Read each of the statements below and for each one place a check mark (√) to the left of the alternative which seems to best describe you. Your answers will not be seen by any of the school authorities, so please try to be as accurate as possible.

1. Compared to the other students in my French class, I think I:

   ______ a) do less studying than most of them

   ______ b) study about as much as most of them

   ______ c) study more than most of them

2. If French were not taught in high school, I would:

   ______ a) not bother learning French at all

   ______ b) try to obtain lessons in French somewhere else

   ______ c) pick up French in everyday situations (i.e., read French books and newspapers, try to speak it whenever possible, etc. . . . . .)

   ______ d) none of these (explain) ______________________

   ____

   ____

3. I actively think about what I have learned in my French classes:

   ______ a) hardly ever

   ______ b) once in a while

   ______ c) very frequently

4. On the average, I spend about the following amount of time doing home study in French (include all French homework):

_______ a) one hour per week

_______ b) four hours per week

_______ c) seven hours per week

_______ d) none of these (Give approximate number of hours per week; _____ hours).

5. Considering how I study my French, I can honestly say that I:

_______ a) will pass on the basis of sheer luck or intelligence because I do very little work

_______ b) really try to learn French

_______ c) do just enough work to get along

_______ d) none of these (explain) ____________________

____

6. After I finish high school, I will probably:

_______ a) try to use my French as much as possible

_______ b) make no attempt to remember the French I have learned

_______ c) continue to improve my French (e.g., daily practice, night school, etc.)

_______ d) none of these (explain) ____________________

____

7. Compared to my other high school courses, I:

_______ a) do less work in French than any other course

_______ b) work harder on French than any other course

_______ c) do about as much work in French as I do in any other course

5.8.9 Parental Encouragement to Learn French Scale

An overall score may be obtained by assigning a numerical value of, say 1 to 7 (or + 3 to – 3) to the seven positions on each scale and summing over the six items. (Reverse directions for Questions 2 and 4.)

1. My parents encourage me to study French.

very definitely YES ___:___:___:___:___:___:___: very definitely NO

2. My parents think that there are more important things to study in school than French.

very definitely YES ___:___:___:___:___:___:___: very definitely NO

3. My parents have stressed the importance that French will have for me when I leave high school.

very definitely YES ___:___:___:___:___:___:___: very definitely NO

4. My parents feel that studying French is a waste of time.

very definitely YES ___:___:___:___:___:___:___: very definitely NO

5. Whenever I have homework in French, my parents make sure I do it.

very definitely YES ___:___:___:___:___:___:___: very definitely NO

6. My parents feel that I should really try to learn French.

very definitely YES ___:___:___:___:___:___:___: very definitely NO

5.8.10 Attitude Toward Learning FLs Scale

The higher the score obtained on these seven items, the more favorable the attitude is expected to be toward studying a FL. (Reverse direction of scoring where appropriate.)

1. I would study a foreign language in school even if it were not required.
   a) definitely
   b) probably
   c) possibly
   d) probably not
   e) definitely not

2. I would enjoy going to see foreign films in the original language.
   a) some
   b) not much
   c) quite a bit
   d) not at all
   e) a great deal

3. Our lack of knowledge of foreign languages accounts for many of our political difficulties abroad.
   a) strongly disagree
   b) disagree
   c) doubtful
   d) agree
   e) strongly agree

4. I want to read the literature of a foreign language in the original.
   a) strongly agree
   b) doubtful
   c) agree
   d) strongly disagree
   e) disagree

5. I wish I could speak another language perfectly.
   a) a great deal
   b) quite a bit
   c) some
   d) not much
   e) not at all

6. If I planned to stay in another country, I would make a great

effort to learn the language even though I could get along in English.
a) definitely not
b) probably not
c) possibly
d) probably
e) definitely

7. Even though Canada is relatively far from countries speaking other languages, it is important for Canadians to learn foreign languages.
a) strongly agree
b) doubtful
c) agree
d) disagree
e) strongly disagree

5.8.11 Study Habits Questionnaire

These 25 items are designed to give the teacher an indication of the student's study habits. The form may be used as a diagnostic device with students who seem to have trouble in FL study.

1. Whether I like a course or not, I still work hard to make a good grade.
a) rarely
b) sometimes
c) frequently
d) generally
e) almost always

2. I lose interest in my studies after the first few days or weeks.
a) almost always
b) mostly
c) frequently
d) sometimes
e) rarely

3. I memorize grammatical rules, definitions of technical terms, formulas, etc., without really understanding them.
   a) almost always
   b) mostly
   c) frequently
   d) generally
   e) rarely

4. When I get behind in my school work for some unavoidable reason, I make up back assignments without prompting from the teacher.
   a) rarely
   b) sometimes
   c) frequently
   d) generally
   e) almost always

5. Daydreaming about dates, future plans, etc., distracts my attention from my lesson while I am studying.
   a) almost always
   b) mostly
   c) frequently
   d) sometimes
   e) rarely

6. Even though an assignment is dull and boring, I stick to it until it is completed.
   a) rarely
   b) sometimes
   c) frequently
   d) generally
   e) almost always

7. I keep all the notes for each subject together, carefully arranging them in some logical order.
   a) rarely
   b) sometimes
   c) frequently

d) generally
e) almost always

8. When I am having difficulty with my school work, I try to talk over the trouble with the teacher.
   a) rarely
   b) sometimes
   c) frequently
   d) generally
   e) almost always
9. I keep my place of study business-like and cleared of unnecessary or distracting items such as pictures, letters, etc.
   a) rarely
   b) sometimes
   c) frequently
   d) generally
   e) almost always
10. It takes a long time for me to get warmed up to the task of studying.
    a) almost always
    b) mostly
    c) frequently
    d) sometimes
    e) rarely
11. When I sit down to study, I find myself too tired, bored, or sleepy to study efficiently.
    a) almost always
    b) mostly
    c) frequently
    d) sometimes
    e) rarely
12. Prolonged reading or study gives me a headache.
    a) almost always
    b) mostly
    c) frequently
    d) sometimes
    e) rarely

13. After reading several pages of an assignment, I am unable to recall what I have just read.
    a) almost always
    b) mostly
    c) frequently
    d) sometimes
    e) rarely

14. I waste too much time "chewing the fat," reading magazines, listening to the radio, going to the movies, etc., for the good of my studies.
    a) almost always
    b) mostly
    c) frequently
    d) sometimes
    e) rarely

15. My studying is done in a random, unplanned manner, and is impelled mostly by the demands of approaching classes.
    a) almost always
    b) mostly
    c) frequently
    d) sometimes
    e) rarely

16. I utilize the vacant hours between classes for studying so as to reduce the evening's work.
    a) rarely
    b) sometimes
    c) frequently
    d) generally
    e) almost always

17. I am on time with written assignments.
    a) rarely
    b) sometimes
    c) frequently
    d) generally
    e) almost always

18. I like to have the radio playing while I am doing my homework.
    a) almost always
    b) mostly
    c) frequently
    d) sometimes
    e) rarely

19. When reading a long assignment, I stop periodically and mentally review the main facts and ideas that have been presented.
    a) rarely
    b) sometimes
    c) frequently
    d) generally
    e) almost always

20. I seem to accomplish very little in relation to the amount of time I spend studying.
    a) almost always
    b) mostly
    c) frequently
    d) sometimes
    e) rarely

21. I prefer to sit in the back of the classroom.
    a) almost always
    b) mostly
    c) frequently
    d) sometimes
    e) rarely

22. With me, studying is a hit-or-miss proposition, depending on the mood I'm in.
    a) rarely
    b) sometimes
    c) frequently
    d) generally
    e) almost always

23. I study three or more hours per day outside of class.
    a) rarely
    b) sometimes
    c) frequently
    d) generally
    e) almost always

24. Before each study period I set up a goal as to how much material I will cover.
    a) rarely
    b) sometimes
    c) frequently
    d) generally
    e) almost always

25. I keep my assignments up to date by doing my work regularly from day to day.
    a) rarely
    b) sometimes
    c) frequently
    d) generally
    e) almost always

5.8.12 through 5.8.19 Parental Attitudes

These questionnaire forms parallel those designed for the students and need not be discussed further. There is evidence that children's and parents' attitudes correlate with each other, and this is, of course, no surprise although the extent of parental influence on the development of attitudes in children can be underestimated in this age of the so-called "generation gap." The parental questionnaire forms are presented here for the sake of completeness, but I am aware that in the majority of situations the teacher's access to parents for testing purposes is no doubt very restricted, especially when dealing with such a sensitive area as ethnocentrism and authoritarianism. On the other hand the teacher and school administrator may wish to fill out themselves these questionnaire forms so as to become more explicitly aware of their own attitudes.

5.8.12 Parental French Attitude Scale

The following statements are ones with which many people agree, and many people disagree. There are no right or wrong answers since many people have different opinions. Please indicate your agreement or disagreement by writing on the line preceding each statement the number from the following scale which best describes your feelings:

+1 slight support, agreement
+2 moderate support, agreement
+3 strong support, agreement

–1 slight opposition, disagreement
–2 moderate opposition, disagreement
–3 strong opposition, disagreement

______ 1. The French who have moved to this country have made a great contribution to the richness of our society.

______ 2. The more I get to know French-speaking people, the more I want to be able to speak their language.

______ 3. French-speaking people are very democratic in their politics and philosophy.

______ 4. French-speaking people have produced outstanding artists and writers.

______ 5. By bringing the old French folkways to our society, they have contributed greatly to our way of life.

______ 6. French-speaking people's undying faith in their religious beliefs is a positive force in this modern world.

______ 7. The French-speaking person has every reason to be proud of his race and traditions.

______ 8. If Canada should lose the influence of French-speaking people, it would indeed be a deep loss.

______ 9. French-speaking people are much more polite than many Canadians.

______10. We can learn better ways of cooking, serving food, and entertaining from the French-speaking people.

______11. French-speaking people are very dependable.

______12. Canadian children can learn much of value by associating with French-speaking playmates.

______13. French-speaking people set a good example for us by their family life.

______14. French-speaking people are generous and hospitable to strangers.

______15. Canadians should make a greater effort to meet more French-speaking people.

______16. It is wrong to try to force the French-speaking person to become completely Canadian in his habits.

______17. London would be a much better city if more French-speaking people would move there.

______18. French-speaking people are generally more friendly, sincere, and likeable than any other group of people.

______19. The French-speaking people show great understanding in the way they adjust to the way of life of other Canadians.

______20. In general, Canadian industry tends to benefit from employment of French-speaking people.

5.8.13 Parental Anomie Scale

The following statements are ones with which many people agree, and many people disagree. There are no right or wrong answers since many people have different opinions. Please indicate your agreement or disagreement by writing on the line preceding each statement the number from the following scale which best describes your feelings:

+1 slight support, agreement
+2 moderate support, agreement
+3 strong support, agreement

–1 slight opposition, disagreement
–2 moderate opposition, disagreement
–3 strong opposition, disagreement

_____ 1. In Canada today, public officials aren't really very interested in the problems of the average man.

_____ 2. Our country is by far the best country in which to live.

_____ 3. The state of the world being what it is, it is very difficult for the student to plan for his career.

_____ 4. In spite of what some people say, the lot of the average man is getting worse, not better.

_____ 5. These days, a person doesn't really know whom he can count on.

_____ 6. It is hardly fair to bring children into the world with the way things look for the future.

_____ 7. No matter how hard I try, I seem to get a "raw deal" in my work.

_____ 8. The opportunities offered young people are far greater than they ever have been.

_____ 9. Having lived this long in this culture, I'd be happier living in some other country now.

_____10. In this country, it's whom you know, not what you know, that makes for success.

_____11. The big trouble with our country is that it relies, for the most part, on the law of the jungle: "get him before he gets you."

_____12. Sometimes I can't see much sense in putting so much time into education and learning.

5.8.14 Parental Ethnocentrism Scale

The following statements are ones with which many people agree, and many people disagree. There are no right or wrong answers since many people have different opinions. Please indicate your agreement or disagreement by writing on the line preceding each statement the number from the following scale which best describes your feelings:

+1 slight support, agreement
+2 moderate support, agreement
+3 strong support, agreement

–1 slight opposition, disagreement
–2 moderate opposition, disagreement
–3 strong opposition, disagreement

______ 1. The worst danger to real Canadians during the last 50 years has come from foreign ideas and agitators.

______ 2. Certain people who refuse to salute the flag should be forced to conform to such a patriotic action, or else be imprisoned.

______ 3. Canada may not be perfect, but the Canadian way has brought us about as close as human beings can get to a perfect society.

______ 4. It is only natural and right for each person to think that his family is better than any other.

5.8.15 Parental Cultural Allegiance Scale

The following statements are ones with which many people agree, and many people disagree. There are no right or wrong answers since many people have different opinions. Please indicate your agreement or disagreement by writing on the line preceding each statement the number from the following scale which best describes your feelings:

+1 slight support, agreement
+2 moderate support, agreement
+3 strong support, agreement

–1 slight opposition, disagreement
–2 moderate opposition, disagreement
–3 strong opposition, disagreement

______ 1. Compared to French-speaking people, other Canadians are more sincere and honest.

_____ 2. Family life is less important to French-speaking people than it is to other Canadians.

_____ 3. Canadian children are better mannered than French-speaking children are.

_____ 4. Canadians appreciate and understand the arts better than do most people in France.

_____ 5. Compared to other Canadians, the French are a very unimaginative people.

_____ 6. The French way of life seems crude when compared to ours.

_____ 7. The French would benefit greatly if they adopted many aspects of the Canadian culture.

_____ 8. People are much happier in France than they are here.

_____ 9. If I had my way, I would rather live in France than in this country.

_____10. The opportunities offered young people in Canada are far greater than in France.

5.8.16 Parental California F–Scale

The following statements are ones with which many people agree, and many people disagree. There are no right or wrong answers since many people have different opinions. Please indicate your agreement or disagreement by writing on the line preceding each statement the number from the following scale which best describes your feelings:

+1 slight support, agreement
+2 moderate support, agreement
+3 strong support, agreement

–1 slight opposition, disagreement
–2 moderate opposition, disagreement
–3 strong opposiiton, disagreement

_____ 1. Obedience and respect for authority are the most important virtues children should learn.

______ 2. What youth needs most is strict discipline, rugged determination, and the will to work and fight for family and country.

______ 3. Nowadays when so many different kinds of people move around and mix together so much, a person has to protect himself especially carefully against catching an infection or disease from them.

______ 4. What this country needs most, more than laws and political programs, is a few courageous, tireless, devoted leaders in whom the people can put their faith.

______ 5. No weakness or difficulty can hold us back if we have enough will power.

______ 6. Human nature being what it is, there will always be war and conflict.

______ 7. A person who has bad manners, habits and breeding can hardly expect to get along with different people.

______ 8. People can be divided into two distinct classes: the weak and the strong.

______ 9. There is hardly anything lower than a person who does not feel a great love, gratitude, and respect for his parents.

______10. The true Canadian way of life is disappearing so fast that force may be necessary to preserve it.

______11. Nowadays more and more people are prying into matters that should remain personal and private.

______12. If people would talk less and work more, everybody would be better off.

______13. Most people don't realize how much our lives are controlled by plots hatched in secret places.

5.8.17 Parental Orientation Index

Below are eight reasons which might be given for studying French. Please read each reason carefully and rate it, indicating the extent to which it is descriptive of your own case. Circle the letter in front of the answer that best represents your feelings.

THE STUDY OF FRENCH CAN BE IMPORTANT TO MY CHILD BECAUSE HE (SHE)

1. Needs it in order to finish high school.
   a) definitely my feeling
   b) pretty much my feeling
   c) slightly by feeling
   d) not very much my feeling
   e) definitely not my feeling

2. Will be able to gain *good* friends more easily among French-speaking people.
   a) definitely my feeling
   b) pretty much my feeling
   c) slightly my feeling
   d) not very much my feeling
   e) definitely not my feeling

3. Needs a good knowledge of French to merit social recognition.
   a) definitely my feeling
   b) pretty much my feeling
   c) slightly my feeling
   d) not very much my feeling
   e) definitely not my feeling

4. Will better understand French-speaking people and their way of life.
   a) definitely my feeling
   b) pretty much my feeling
   c) slightly my feeling
   d) not very much my feeling
   e) definitely not my feeling

5. Will need it to get a job.
   a) definitely my feeling
   b) pretty much my feeling
   c) slightly my feeling
   d) not very much my feeling
   e) definitely not my feeling

6. Will be able to meet and converse with more and varied people.
   a) definitely my feeling
   b) pretty much my feeling
   c) slightly my feeling
   d) not very much my feeling
   e) definitely not my feeling

7. Will not be really educated unless he (she) is fluent in French.
   a) definitely my feeling
   b) pretty much my feeling
   c) slightly my feeling
   d) not very much my feeling
   e) definitely not my feeling

8. It should enable him (her) to think and behave as do French-speaking people.
   a) definitely my feeling
   b) pretty much my feeling
   c) slightly my feeling
   d) not very much my feeling
   e) definitely not my feeling

5.8.18 Parental Encouragement to Learn French

1. We, as parents, encourage our child to study French.

Very Definitely YES ___: ___: ___: ___: ___: ___: ___: Very Definitely NO

2. We think that there are more important things to study in school than French.

Very Definitely YES ___:___:___:___:___:___:___: Very Definitely NO

3. We have stressed the importance that French will have for our child when he (she) leaves high school.

Very Definitely YES ___: ___: ___: ___: ___: ___: ___: Very Definitely NO

4. We feel that studying French is a waste of time.

Very Definitely YES ___:___:___:___:___:___:___: Very Definitely NO

5. When our child has homework in French, we make sure he (she) does it.

Very Definitely YES ___:___:___:___:___:___:___: Very Definitely NO

6. We feel that our child should really try to learn French.

Very Definitely YES ___:___:___:___:___:___:___: Very Definitely NO

5.8.19 Parental Perceived Study Habits

1. We feel that our child wastes too much time "chewing the fat," reading magazines, listening to the radio, watching TV, etc., for the good of studies.

Very Definitely YES ___:___:___:___:___:___:___: Very Definitely NO

2. Our child likes to have the radio playing while he (she) is doing his (her) homework.

Very Definitely YES ___:___:___:___:___:___:___: Very Definitely NO

3. Our child seems to accomplish very little in relation to the amount of time he (she) spends studying.

Very Definitely YES ___:___:___:___:___:___:___: Very Definitely NO

4. With our child, studying is a hit-or-miss proposition, depending upon his (her) mood.

Very Definitely YES ___:___:___:___:___:___:___: Very Definitely NO

5. Our child is easily distracted when he (she) is studying.

Very Definitely YES ___:___:___:___:___:___:___: Very Definitely NO

6. Our child keeps his (her) assignments up to date by working regularly from day to day.

Very Definitely YES ___:___:___:___:___:___:___: Very Definitely NO

7. When our child has difficulties with school work, he (she) tries to talk over the trouble with the teacher.

Very Definitely YES ___:___:___:___:___:___:___: Very Definitely NO

8. Even though an assignment is dull and boring, our child sticks to it until it is completed.

Very Definitely YES ___:___:___:___:___:___:___: Very Definitely NO

9. It takes a long time for our child to get warmed up to the task of studying.

Very Definitely YES ___:___:___:___:___:___:___: Very Definitely NO

5.9 ILLINOIS FOREIGN LANGUAGE ATTITUDE QUESTIONNAIRE FORMS S_1 and S_2

Instructions to the Teacher. . . . This questionnaire, completed in October of 1969, was undertaken upon request of Committee 1 of the 1970 Northeast Conference on the Teaching of Foreign Languages: "The Relevant Curriculum." This Preface is intended as a guide to the teacher in the use of the questionnaire and the interpretation of the data. It should be pointed out at the outset that this questionnaire is not to be construed as a "standardized test." The items that are included have been carefully selected from previous studies on student attitudes.

The questionnaire should be administered in an atmosphere that does not put pressure upon the student to give "acceptable" answers as opposed to "true feelings." It is a good idea to maintain the anonymity of the respondent, unless there are valid reasons for knowing his identity. Under conditions of freedom and anonymity, there is much less likelihood that the student would qualify his answers. Where the teacher has strong reasons to suspect that respondents are not entirely candid, the data can still be useful as an indication of what students feel to be the "official" or "acceptable" line.

The questionnaire data will be useful to the teacher for three principal reasons: (a) to find out how students really feel about various aspects of the foreign language curriculum; (b) to change aspects of the instruction process to the extent that these are pedagogically feasible and desirable; and (c) to help correct erroneous ideas, unrealistic expectations, or negative attitudes that students may hold. In connection with this last aim, providing information to the students about the results of the questionnaire may be helpful by showing how they agree or disagree with each other.

The questionnaire contains two sections. The first (S_1) is intended for students who are currently enrolled in a foreign language course, or have been at one time. Section 2 (S_2) is intended for students who have never taken a foreign language course. The following is a brief explanation of the factors the questions are intended to index and their potential significance.

Section 1: Form S_1

Questions 1–3: Information about the respondent's foreign language background. The student's ethnic-linguistic background may be an important source of his attitude toward foreign language study. One should not expect a simple relationship here, for to the individual the ethnicity of his parents may be a disturbing source of estrangement or loss of identity in the American setting ("anomie"). On the other hand his ethnic background may be a source of pride that intensifies his interest in the family's culture and language of origin.

Questions 4 and 5: Information concerning the choice of the foreign language being studied. The attitude of the parents towards foreign languages is likely to exert significant influence upon the student (see also 5.8.12 through 5.8.19). It should be pointed out that the "real" reasons that have influenced the student in his language choice may in fact be other than those stated by him here. This is not the issue. However, the reasons he publicly claims (actually, his "rationalizations") are likely to be most salient in his mind at the present time and, therefore, to influence his current efforts.

Question 6: The student's publicly stated claims about the language skills he is most interested in. It is not suggested here that the teacher ought automatically to give the student what he wants (this may be either foolish or impossible, or both). Rather, the purpose of this question (and 7-14 as well) is to provide information to the teacher concerning disagreements between his ideas and those of the students, disagreements which should not be ignored. If the students have unrealistic expectations frank discussion may lead to a more mature attitude. If their expectations are justifiable within the context of a particular school, changes ought to be instituted, if feasable.

Questions 7-14: Direct feedback from the student to the teacher concerning specific aspects of the instruction process. Most students evaluate and pass judgment on the teacher and what goes on in the school. At issue here is whether such critical activity is to be given legitimate expression or whether it is to be squelched in an authoritarian manner. Suppression of feelings simply drives them underground, rather than resolves them. It is better to face them openly and realistically. Even where resolution is not possible (for a multiplicity of reasons), legitimization of these feelings through acceptable overt expression is psychologically beneficial in reducing their destructive effects. Question 11 is included to assess whether students generally feel they want to have more say in the content of courses, or whether this feeling is restricted to foreign language courses.

Questions 15–28: Interest in foreign language study and degree of personal involvement in it. These questions not only tap various sources of direct motivation (e.g., enjoyment, importance, benefit) but attempt also to get at some factors that are indirectly but importantly related to motivation, e.g., perceived support from others (19), extent of desirable training (20), sources of unease (23 and 27), self attribution of talent, (24-26). It is possible to sum the answers to several of the questions and to come up with an over-all and rough interest or motivation score. If this is done caution should be exerted in the interpretation of the magnitude of difference between respondents since there is no evidence that the answers are linearly related as indices of interest (some questions may be more crucial than others).

Questions 29–31: Anomie related to language study. Agreement with these statements indicates the presence of anomie, which is a clue to the teacher that the student is experiencing feelings of doubt and conflict. The presence of anomie may be a source of resistance to progress in foreign language study, but on the other hand if it is successfully resolved, it may be the source of positive motivational drive since it indicates the student is "involved." The teacher through class discussion and choice of content of readings can play a through class discussion and choice of content of readings can play a crucial role in helping the student to manage anomie.

Question 32: This information may be used to construct additional questions in future forms of the questionnaire.

Section 2: S_2

There is little need for additional explanations here.

Note that there is a good deal of overlap between the two sections and comparisons can be made between foreign language students and those who did not choose such study on factors such as interest and involvement (Questions 8–18 in this section), anticipated anomie (Questions 19–20 in this section) and ideas about course content (Questions 4–7 in this section). Information obtained on reasons for not taking foreign languages (Question 3) can conceivably be used to prepare students for thinking about their future foreign language study plans in realistic and relevant terms.

5.9.1 Analysis of the Questionnaire Data

The data obtained by means of these questionnaires can be analyzed in at least three ways. These are discussed below.

A. Simple Class Profile.

This method consists of simply summing the answers given for each question to get an indication of the prevalent attitudes of students in a particular class. A convenient procedure is to use a blank form of the Questionnaire to record the summary data. Here are some examples:

4. Indicate whether or not each of the following persons influenced you in the choice of the foreign language you are studying:

   a. your parents Yes 40 No 20
   b. your friend(s) Yes 10 No 50
   c. your high school teacher or counselor Yes 25 No 35
   d. someone else? please specify 10

[*Note:* this example indicates that of the 60 students in the class, 40 of them indicated that their parents influenced their choice, 20 indicated that their parents did not influence their choice; and so on. The answer to (d) shows that 10 students indicated a fourth source of influence, but the identity of the source is not recorded in this summary; it may be done so on a separate sheet, if it is of any interest.]

19. In your judgment, to what extent do the following people consider foreign language study important? In each case, circle one of the three numbers:

3 = extremely important
2 = important
1 = not so important

a. your parents: 3 2 1 [30, 30, 0]
b. your friends: 3 2 1 [25, 5, 20]
c. your high school teachers *other than* the foreign language teacher: 3 2 1 [5, 10, 45]
e. yourself: 3 2 1 [40, 20, 0]

[*Note:* this example indicates that, in the case of subpart (a), for instance, 30 students indicated that their parents consider foreign language study extremely important, 30 indicated "important," and none indicated "not so important"; and so on.]

29. Our lack of knowledge of foreign languages accounts for many of our political difficulties abroad:

4 3 2 1 0 [5, 10, 15, 20, 10]

B. Relating Answers to Outside Factors.

In this method the teacher or administrator is interested in a comparison between different Simple Class Profiles (Method A) when classes are distinguished on the basis of some outside criterion. For instance, what is the distribution of answers to question 18 between Class X and Class Y when both were taught by the same teacher but different instructional procedures were used in the two instances? Or, between two classes taught by the same teacher in different semesters? Or, between a class at level 4 and a class at level 1? Another example would be this: what is the difference in distribution to question 7 between two subgroups of students in Class X, those that obtained grades A or B versus those who obtained C or D? And so on.

C. Interrelating Answers to Each Other:

Here the teacher may be interested in making up subgroups on the basis of the distribution of answers on one question, and seeing the difference on the distribution of answers to another question. For instance, on the basis of question 1, three subgroups in the school can be made up: (i) all those studying Latin at level 1; (ii) all those studying French at level 1; (iii) all those studying Russian at level 1; now a comparison can be made between those three subgroups with respect to the distribution of answers to question 7. Another example, would be the following: Two subgroups of students can be made up on the basis of the answers to questions 29 to 31 such that group (i) is made up of students who experience anomie (those who check alternatives 4 or 3) and group (ii) is made up of students who do not experience anomie (those who check alternatives 2 or 1); now these two groups can be compared with respect to their answers to any of the other questions.

5.9.2 Recording the Data

It is suggested that a Summary Transcription Form be used to record the data contained in the individual questionnaire booklets. These forms are available from the Northeast Conference and may be obtained along with the Attitude Questionnaire forms. All three of the methods of analysis here described may be carried out using the Summary Transcription Forms. Teachers and administrators who wish to cooperate with the surveys carried out by the Northeast Conference and the author are asked to send along the Summary Transcription Forms or a copy thereof. In return, they will be entitled to receiving a statistical analysis of the data as well as any summary reports based on data sent in by the other cooperative participants.

Illinois Foreign Language Attitude Questionnaire
Form S_1
Summary Transcription Form: Page 1

Name, level and location of school: ____________________

Student I.D. Number: __________ Level of study: __________

Q.1. __________ __________ __________ __________

Q.2. __________; ____________________

Q.3. __________; ____________________

Q.4. a. ______	Q.5. a. ______	Q.6. a. ______
b. ______	b. ______	b. ______
c. ______	c. ______	c. ______
d. ______	d. ______	d. ______
Q.7. a. ______	e. ______	e. ______
b. ______	f. ______	f. ______
c. ______	g. ______	g. ______
d. ______	h. ______	h. ______
e. ______	i. ______	
f. ______	j. ______	
g. ______	k. ______	
h. ______	l. ______	
i. ______	Q.8. ______	Q.9. ______
j. ______	Q.10. ______	Q.11. ______
k. ______	Q.12. ______	Q.13. ______
l. ______		______
m. ______	Q.14. ______	Q.15. ______
n. ______	Q.16. ______	Q.17. ______
o. ______	Q.18. ______	

Illinois Foreign Language Attitude Questionnaire
Form S_1
Summary Transcription Form: Page 2

Q.19. a. ________ Q.20. a. ________ Q.21. ________
b. ________ b. ________ Q.22. ________
c. ________ c. ________ Q.23. ________
d. ________ d. ________
e. ________

a. ________
b. ________
c. ________
d. ________

Q.24. ________; ________

Q.25. ________ Q.26. ________ Q.27. ________

Q.28. a. ________ Q.29. ________ Q.30. ________
b. ________
c. ________ Q.31. ________; ________; ________;
d. ________ ________

Instructions: Fill in blanks so as to reproduce unambiguously the student's answers. *Examples:* For Q.1, fill in "1" for "Yes" and "2" for "No." For Q.5, fill in the number circled by the student. For Q.9, fill in "1" for "Yes," "2" for "No," "3" for "Can't say." For Q.15, fill in "1" for "Very much so," "2" for "Yes," "3" for "Maybe." And so on. Add comments where you think transcription may be ambiguous.

Illinois Foreign Language Attitude Questionnaire
Form S_2
Summary Transcription Form

Name, level, and location of school: ______________________

Student I.D. Number: __________ Level of study: ________

Q.1. ________; ______________________________

Q.2. ________; ______________________________

Q.3. a. ________
b. ________
c. ________
d. ________
e. ________
f. ________
g. ________
h. ________
i. ________
j. ________
k. ________
l. ________
m. ________

Q.4. a. ________
b. ________
c. ________
d. ________
e. ________
f. ________
g. ________
h. ________

Q.5. ________
Q.6. ________
Q.7. ________
Q.8. ________

Q.9. ________
Q.10. ________
Q.11. a. ________
b. ________
c. ________
d. ________
e. ________

Q.12. a. ________
b. ________
c. ________
d. ________

Q.13. a. ________
b. ________

Q.14. ________
Q.15. a. ________
b. ________
c. ________
d. ________

Q.16. ________;
____
Q.17. ________
Q.18. ________
Q.19. ________
Q.20. ________

Instructions: Fill in blanks so as to reproduce unambiguously the student's answers. *Examples:* For Q.1, fill in "1" for "Yes" and "2" for "No." For Q.3, check those that were checked off by the student. For Q.4, fill in the number circled by the student. For Q.5, fill in "1" for "Yes," "2" for "No," "3" for "Maybe." For Q.16, fill in "1" for "Yes," "2" for "No," "3" for "Don't know"–first part; and for second part, fill in "1" for "Above average," "2" for "Average," "3" for "Below average" and "4" for "Don't know." And so on. Add comments where you think transcription may be ambiguous.

Form S_1

Instructions. This is not a test. Your grades will in no way be affected by your answers and you need not put your name on this form. This questionnaire has been designed to find out from you how students feel about foreign language study. Your teacher is honestly interested in improving the quality of the foreign language curriculum and one kind of information that would help him would be an honest expression of student opinion on this matter. If you fail to express your true feelings you are evading the responsibility you have towards yourself, your fellow students, and the school as a whole. This is your chance to "tell it like it is" in your own mind.

There are two sections to this questionnaire. This is Section 1 and it is intended for students who are now, or have previously been, enrolled in a foreign language course. (Section 2 is to be filled out by students who have never taken a foreign language course.)

Thank you for your cooperation.

[*Note:* Many of the questions make reference to speaking the foreign language and its use in travel, etc. If the foreign language you are studying is Latin or Greek, these questions may not apply to you. You may skip them and answer the other questions that are relevant.]

Circle the appropriate information.

Present Level or Year of Study: 1 2 3 4 FLES
J H S
S H S
College
Graduate

1. Which foreign language(s) are you studying now (or have studied in the past) in school?

____

2. Have you ever studied a language other than English *outside* school?

Yes ________ No ________

If "Yes," which language(s) and under what circumstances (e.g. while living abroad, in a "language camp," at home, through T.V., etc.)?

____

3. Do you personally know anyone (other than your language teacher) who can speak a language other than English?

Yes ________ No ________

If "Yes," please specify your relationship to that person (e.g. grandfather, friend, neighbor, etc.): ________________________

____

4. Indicate whether or not each of the following persons influenced you in the choice of the foreign language you are studying:

a. your parents	Yes ________	No ________
b. your friend(s)	Yes ________	No ________
c. your high school teacher or counselor	Yes ________	No ________

d. someone else? please specify ________________________

5. What were your reasons for choosing the foreign language you are studying? For each item given, rate the importance it had *for you* by circling one of the three numbers as follows:

3 = very important
2 = slightly important
1 = unimportant

a. There was no other language available for study: True ____
False ____

[*Note:* If you check "True," skip to question 6.]

b. This language is prettier (sounds better, is more musical, etc.) than others I could have taken: 3 2 1

c. This language seemed easier than others I could have taken: 3 2 1

d. This language seemed of great importance in today's world: 2 1

e. This language will probably be useful in getting a good job some day: 3 2 1

f. This language will be useful in my probable field of study (e.g. medicine, law, graduate work, etc.): 3 2 1

g. I want to visit the country where the language is spoken: 3 2 1

h. I want to understand better the people who speak that language and their way of life: 3 2 1

i. This language will enrich my background and broaden my cultural horizons: 3 2 1

j. This language is (or was at one time) spoken by my relatives or persons who are (or were) close to me: 3 2 1

k. Knowledge of this language will add to my social status: 3 2 1

1. Any other reason? Please state briefly:

____

____

6. The following are various skills that a foreign language course can emphasize. Rate the extent to which you are interested in each of them by circling one of the three numbers as follows:

3 = great interest
2 = some interest
1 = very little interest

a. being able to engage in an everyday conversation with native speakers of that language: 3 2 1

b. being able to listen to news broadcasts in that language: 3 2 1

c. being able to enjoy films in the original language: 3 2 1
d. being able to read the classical literature in that language:
3 2 1
e. being able to read the current literature in that language (e.g. newspapers, magazines, best sellers, etc.): 3 2 1
f. being able to write letters in that language for various purposes (e.g. business, social, etc.): 3 2 1
g. being able to write stories, articles, etc. in that language:
3 2 1
h. any others? ____

____

7. Indicate the extent to which you are satisfied with each of the following aspects of your foreign language courses by circling one of the three numbers as follows:

3 = quite satisfied
2 = fairly satisfied
1 = dissatisfied

a. the type of skills you were taught in the course: 3 2 1
b. the text you have used: 3 2 1
c. the classroom activities: 3 2 1
d. the language laboratory: 3 2 1 (leave blank if no language laboratory in your school)
e. the homework you were assigned: 3 2 1
f. the readings you were assigned: 3 2 1
g. the outside opportunities you have had to practice the language (e.g. conversing with native speakers, listening to radio broadcasts, reading magazines, etc.): 3 2 1
h. the information you received from your teacher as to how you were progressing in the language course: 3 2 1
i. the way your progress and achievement were evaluated (e.g. grades): 3 2 1
j. the overall amount of time you were given for study:
3 2 1
k. the teacher's personality: 3 2 1
l. the teacher's ability to speak the language: 3 2 1

m. the teacher's ability to help you learn (his helpfulness):
3 2 1
n. the teacher's availability for consultation outside the regular classroom hour: 3 2 1
o. any other aspects of the course for which you wish to indicate your satisfaction or dissatisfaction: ________________

____

____

8. Do you feel the teacher placed too much emphasis on speaking correctly at all times?
Yes ________ No ________ ________

9. Would you have found it helpful to be able to use the language more to express your thoughts even if it meant speaking incorrectly?
Yes ________ No ________ Can't say ________

10. Do you think it's necessary to be able to speak a language correctly (pronunciation, grammar) in order to be able to communicate in that language?
Yes ________ No ________ No opinion ________

11. Do you think students should have a greater say in the content and method of courses in mathematics or the sciences?
Yes ________ No ________ No opinion ________

12. Do you think students should have a greater say in the content and method of foreign language courses?
Yes ________ No ________ No opinion ________

13. Would you have liked to spend more time discussing the culture of the people whose language you were studying?
Discussions in the foreign language:
Yes ________ No ________ No opinion ________
Discussions in English:
Yes ________ No ________ No opinion ________

14. Could you have accomplished more if the foreign language you took had been organized in a different way?

Yes ________ No ________ Can't say ________

If "Yes," describe briefly the suggestions you have (e.g., more or less structure in class, more or less explanations in grammar, more or less drills, more or less use of English, etc.): ____________________

____

____

____

15. Do you wish you could speak a foreign language like a native speaker?

Very much so ________ Yes ______ Maybe ________

16. If you had to stay in another country for an extended period of time, would you make a great effort to learn the language spoken there even though you could get along in English?

Definitely ________ Maybe ________ No ________

17. How important is it for Americans to learn foreign languages?

Extremely important ________ Important ________

Not so important ________

18. Would you say that the time you have spent in studying a foreign language has been beneficial to you?

Definitely, yes ________ Yes ________

Not sure ________

19. In your judgment, to what extent do the following people consider foreign language study important? In each case, circle one of the three numbers:

3 = extremely important
2 = important
1 = not so important

a. your parents: 3 2 1
b. your friends: 3 2 1

c. your high school teachers *other than* the foreign language teacher: 3 2 1
d. society as a whole: 3 2 1
e. yourself: 3 2 1

20. To what extent are you in favor of the following? In each case, circle one of the three numbers:

3 = very much in favor
2 = slightly in favor
1 = not in favor

a. beginning the study of a foreign language in elementary school: 3 2 1
b. having four years of foreign language study in high school: 3 2 1
c. eliminating the teaching of foreign languages in our schools: 3 2 1
d. requiring that everyone take a foreign language at some time during his schooling: 3 2 1

21. Would you consider going abroad to increase your skills in the use of a foreign language?

Definitely ________ Maybe ________ No ________

22. How enjoyable do you find the study of a foreign language?

Very enjoyable ________ Slightly enjoyable ________
Not enjoyable ________

23. Do you feel at ease when making use of the skills you are learning in a foreign language?

a. in listening: Yes ________ No ________ Not sure ________
b. in speaking: Yes ________ No ________ Not sure ________
c. in reading: Yes ________ No ________ Not sure ________
d. in writing: Yes ________ No ________ Not sure ________

24. Do you agree with the notion that to be good in a foreign language one must have a special talent for it?

Yes ________ No ________ Don't know ________

If "Yes," how much of this special talent do you think you have?

Above average ________ Average ________
Below average ________ Don't know ________

25. How probable is it, do you think, that you will one day be a fluent speaker of a second language? Place a number "0" (Completely improbable) to "5" (completely probable) to indicate your estimate: ________________________________

26. Do you feel that you have a lack of a special talent for foreign languages to such an extent that it will prevent you from gaining any benefit whatsoever from foreign language study?

Yes ________ No ________ Not applicable ________

27. Some people feel uneasy, or are afraid to make mistakes, or to sound ridiculous when they try to speak a foreign language they are studying. Rate the extent to which you tend to feel this way yourself: "0" (not at all, never) to "5" (very much so, all the time): ____

28. In these situations, to whom do you attribute any uneasiness? Check all those that apply to you:

a. ________ mostly to yourself
b. ________ mostly to the teacher
c. ________ mostly to the other students in the class
d. ________ don't know

Please indicate your agreement or disagreement with each of the following statements by circling one of the five numbers as follows:

4 = strongly agree
3 = agree
2 = disagree
1 = strongly disagree
0 = no opinion

29. Our lack of knowledge of foreign languages accounts for many of our political difficulties abroad: 4 3 2 1 0

30. A whole-hearted commitment to the study of a foreign language and the culture of its people endangers one's own cultural identity:
4 3 2 1 0

31. Through my exposure to the foreign culture of the language I am studying, I have discovered that some aspects of American culture are not as good as I had previously thought:
4 3 2 1 0

This realization has caused me concern and worry:
4 3 2 1 0

This realization has interfered with my progress in the study of that language: 4 3 2 1 0
Because of the possibility of such conflict, it would be better if foreign language courses concentrated on the language itself rather than the culture of the people who speak it:
4 3 2 1 0

32. Please add any comments you might wish to make about foreign languages or about this questionnaire:

Foreign Language	Questionnaire
______________________	______________________
______________________	______________________
______________________	______________________
______________________	______________________
______________________	______________________
______________________	______________________
______________________	______________________
______________________	______________________
______________________	______________________
______________________	______________________
______________________	______________________
______________________	______________________

Form S_2

Instructions. This questionnaire is intended for students who have never been enrolled in a foreign language course. This is not a test. Your grades will in no way be affected by your answers and you need not put your name on this form. You are being asked to fill out this questionnaire to help foreign language educators improve the quality of the foreign language curriculum. One kind of information that would help them is an honest expression of student opinion on this matter. You owe it to yourself, your fellow students, and the school as a whole to let your true feelings be known. This is your chance to "tell it like it is" in your own mind.

Thank you for your cooperation.

1. Have you ever studied a language other than English *outside* school?

Yes ________ No ________

If "Yes," which language(s) and under what circumstances (e.g. while living abroad, in a "language camp," at home, through T.V., etc.)?

____

____

2. Do you personally know anyone (other than your language teacher) who can speak a language other than English?

Yes ________ No ________

If "Yes," please specify your relationship to that person (e.g. grandfather, friend, neighbor, etc.): ______________________________

____

3. What are the reasons you have never studied a foreign language in school? Check *all* of the reasons that apply to you.

a. None of the schools I ever attended offered a foreign language course: ________

b. I already know a language other than English, so there was no need to study one in school: ________

c. I postponed taking a foreign language to the future, perhaps later in high school or even in college: ____________

d. No one ever told me to take a foreign language: ________

e. It was suggested to me that I take a foreign language but I was never convinced of its value: ________

f. There was not enough time to take a foreign language, as I was busy with too many other courses I had to or wanted to take:______

g. I thought a foreign language course would be too difficult, or, at least, would not be worth the effort: ________

h. Getting involved with the study of a foreign language and foreign culture might have endangered my American identity: ________

i. I did not like the foreign language teachers: ________

j. I did not like the way in which foreign languages were taught in my school:________

k. I wanted to take a foreign language, but the one I was interested in was not offered in my school: ________

If so, which language was it? ________

l. People whose judgment I trust were against it: ________

If so, specify your relationship to those persons (*e.g.* father, friend, teacher, etc.): ______________________________________

____

m. Any other reasons you might like to specify? ______________

____

____

4. The following are various skills that a foreign language course can emphasize. Assuming that one day you might wish to take a foreign language course, which of these skills would you be interested in learning? Rate each of them by circling one of the three numbers as follows:

3 = great interest
2 = some interest
1 = very little interest

a. being able to engage in an everyday conversation with native speakers of that language: 3 2 1

b. being able to listen to news broadcasts in that language: 3 2 1

c. being able to enjoy films in the original language: 3 2 1

d. being able to read the classical literature in that language: 3 2 1

e. being able to read the current literature in that language (e.g. newspapers, magazines, best sellers, etc.): 3 2 1

f. being able to write letters in that language for various purposes (e.g. business, social, etc.): 3 2 1

g. being able to write stories, articles, etc. in that language: 3 2 1

h. any others? ____

____

5. If a special foreign language course had been available in which almost all the time had been spent on the study of foreign culture in English, would you have taken it?

Yes ________ No ________ Maybe ________

6. Do you think students should have a greater say in the content and method of courses in mathematics or the sciences?

Yes ________ No ________ No opinion ________

7. Do you think students should have a greater say in the content and method of foreign language courses?

Yes ________ No ________ No opinion ________

8. Do you wish you could speak a foreign language like a native speaker?

Very much so ________ Yes ________ Maybe ________

9. If you had to stay in another country for an extended period of time, would you make a great effort to learn the language spoken there even though you could get along in English?

Definitely ________ Maybe ________ No ________

10. How important is it for Americans to learn foreign languages?

Extremely important ________ Important ________

Not so important ________

11. In your judgment to what extent do the following people consider foreign language study important? In each case circle one of the three numbers:

3 = extremely important
2 = important
1 = not so important

a. your parents: 3 2 1
b. your friends: 3 2 1
c. your high school teachers *other than* the foreign language teacher: 3 2 1
d. society as a whole: 3 2 1
e. yourself: 3 2 1

12. To what extent are you in favor of the following? In each case circle one of the three numbers:

3 = very much in favor
2 = slightly in favor
1 = not in favor

a. beginning the study of a foreign language in elementary school: 3 2 1
b. having four years of foreign language study in high school: 3 2 1
c. eliminating the teaching of foreign languages in our schools: 3 2 1
d. requiring that everyone take a foreign language at some time during their schooling: 3 2 1

13. Would you consider going abroad:
a. to acquire the skills in the use of a foreign language?
Definitely ________ Maybe ________ No ________
b. to increase your skills in the use of a foreign language you are already familiar with?
Definitely ________ Maybe ________ No ________

14. If you took a foreign language course how enjoyable do you think you would find it?
Very enjoyable ________ Slightly enjoyable ________
Not enjoyable ________

15. If you took a foreign language course would you feel at ease when making use of the skills you would be learning?

a. in listening: Yes ______ No ________ Not sure ________
b. in speaking: Yes ______ No ________ Not sure ________
c. in reading: Yes ______ No ________ Not sure ________
d. in writing: Yes ______ No ________ Not sure ________

16. Do you agree with the notion that to be good in a foreign language one must have a special talent for it?

Yes ________ No ________ Don't know ________

If "Yes," how much of this special talent do you think you have?

Above average ________ Average ________
Below average ________ Don't know ________

17. How probable is it, do you think, that you will one day be a fluent speaker of a second language? Place a number "0" (completely improbable) to "5" (completely probable) to indicate your estimate:

____

18. Do you feel that you have a lack of a special talent for foreign languages to such an extent that it will prevent you from gaining any benefit whatsoever from foreign language study?

Yes ________ No ________ Not applicable ________

Please indicate your agreement or disagreement with each of the following statements by circling one of the five numbers as follows:

4 = strongly agree
3 = agree
2 = disagree
1 = strongly disagree
0 = no opinion

19. Our lack of knowledge of foreign languages accounts for many of our political difficulties abroad: 4 3 2 1 0

20. A whole-hearted commitment to the study of a foreign language and the culture of its people endangers one's own cultural identity:
4 3 2 1 0

21. Please add any comments you might wish to make about foreign languages or about this questionnaire:

Foreign Language	Questionnaire
____________________	____________________
____________________	____________________
____________________	____________________
____________________	____________________
____________________	____________________
____________________	____________________
____________________	____________________
____________________	____________________
____________________	____________________
____________________	____________________
____________________	____________________
____________________	____________________

REFERENCES

Alkonis, N. V. and M. H. Brophy. "A Survey of FLES Practices," in *Reports and Surveys of Studies in the Teaching of Modern Foreign Languages,* New York, (1961), 213-217.

Anderson, Theodore. "The Optimum Age for Beginning the Study of Modern Languages," *International Review of Education,* VI (1960), 298-306.

Belasco, Simon. "The Plateau or the Case for Comprehension: The 'Concept' Approach," *Modern Language Journal,* LI (1967), 82-88.

——. "Nucleation and the Audiolingual Approach," *The Modern Language Journal,* XLIX (1965), 485.

Bellugi, Ursulla and Roger Brown (eds.), "The Acquisition of Language," *Monographs of the Society for Research in Child Development,* XXIX (1964).

Berlyne, D. E. "Mediating Responses: A Note on Fodor's Criticisms," *Journal of Verbal Learning and Verbal Behavior,* V (1966), 408-411.

Betts, Mary L. B. "Relationships among Learning, Practice, and Recall," Final Report, Cooperative Research Project No. S-169, Laboratory for Research in Instruction, Harvard University (1966). (Mimeo.)

Bever, T. G., J. A. Fodor and Merrill Garrett. "A Formal Limitation of Associanism," in T. R. Dixon and D. L. Horton (eds.), *Verbal Behavior and General Behavior Theory.* Prentice-Hall, Englewood Cliffs, N.J., 1968.

Birkmaier, Emma M. and D. L. Lange. "A Selective Bibliography on the Teaching of Foreign Languages, 1920-1966," *Foreign Language Annals,* I (1968), 318-353.

Brown, Roger. *Social Psychology,* The Free Press, New York, (1965).

Bugelski, B. R. *The Psychology of Learning.* Holt, New York, (1956).

Burling, Robbins. "Some Outlandish Proposals for the Teaching of Foreign Languages," *Language Learning,* XVIII (1968), 61-75.

Carroll, J. B. "Foreign Language Proficiency Levels Attained by Language Majors near Graduation from College," *Foreign Language Annals,* I (1968), 318-353.

____. "Foreign Language Proficiency Levels Attained by Language Majors near Graduation from College, *Foreign Language Annals,* I (1967), 131-151.

____. "The Contribution of Psychological Theory and Educational Research to the Teaching of Foreign Languages," in Valdman (1966a), 93-106.

____. "Research in Foreign Language Teaching: The Last Five Years," in Robert G. Mead, Jr. (ed.), *Language Teaching: Broader Contexts, Northeast Conf. on the Teaching of Foreign Languages: Reports of the Working Committees.* MLA Materials Center, New York, (1966), 12-42.

____. "Individual Differences in Foreign Language Learning," Thirty-Second Annual Foreign Language Conference, New York University School of Education, (1966).

____. "The Prediction of Success in Intensive Foreign Language Training," in Robert Glazer (ed.), *Training Research and Education,* Wiley, New York, (1965).

____. "Research on Teaching Foreign Languages," in N. L. Gage (ed.), *Handbook of Research on Teaching.* Rand McNally, Chicago, (1963), pp. 1060-1100.

____. "A Model of School Learning," *Teachers College Record,* LXIV (1963), 723-733.

____. "Linguistic Relativity, Contrastive Linguistics, and Language Learning," *International Review of Applied Linguistics*, I (1963), 1-20.

____. Foreign Languages for Children: What Research Says," *National Elementary Principal,* XXXIX (1960), 12-15.

____ and S. M. Sapon. *Modern Language Aptitude Test, MLAT Manual, 1959 edition.* The Psychological Corporation, New York.

Center for Comparative Psycholinguistics. *An Atlas of Affective Meaning.* University of Illinois Press, Urbana, in press.

Chomsky, Noam. *Language and Mind.* Harcourt, New York, (1968).

____. *Aspects of the Theory of Syntax.* M.I.T. Press, Cambridge, (1965).

____. Review of Skinner's "Verbal Behavior," *Language,* XXXV (1959), 26-58. (Also reprinted in Jakobovits & Miron, 1967).

____. *Syntactic Structures.* Mouton, The Hague, (1957).

Cleveland, H., G. J. Mangone, and J. C. Adams. *The Overseas Americans.* McGraw-Hill, New York (1960).

Cofer, C. N. "On Some Factors in the Organizational Characteristics of Free Recall." *American Psychologist,* XX (1965), 261-272.

Crothers, Edward and Patrick Suppes. *Experiments in Second Language Learning.* Academic Press, New York, (1967).

DeCamp, David. "The Current Discrepancy between Theoretical and Applied Linguistics," a paper delivered at the 1968 TESOL Convention, San Antonio.

Deese, James. "Behavior and Fact." Paper given as invited address to Division 3 at the meetings of the American Psychological Ass'n., San Francisco, Calif., Sept., 1968. (Dept. of Psych., The Johns Hopkins Univ., Mimeo.)

____. "The Structure of Associations in Language and Thought." The Johns Hopkins Press, Baltimore, (1965).

Diebold, A. R., Jr. "Incipient Bilingualism." *Language,* XXXVII (1961), 97-112.

Edgerton, M. F., Dwight Bolinger, T. W. Kelley, Gail E. Montgomery, and D. G. Reiff. "Liberated Expression," in Thomas E. Bird (ed.), *Foreign Language Learning: Research and Development: An Assessment. Northeast Conference on the Teaching of Foreign Languages.* Mary S. Rosenberg, Inc., New York, (1968).

Ervin-Tripp, Susan. "Sociolinguistics." Working Paper No. 3, Language-Behavior Research Laboratory, (1967), Univ. of California, Berkeley. (Mimeo.)

____. "An Issei Learns English," *Journal of Social Issues,* XXIII (1967), 78-90.

____. "The Verbal Behavior of Bilinguals: The Effects of Language of Response upon the T.A.T. Scores of Adult French Bilinguals," *American Psychologist,* X (1955), 391.

____ and C. E. Osgood. "Second Language Learning and Bilingualism," in C. E. Osgood and T. Sebeok (eds.), *Psycholinguistics* (Suppl.), *Journal of Abnormal and Social Psychology,* XXXXIX (1954), 139-146.

Feenstra, H. J. "Aptitude, Attitude, and Motivation in Second Language Acquisition." Unpublished doctoral dissertation, University of Western Ontario, London, Ontario, (1968).

Ferguson, C. A. "On Sociolinguistically Oriented Language Surveys," *The Linguistic Reporter,* VIII (1966), 1-3.

____. "Diglossia," in Dell Hymes (ed.), *Language in Culture and Society.* Harper, New York, (1964), pp. 429-439.

____. "On Transfer and the Abilities of Man," *Canadian Journal of Psychology,* X (1956), 121-131.

Fishman, J. A. *Language Loyalty in the United States.* Mouton, The Hague, (1966).

____. "The Implications of Bilingualism for Language Teaching and Language Learning," in Valdman, (1966a), 121-132.

Flaughter, Ronald. "Intercorrelations of Freshman Grades from Nine Academic Areas," Research Memorandum No. 24, Office of Instructional Resources, University of Illinois, April 13, 1967 (Mimeo.)

Fodor, J. A. *Psychological Explanation.* Random House, New York, (1968).

____. "Could Meaning Be an r_m?" *Journal of Verbal Learning and Verbal Behavior,* IV (1965), 75-81.

Fraser, C., Ursula Bellugi, and Roger Brown. "Control of Grammar in Imitation, Comprehension, and Production." *Journal of Verbal Learning and Verbal Behavior,* II (1963), 121-135.

Gaardner, A. B. "The Basic Course in Modern Foreign Languages," in *Reports of Surveys and Studies in the Teaching of Modern Foreign Languages.* New York, (1961).

Gardner, R. C., and W. E. Lambert. "Language Aptitude, Intelligence and Second Language Achievement," Department of Psychology, University of Western Ontario, 1961 (Mimeo). (Date uncertain.)

Harmon, J. T. "Annual Bibliography on the Teaching of Foreign Languages: 1967," *Foreign Language Annals,* I 1967-1968, Numbers 1-4.

Haukebo, G. K. "The Next Best Thing to Being There: Language Camps," in Levenson and Kendrick, (1967), 471-473.

Hayes, Alfred S. "New Directions in Foreign Language Teaching." *Modern Language Journal,* XXXXIX (1965), 281-293.

____. "Paralinguistics and Kinesics: Pedagogical Perspectives," in Sebeok, Hayes, and Bateson, (1964), 145-172.

____. "Procedures for Language Laboratory Planning," *Bulletin* of the National Association of Secondary School Principals, XXXXVI (1962), 123-135.

____, W. E. Lambert, and G. R. Tucker. "Evaluation of Foreign Language Teaching," *Foreign Language Annals,* I (1967), 22-44.

____ , H. Lane, T. Mueller, and W. E. Sweet. "A New Look at Learning," in W. F. Bottiglia (ed.), *Current Issues in Language Teaching Reports, Northeast Conference on the Teaching of Foreign Languages.* Manchester, N.H., (1962), 19-60.

Hoeningswald, H. M. "A Proposal for the Study of Folk-Linguistics," in William Bright (ed.), *Sociolinguistics.* Mouton, The Hague, (1966), 16-20.

Holby, Dorothy J. "Self-evaluation and Foreign Language," *Peabody Journal of Education,* XXXXIV (1967), 239-241.

Howell, R. W. "Linguistic Choice and Social Change," manuscript to be published; Richmond College, City University of New York, (1968).

Hull, C. L. *Principles of Behavior.* Appleton-Century-Crofts, New York, (1943).

Hutchison, J. C. "Modern Foreign Languages in High School: The Language Laboratory," U.S. Department of Health, Education, and Welfare. OE-27043, Bulletin No. 23, (1961).

Jakobovits, L. A. Introduction to "Foundations of Foreign Language Teaching and Learning: Psychological Aspects," in Eberhard Reichmann (ed.), *The Teaching of German: Problems and Methods.* Published by the National Carl Schutz Association–Teaching Aid Project; Winchell Company, Philadelphia, (1970). (Part II, Ch. 1)

———. "Motivation and Foreign Language Learning: Part A. Motivation and Learner Factors." *Report to the 1970 Northeast Conference on the Teaching of Foreign Languages.*

———. "Illinois Foreign Language Attitude Questionnaire: Forms S_1 and S_2." Report of Working Committee 1. Northeast Conference on the Teaching of Foreign Languages, (1970).

———. "The Physiology and Psychology of Second Language Learning," in Emma Birkmaier (ed.), *Britannica Review of Foreign Language Education.* Encyclopaedia Britannica, Chicago, (1969).

———. "A Functional Approach to the Assessment of Language Skills," *Journal of English as a Second Language,* IV (1969), 63-76.

———. "Research Findings and FL Requirements in Colleges and Universities," *Foreign Language Annals,* II (1969), 436-456.

———. "Second Language Learning and Transfer Theory: A Theoretical Assessment," *Language Learning,* XIX (1969), 55-86.

———. "Rhetoric and Stylistics: Some Basic Issues in the Analysis of Discourse," *College Composition and Communication,* XX (1969), 314-328.

———. "Some Potential Uses of the Cross-Cultural Atlas of Affective Meanings." *Proceedings of the XI Congress of the Inter-American Society of Psychology,* February 1969, No. 40, 1-16. (Originally presented in Mexico City, December 1967.)

———. "Dimensionality of Compound-coordinate Bilingualism." *Language Learning* (Special Issue No. 3), August 1968, 29-49.

———. "Implications of Recent Psycholinguistic Developments for the Teaching of a Second Language." *Language Learning,* XVIII (1968), 89-109.

——— . "The Act of Composition: Some Elements in a Performance Model of Language." Conference on the Composing Process, Colorado Springs, November 1968. (The National Council of Teachers of English, Champaign, Ill., proceedings forthcoming.)

——— . "Comments on Macnamara's 'How Can One Measure the Extent of a Person's Bilingual Proficiency?' " *Proceedings of the International Seminar on the Description and Measurement of Bilingualism.* University of Mouton, New Brunswick (1967).

———. "Comparative Psycholinguistics in the Study of Cultures." *International Journal of Psychology,* I (1966), 15-37.

———. "Mediation Theory and the Single-stage S-R Model: Different?" *Psychological Review,* LXXIII (1966), 376-381.

——— and C. E. Osgood. "Connotations of Twenty Psychological Journals to Their Professional Readers." *American Psychologist,* XXII (1067), 792-800.

——— and M. S. Miron (eds.) *Readings in the Psychology of Language.* Prentice-Hall, Englewood Cliffs, N.J., (1967).

___ and W. E. Lambert. "Semantic Satiation among Bilinguals." *Journal of Experimental Psychology,* LXII (1961), 576-582.

Jenkins, J. J. "The Challenge to Psychological Theorists." In T. R. Dixon and D. L. Horton (eds.), Verbal Behavior and General Behavior Theory. Prentice-Hall, Englewood Cliffs, N.J., (1968).

___ and W. A. Russell. "Systematic Changes in Word Association Norms: 1910-1952." *Journal of Abnormal and Social Psychology,* LX (1960), 293-304.

___ and W. A. Russell. "Associative Clustering during Recall." *Journal of Abnormal and Social Psychology* XXXXVII (1952), 818-821.

Jung, John. *Verbal Learning.* Holt, New York, (1968).

Kansas State Teachers College of Emporia, Service Bureau for Modern Language Teachers. The French Club. ERIC Documentation Service, U.S. Office of Education, ED-01H84, (1967). (Date uncertain.)

Katz, J. J. *The Philosophy of Language.* Harper & Row, New York, (1966).

___ and J. A. Fodor. "The Structure of a Semantic Theory," *Language,* XXXIX (1963), 170-210.

Kirsch, M. S. "At What Age Elementary School Language Teaching?" *The Modern Language Journal,* XXXX (1956), 399-400.

Kolers, P. A. "Interlingual Word Associations." *Journal of Verbal Learning and Verbal Behavior,* II (1963), 291-300.

Kuusinen, Jorma. "Correspondence between the Group and the Individual in the Factor Structure of Personality Ratings." Paper prepared for the Second International Conference of Affective Meaning Systems, Tehran, Iran, August 1967.

Lado, Robert. *Language Testing.* Longmans, London, (1961).

Lambert, W. E. "A Social Psychology of Bilingualism." *The Journal of Social Issues,* XXIII (1967), 91-109.

___. "Psychological Approaches to the Study of Language: II. On Second Language Learning and Bilingualism." *The Modern Language Journal,* XXXXV (1961), 203-206.

___, R. C. Gardner, H. C. Barik, and K. Tunstall. "Attitudinal and Cognitive Aspects of Intensive Study of a Second Language." *Journal of Abnormal and Social Psychology,* LXVI (1963), 358-368.

___, J. Havelka, and C. Crosby. "The Influence of Language-Acquisition Contexts on Bilingualism." *Journal of Abnormal and Social Psychology,* LVI (1958), 239-244.

___, J. Havelka, and R. C. Gardner. "Linguistic Manifestations of Bilingualism." *American Journal of Psychology,* LXXII (1959), 77-82.

___ and L. A. Jakobovits. "Verbal Satiation and Changes in the Intensity of Meaning." *Journal of Experimental Psychology,* LX (1960), 376-383.

____ and Nancy Moore. "Word-association Responses: Comparisons of American and French Monolinguals with Canadian Monolinguals and Bilinguals." *Journal of Verbal Learning and Verbal Behavior,* III (1966), 313-320.

Larew, L. A. "The Optimum Age for Beginning a Foreign Language." *The Modern Language Journal,* XXXXV (1961), 203-206.

Lashley , K. S. "The Problem of Serial Order in Behavior," in L.A. Jeffress (ed.), *Cerebral Mechanisms in Behavior: The Hixon Symposium.* Wiley, New York, (1951).

Lee, W. R. *Language-Teaching Games and Contests.* Oxford University Press, England, (1965).

Lenneberg, E. H. *Biological Foundations of Language.* Wiley, New York, (1967).

____. "The Natural History of Language," in Smith and Miller, (1966), 219-252.

Levenson, Stanley and William Kendrick (eds.) *Readings in Foreign Languages for the Elementary School.* Blaisdell, Waltham, Mass., (1967).

Levin, Joseph. "Three-mode Factor Analysis." *Psychological Bulletin,* LXIV (1965), 442-452.

Lieberson, Stanley. *Bilingualism in Canada.* Wiley, New York, (1969), *in press.*

Mackey, W. F. "The Measurement of Bilingual Behavior," *The Canadian Psychologist,* VIIa (1966), 75-92.

____. "Bilingual Interference: It's Analysis and Measurement." *The Journal of Communication,* XV (1965), 239-249.

____. *Language Teaching Analysis.* Longmans, London, (1965).

____. "The Description of Bilingualism." *Canadian Journal of Linguistics,* VII (1962), 51-85.

____. "Toward a Redefinition of Bilingualism." *Journal of the Canadian Linguistic Association,* III (1956), 2-11.

____ and J. G. Savard. "The Indices of Coverage." *International Review of Applied Linguistics,* (1967), 71-121.

Macnamara, John. "The Bilingual's Linguistic Performance: A Psychological Overview." *The Journal of Social Issues,* XXIII (1967), 58-97.

____. "How Can One Measure the Extent of A Person's Bilingual Proficiency?" *Proceedings of the International Seminar on the Description and Measurement of Bilingualism.* New Brunswick: University of Moncton, 1967.

____ . *"Bilingualism and Primary Education: A Study of Irish Experience."* University of Edinburgh Press, Edinburgh, (1966).

Mandler, George. "Organization and Memory," in K. W. Spence and Janet T. Spence (eds.), *The Psychology of Learning and Motivation:* Advances in Research and Theory. Academic Press, New York, (1966).

McNeill, David. "Developmental Psycholinguistics," in Frank Smith & G. A. Miller (eds.), *The Genesis of Language: A Psycholinguistic Approach.* The M.I.T. Press, Cambridge, Mass, (1966).

Meckel, H. C. "Research on Teaching Composition and Literature," in N. L. Gage (ed.), *Handbook of Research on Teaching.* Rand McNally, Chicago, (1963), pp. 966-1006.

Michel, Joseph (ed.). *Foreign Language Teaching: An Anthology.* Macmillan, New York, (1967).

Mildenberger, Andrea S. and Allen Yvan-heng Liao. ERIC documents on the teaching of foreign languages; List Number 1. *Foreign Language Annals,* II (1968), 1-26.

Miller, G. A. "Some Preliminaries to Psycholinguistics." *American Psychologist,* XX (1965), 15-20.

____. "Some Psychological Studies of Grammar." *American Psychologist,* XVII (1962), 748-762.

Milner, P. M. Book review of "Speech and Brain Mechanisms" by W. Penfield and L. Roberts. *Canadian Journal of Psychology,* XIV (1960), 140-143.

Modern Language Association. "Advice to the Language Learner." *Modern Language Journal,* L, (1966), 260-263.

Monot-Cassidy, Helene. "The New Audiovisual Student." *Modern Language Journal,* L (1966), 15-18.

Moran, L. J. "Generality of Word-association Response Sets." *Psychological Reports,* LXXX (1966).

Morgan, D. Y. "Game and Playacting." *English Language Teaching,* XXI (1967), 182-185.

Moulton, W. G. "Linguistics and Language Teaching in the United States: 1940-1960." In *Trends in European and American Linguistics.* Spectrum Publishers, Utrecht, Netherlands, (1962).

Mueller, Klaus. "The Army Language School and its Implications," in Levenson and Kendrick, (1967), 479-485.

Mueller, T. H. and Robert Harris. "The Effect of an Audiolingual Program on Drop-out Rate." *Modern Language Journal,* L (1966), 133-137.

____ and R. R. Leutenegger. "Some Inferences about An Intensified Oral Approach to the Teaching of French Based on a Study of Course Drop-outs." *The Modern Language Journal,* XLVIII, (1964), 91-94.

Nelson, R. and L. A. Jakobovits (eds.). "Motivation and Foreign Language Learning: Report of Working Committee 3," in *Northeast Conferences on the Teaching of Foreign Languages,* (1970).

Noble, C. E. "An Analysis of Meaning." *Psychological Review,* LIX (1952), 421-430.

Nostrand, H. L. "A Shared Repertory of Audiovisual Materials for Foreign Languages, Language Arts and Social Studies?" *Audiovisual Instruction,* XI (1966), 624-626.

Ollman, M. L. (ed.). *MLA Selective List of Materials.* New York, (1962).

Osgood, C. E. "Interpersonal Verbs and Interpersonal Behavior." Institute of Communications Research, The University of Illinois, Urbana, (1968). (Mimeo.)

———. "Speculation on the Structure of Interpersonal Intentions." Department of Psychology, University of Illinois, (1966). (Mimeo.)

———. "Meaning Cannot Be r_m?" *Journal of Verbal Learning and Verbal Behavior,* V (1966), 402-407.

———. "Semantic Differential Technique in the Comparative Study of Cultures." *American Anthropologist,* LXVI (1964), 171-200.

———. "Studies of the Generality of Affective Meaning Systems." *American Psychologist,* XVII (1962), 10-28.

———. *Method and Theory in Experimental Psychology.* Oxford University Press, New York, (1953).

———, W. H. May, and M. S. Miron. *The Structure of Affective Meaning: A Multi-cultural Application of Semantic Differential Technique.* University of Illinois Press, Urbana, (forthcoming).

———, W. K. Archer, and M. S. Miron. "The Cross-cultural Generality of Meaning Systems." Progress Report: January 1960-September 1962. Institute of Communications Research, University of Illinois, (1962). (Mimeo.)

———, G. J. Suci, and P. H. Tannenbaum. *The Measurement of Meaning.* University of Illinois Press, Urbana, (1957).

——— and Zella Luria. "A Blind Analysis of a Case of Multiple Personality Using the Semantic Differential." *Journal of Abnormal and Social Psychology,* XXXXIX (1954), 579-591.

Peal, Elizabeth and W. E. Lambert. "The Relation of Bilingualism to Intelligence." *Psychological Monographs,* LXXVI (1962), No. 27. (Whole Issue No. 546).

Penfield, Wilder. "A Consideration of the Neurophysiological Mechanism of Speech and Some Educational Consequences." *Proceedings of the American Academy of Arts and Sciences,* LXXXII (1953), 201-214.

——— and Lamar Roberts. *Speech and Brain Mechanisms.* Princeton University Press, Princeton, (1959).

Pimsleur, Paul and R. J. Bonkowski. "The Transfer of Verbal Material across Sense Modalities." *Journal of Educational Psychology,* LII (1961), 104-107.

———, D. M. Sundland, and Ruth D. McIntyre. "Underachievement in Foreign Language Learning." *International Review of Applied Linguistics,* II (1964), 113-150.

Politzer, R. L. "Student Motivation and Interest in Elementary Language Courses." *Language Learning,* V (1953-54), 15-21.

Postman, Leo. "The Present Status of Interference Theory," in C. N. Cofer and Barbara S. Musgrave (eds.), *Verbal Learning and Verbal Behavior.* McGraw-Hill, New York, (1961), 152-179.

Preston, M. S. "Interlingual Interference in a Bilingual Version of the Stroop Color-word Test." Unpublished doctoral dissertation, McGill University, Montreal, Canada, (1965).

Reid, J. R. "An Exploratory Survey of Foreign Language Teaching by Television in the United States," in *Reports of Surveys and Studies in the Teaching of Modern Foreign Languages.* New York, (1961), 197-211.

Rice, Frank. *In the Linguistic Reporter,* May 1959.

Rivers, Wilga M. *The Psychologist and the Foreign Language Teacher.* University of Chicago Press, Chicago, (1964).

Rogers, Adrienne. "Motivation: The Forgotten Word." *French Review,* XXXIX (1969), 906-909.

Rosenzweig, M. R. "Comparisons among Word Association Responses in English, French, German and Italian." *American Journal of Psychology,* LXXIV (1961), 347-360.

Rutherford, W. E. "Deep and Surface Structure, and the Language Drill." *TESOL Quarterly,* II (1968), 71-79.

Scherer, G. A. C., and Michael Wertheimer. "The German Teaching Experiment at the University of Colorado." *German Quarterly,* XXXV (1962), 298-308.

Sebeok, T. A., A. S. Hayes, and Mary C. Bateson, (eds.) *"Approaches to Semiotics: Cultural Anthropology, Education, Linguistics, Psychiatry, Psychology."* Mouton, The Hague, (1964).

Selinker, Larry. "The Psychologically-relevant Data of Second Language Learning." Paper read at the Second International Congress of Applied Linguistics, Cambridge, England, September 8-12, 1969.

Skinner, B. F. *Verbal Behavior.* Appleton-Century-Crofts, New York, (1957).

Slobin, D. I. "The Acquisition of Russian as a Native Language," in Smith and Miller, (1966).

Smith, Frank and G. A. Miller, (eds.). *The Genesis of Language.* M.I.T. Press, Cambridge, (1966).

Snider, J. G. and C. E. Osgood, (eds.), *Semantic Differential Technique.* Aldine, Chicago, (1969).

Spolsky, Bernard. "Language Testing: The Problem of Validation." *TESOL Quarterly,* II (1968), 88-94.

____. "What Does it Mean to Know a Language, Or How Do You Get Someone to Perform His Competence?" Paper prepared for presentation at the Second Conference on Problems in Foreign Language Testing, University of Southern California, November 7-9, 1968.

____, B. Sigurd, M. Sato, E. Walker, and Catherine Arterburn. "Preliminary Studies in the Development of Techniques for Testing Overall Second Language Proficiency." Indiana Language Program, Indiana University, Bloomington, Ind., (1966) (Mimeo.).

———. "A Psycholinguistic Critique of Programed Foreign Language Instruction." *International Review of Applied Linguistics,* IV (1966), 119-129.

Steinberg, D. and L. A. Jakobovits, (eds.). *"Semantics: An Interdisciplinary Reader in Philosophy, Linguistics, and Psychology."* Cambridge University Press, Cambridge, England, in press.

Stephens, J. M. "Transfer of Learning," in C. W. Harris and Marie R. Liba (eds.), *Encyclopedia of Educational Research,* Macmillan, New York, pp. 1535-1543.

Stern, H. H. *"Foreign Languages in Primary Education: The Teaching of Foreign or Second Languages to Younger Children.* UNESCO Institute for Education, Hamburg, (1963).

Suppes, P., E. Crothers, Ruth Weir, and Edith Trager. "Some Quantitative Studies of Russian Consonant Phoneme Descrimination." Institute for Mathematical Studies in the Social Sciences, Technical Report No. 49, Stanford, Calif. (1962).

Taylor, W. L. "Cloze Procedure: A New Tool for Measuring Readability." *Journalism Quarterly,* XXX (1953), 415-433.

Underwood, B. J., and R. W. Schulz. *Meaningfulness and Verbal Learning.* Lippincott, Chicago, (1960).

Upshur, J. A. "Measurement of Oral Communication." Second Conference on Language Testing, University of Southern California, November 1968. (Mimeo.)

Valdman, Albert (ed.). *Trends in Language Teaching.* McGraw-Hill, New York, (1966).

———. "Programed Instruction and Foreign Language Teaching," in Valdman (1966a), 133-158.

———. "Toward Self-instruction in Foreign Language Learning." *International Review of Applied Linguistics,* II (1964), 1-36.

Wagner, Grace D. "Parental Negative Reaction to Current Methods of Foreign Language Teaching: Encounter and Alternative." ERIC Documentation Service, U.S. Office of Education, ED-012-546, (1966).

Weinreich, Uriel. *Languages in Contact.* Mouton, The Hague, (1968).

Willbern, Glen. "Foreign Language Enrollments in Public Secondary Schools, 1965." *Foreign Language Annals,* I (1968), 239-253.

Whorf, B. L. *Language, Thought, and Reality: Selected Writings of Benjamin Lee Whorf,* ed. J. B. Carroll, M.I.T. Press, Cambridge, Mass. (1956).

Wolfe, David L. "Some Theoretical Aspects of Language Learning and Language Teaching." *Language Learning,* XVII (1967), 173-188.

Yeni-Komshian, Grace, D. A. Zubin, and Evangelos Afendras. "A Pilot Study on the Ability of Young Children and Adults to Identify and Reproduce Novel Speech Sounds," in *Annual Report* of the Neurocommunications Laboratory of the Johns Hopkins University School of Medicine, Baltimore, Md., (1968), 288-305. (Mimeo.)

——. "Personal Communication," (1962).

INDEX